Trustworthy Cyber-Physical Systems

Nazila Gol Mohammadi

Trustworthy Cyber-Physical Systems

A Systematic Framework towards Design and Evaluation of Trust and Trustworthiness

With Forewords by Prof. Dr. Maritta Heisel, Prof. Dr. Karin Bernsmed and Prof. Dr. Sachar Paulus

 Springer Vieweg

Nazila Gol Mohammadi
paluno – The Ruhr Institute for
Software Technology
University of Duisburg-Essen
Duisburg, Germany

Dissertation, University of Duisburg-Essen, 2018

ISBN 978-3-658-27487-0   ISBN 978-3-658-27488-7   (eBook)
https://doi.org/10.1007/978-3-658-27488-7

Springer Vieweg

This Springer Vieweg imprint is published by the registered company Springer Fachmedien Wiesbaden
GmbH part of Springer Nature.
The registered company address is: Abraham-Lincoln-Str. 46, 65189 Wiesbaden, Germany

To my parents

Foreword

This book is about the trustworthiness of cyber-physical systems (CPS). Cyber-physical systems are, on the one hand, physical, which means that they contain technical devices that interact with the physical world. On the other hand, such systems are connected to the Internet, i.e. the cyberspace. Cyber-physical systems make it possible to provide services that have been unimaginable in the past. For example, ambient-assisted living systems can sense when an elderly person has fallen to the ground and can call for help when that happens; or smart grids can optimize the power consumption of private households and industry. Because of the potential to enhance the power of technical systems significantly, CPS will gain much in importance for our daily lives in the future. The downside of these developments, however, is that CPS come with new risks for safety, security, and privacy of their users. For example, in a smart home scenario, an attacker could remotely switch on the stove and set the house on fire. And in a smart mobility scenario, the location data of a person could be used to reveal private information, for example when a person regularly is detected near a dialysis station.

To deal with such risks, CPS have to be designed to be trustworthy, i.e. such that it is justified to trust such a system. Nazila Gol Mohammadi addresses this problem in great depth and breadth. She elaborates the difference between trust and trustworthiness. Trustworthiness properties can be built into a system, whereas trust needs to be developed by its users, based on and supported by trustworthiness properties. But what properties of CPS should we base our trust on? All properties contributing to foster the trust of users in a CPS are trustworthiness properties. Thus, trustworthiness is not a single quality of a CPS, but a set of different quality properties. What complicates the situation even more is the fact that different user groups may consider different trustworthiness properties as relevant, and that for different CPS different properties may contribute to their trustworthiness.

This book focuses on the software engineering aspects of developing trustworthy CPS. Nazila Gol Mohammadi investigates all the different facets of trustworthiness during the software development lifecycle, from the elicitation of trustworthiness requirements based on users' concerns, and assessing the design of a CPS with respect to trustworthiness, to maintaining the trustworthiness of a CPS at run-time. Most important from a software engineering point of view, this work does not propose a brand-new software development process that would have little chances to be applied by professional software engineers who are used to work with specific processes specialized to their area of expertise or their working context. Instead, the approach is to enhance existing methods with process chunks that support trustworthiness. To this end, a number of trustworthiness capability patterns are defined, which are based on the notion of capability patterns as proposed by the Software Process Engineering Meta-model (SPEM) developed by the Object Management Group. Such patterns represent process chunks that can be incorporated into other processes to enhance them. Thus, it is made as easy as possible to incorporate trustworthiness aspects into routine software engineering practice.

Nazila Gol Mohammadi also provides metrics that can be used to compare different design alternatives with respect to their trustworthiness properties. In addition, the book contributes a process for run-time maintenance, and the concept of a trustworthiness case. As safety cases demonstrate the safety of a system, trustworthiness cases serve to demonstrate the trustworthiness of a CPS, for example, for the purpose of certification.

The contributions presented in this book constitute a signification step forward in the direction of engineering trustworthy CPS in a systematic fashion. They have been validated using a case study of high practical importance, namely an ambient assisted living system. All in all, they provide a comprehensive framework to address trustworthiness of CPS.

Dusiburg, Germany   Prof. Dr. Maritta Heisel

Foreword

We first met Dr. Gol Mohammadi in 2012, at the kick-off of the European Union's Seventh Framework Programme project "OPTET" (OPerational Trustworthiness Enabling Technologies). She was a young, very ambitious PhD student who quickly became one of the key technical persons in the project, leading the research activities on design and validation of trustworthy socio-technical systems. For three years, we cooperated intensively on developing methodology and technology to enhance system development towards producing trust and trustworthiness evidence. It was a challenging and, at the same time, very productive time.

So, why are trust and its counterpart trustworthiness so important? As Dr. Gol Mohammadi explains it in her book, trustworthiness is a key aspect of cyber-physical systems aiming at being trusted by users and therefore a main driver for user acceptance of new technologies and services in their daily lives. As a user of today's online apps and services, it has become increasingly difficult to understand what data these services collect and what they do with the data. In addition, there is often a mismatch between the trust that users put into such services and to what degree they really can – or should – be trusted. In her book, Dr. Gol Mohammadi presents a framework for requirements engineering and design methods for considering trustworthiness during the design-time of such systems. More specifically, the book delivers design methodologies, architectures and specific service definitions for balancing trust and trustworthiness in systems, together with elements to verify/validate the trustworthiness propositions. This is a highly relevant and timely topic, which addresses one of the fundamental challenges that the European software industry faces today. The current discussion about software security certifications as part of the upcoming Cybersecurity legal framework shows the practical relevance of Dr. Gol Mohammadi's work. The scope of this book is very ambitious; it covers all parts of a software development lifecycle, and it can be applied independently of the development methodology that is being used. The results presented in this book are hence an important step towards a more trustworthy digital society.

The OPTET project has now ended, but Dr. Gol Mohammadi's footprint remains. In this book, she has addressed one of most important and fundamental problems in the digital society of today. The book is an outstanding research contribution, which drills into the different parts of the software development lifecycle and proposes several different methods, which can be integrated into existing software development processes, hence facilitating for smooth integration of trustworthiness as a key concept in digital software and services. We highly recommend the book to anyone interested in the state-of-the-art of research on trust and trustworthy system development.

Trondheim, Norway   Prof. Dr. Karin Bernsmed

Mannheim, Germany   Prof. Dr. Sachar Paulus

Preface

In the era of cyber-physical systems (CPS), almost all activities of our daily life are supported by a multitude of heterogeneous, loosely coupled systems communicating over the Internet. These systems are increasingly enabling the digitalization of complex business processes. We use them every day for e-commerce, information access, and in our social life where we have inter-personal interactions. As entities of these systems, humans, processes and organizations are dependent on each other as well as on the CPS. This dependence entails the need for a high degree of *trust*. The adoption and acceptance of CPS by end-users are dependent on whether users have trust in these systems. In recent years, many researchers contributed to addressing the lack of trust. Trust is subject to individual interpretation, e.g. organizations require confidence about how their business-critical data is handled, whereas end-users may be more concerned about the usability of a system. While trust is an act carried out by a person, *trustworthiness* is a quality of the system that has the potential to influence the trust this person has in the system in a positive way. Therefore, CPS should be made trustworthy. They should exhibit objective properties to increase the confidence of their users that placing trust in the system will lead to an expected outcome. Unfortunately, even well-established development methodologies provide little support for the realization of a trustworthy CPS. In this book, we aim at providing several methods that support (i) building trustworthiness into the core of a CPS, (ii) evaluating the trustworthiness of a CPS, and (iii) establishing run-time maintenance of the trustworthiness of a CPS.

The contribution of this book consists in a holistic approach towards trustworthiness assurance. We provide a trustworthiness management framework (TW-Man) that includes several methods to address trustworthiness-related issues throughout the whole development lifecycle. The TW-Man framework aims at addressing trustworthiness, starting with a collection of key concepts of trustworthiness. Using our TW-Man framework, trustworthiness requirements can be elicited, assessed and evaluated according to trust concerns of the end-users. The trustworthiness-by-design methodology that is provided in this book extends the development process in order to address trustworthiness requirements. Our proposed evaluation method, as part of TW-Man, provides evidence-based evaluation of systems' trustworthiness using two existing evaluation techniques: a computational approach and a risk assessment approach. To preserve the overall established trustworthiness during run-time, TW-Man's trustworthiness maintenance reference architecture may be used. We also provide processes for monitoring, management, and mitigation of potential issues. Furthermore, all produced evidence by using a trustworthiness-by-design methodology for trustworthiness of a CPS, can be documented in a structured and systematic way using our trustworthiness cases. The proposed framework has been evaluated with a running example from the ambient assisted living domain. Furthermore, most of the developed methods in this book have been evaluated with other case studies from a European project, called OPTET.

Essen, Germany   Nazila Gol Mohammadi

Acknowledgements

First, I would like to express the deepest gratitude to Prof. Maritta Heisel. She gave me intellectual freedom to pursue this research topic and provided encouragement throughout the whole time. Without her support, scientific advice and wisdom this work would not have been possible. Likewise, I would like to thank Prof. Karin Bernsmed for sharing her expertise, support and constructive comments, which helped me improve my work.

I thank my colleagues from the working group *Software Engineering* at the University of Duisburg-Essen: Azadeh Alebrahim, Angela Borchert, Nicolás Díaz Ferreya, Stefan Faßbender, Ludger Goeke, Denis Hatebur, Rene Meis, Jens Leicht, Jörg Petersen, Nelufar Ulfat-Bunyadi, and Roman Wirtz for the constructive and fruitful discussions and the collaborative work. I especially thank Nelufar who proof-read countless numbers of pages. I would also like to thank Katja Krause as well as Joachim Zumbrägel, who supported me in organizational and technical issues.

I also wish to express my gratitude to my former colleagues and associates from *Software Systems Engineering* working group: Torsten Bandyszak, Marian Daun, Andreas Metzger, Christian Reinartz, Osama Samoodi, Eric Schmieders, Philipp Schmidt, Vanessa Stricker, Bastian Tenbergen, Thorsten Weyer, and many more for the collaborative work. I especially thank Prof. Klaus Pohl who introduced me into the world of research and supported me during my first publications.

I am grateful to all of those with whom I have had the pleasure to work on different scientific papers and in research projects: Pascal Bisson, Francesco Di Cerbo, Abigail Goldsteen, Per Håkon Meland, Costas Kalogiros, Micha Moffie, Bassem I. Nasser, Prof. Sachar Paulus, Stuart Short, Prof. Mike Surridge, and many more who helped me with constructive discussions.

Last but not least, I thank my family for the support, encouragement and unconditional love they gave me along the way. I also express my gratitude to my friends for their patience.

Essen, Germany   Nazila Gol Mohammadi

Contents

List of Acronyms

AAL	Amibient Assited Living
API	Application Programming Interface
BPEL	Business Process Execution Language
BPMN	Business Process Modeling Notation
C	Contribution
CASE	Computer-Aided Software Engineering
CC	Common Criteria
CEP	Complex Event Processing
CMM	Capability Maturity Model
CMMI	Capability Maturity Model Integration
CPS	Cyber-Physical System
CPU	Central Processing Unit
DB	DataBase
DBMS	DataBase Management System
DBLP	Digital Bibliography & Library Project
DSL	Domain Specific Language
DTWC	Digital TrustWorthiness Certificate
E2E	End-to-End
E2E TW	End-to-End TrustWorthiness
E2E TWE	End-to-End TrustWorthiness Evaluation
EAL	Evaluation Assurance Level
EMF	Eclipse Modeling Framework
EMHT	Emergency Monitoring and Handling Tool
EPF	Eclipse Process Framework
EU	European Union
FMS	Fall Management System
GDPR	General Data Protection Regulation
GRL	Goal-oriented Requirement Language
GQM	Goal-Question-Metric
GSN	Goal Structuring Notation
HIPAA	US Health Insurance Portability and Accountability Act
HM	Health Manager application

HMS	Home Monitoring System
HTTP	The Hypertext Transfer Protocol
IBM	International Business Machines
ICT	Information and Communication Technology
IP	Internet Protocol address
JSON	JavaScript Object Notation
KAOS	Knowledge Acquisition in autOmated Specification
MAPE-K	Monitor, Analyze, Plan, Execute, and Knowledge loop
OMG	Object Management Group
PERS	Personal Emergency Response Systems
PriS	Privacy Safeguard method
Proton	the IBM PROactive Technology ONline
OPTET	OPerational Trustworthiness Enabling Technologies
QoS	Quality of Service
RALPH	Resource Assignment Language graPH
RDF	Resource Description Framework
RE	Requirements Engineering
REQ	Requirements
RG	Research Goal
RQ	Research Question
SDM	Strategic Dependency Model
SE	Software Engineering
SecBPMN	Secure BPMN
SLA	Service Level Agreement
SLR	Structured Literature Review
SOA	Service Oriented Architecture
SPEM	Software Process Engineering Meta-Model
SRM	Strategic Rationale Model
SSH	Secure SHell (a cryptographic network protocol)
SSE-CMM	Systems Security Engineering Capability Maturity Model
ToE	Target of Evaluation
TA	Trust Assumption
TC	Trust Concern
TM	Trondheim Municipality
TPA	Trustworthy Process Areas
TSLA	Trustworthiness Service Level Agreement
TSM	Trusted Software Methodology
TW	TrustWorthiness
TWbyD	TrustWorthiness-by-Design
TWE	TrustWorthiness Evaluator

TW-Man	TrustWorthiness Management framework
UCD	User-Centered Design
UML	Unified Modeling Language
VM	Virtual Machine
XML	Extensible Markup Language

Part I

Scope of the Book

1 Introduction

The vast public interest in using cyber-physical systems and relying on them has opened up many new spaces of research. Cyber-physical systems comprise of humans as well as software and hardware components (Broy et al., 2012; Rajkumar et al., 2010). These systems are distributed, software-intensive and highly connected via the Internet, leading to interaction with other software as well as a multitude of physical entities (Lee, 2008). Examples of the application domain of cyber-physical systems include health-care systems, aerospace systems, vehicles and intelligent highways, smart homes and smart grids. We rely on these systems to run daily activities since many of our daily interactions are mediated by, or executed with, a type of cyber-physical system. Online banking can serve as an example for people performing their business online and depending on a cyber-physical system in order to execute a transaction efficiently and reliably. Even our social life is affected by these systems, e.g. entertainment with online multiplayer games, or getting medical advice or supervision through health-care systems without any face-to-face interactions with the health-service providers. In such interactions where human dependencies and reliances on the systems are crucial factors, different types and levels of risks are introduced. Only if the end-users are able to place trust in the cyber-physical system they use to communicate and collaborate, is a successful adoption of cyber-physical system possible.

Trust is a well-known concept that we deal with in every aspect of our daily life. Trust is defined as "a bet about the future contingent actions of others" (Sztompka, 2000). This definition involves concepts like dependency, uncertainty, risk and commitment. In this book, we stick to this definition of trust, while extending it to include cyber-physical systems: *"a bet about the future contingent actions of others, be they individuals or groups of individuals, or entire cyber-physical systems"* (cf. Chapter 2). However, given our chosen definition of trust, we argue that – while trusting is an act carried out by an end-user – trustworthiness is a quality of the system that has the potential to influence the end-users' trust in the system in a positive way. In contrast to trust which is subjective, we consider the concept of trustworthiness as *"objective"*, therefore acting as a measure of probability indicating whether the system will successfully meet all the trustworthiness requirements or trust concerns of an end-user. Trustworthiness, as *"objective"* property, bridges

© Springer Fachmedien Wiesbaden GmbH, part of Springer Nature 2019
N. Gol Mohammadi, *Trustworthy Cyber-Physical Systems*,
https://doi.org/10.1007/978-3-658-27488-7_1

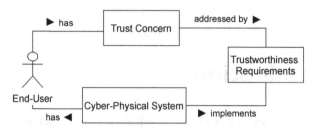

Figure 1.1: The relation of important concepts

the gap between informal trust concerns and formal implementation techniques. Figure 1.1 shows the relation of important concepts in this book.

Trustworthiness of a software, application, service or infrastructure is a key success factor for its use and acceptance by end-users. Furthermore, these systems also need to provide indications to their end-users whether to trust other users and the involved parties. Most importantly, the end-users need to trust the organisations that develop and provide cyber-physical systems.

Reports, like the one provided by Richardson (2011), indicate an increasing number of cyber-crime victims, which leads to a massive deterioration of trust in current cyber-physical systems (e.g. considering transactions with business-critical data). Hence, in the past years, growing interest in trustworthy computing has emerged in both, academia and practice. Additionally, there are reported indications, that in many applications this essential quality has been observed as difficult to obtain, e.g. (Riegelsberger et al., 2005). The so-called *"lack of trust"* is one of the barriers widely recognized in the adoption of new technologies (Princeton Survey Research Associates, 2002; Grabner-Kräuter and Kaluscha, 2003; Camp, 2000; Riegelsberger et al., 2005).

As mentioned before, trustworthiness is the key for any successful software, service, app or infrastructure. The notion of trustworthiness, however, is actually subject to individual interpretation. For instance, organisations require confidence in the secure handling of their business-critical data, whereas end-users may be more concerned about usability.

The role of trust with its social aspects is becoming a prominent topic for research, especially within systems that include humans as social parts as well as technical parts which are both interacting in a larger computing community. This research considers socio-economical as well as technical aspects as the foundation for studying trust and trustworthiness.

The goal of this work is twofold. First, find ways to utilise the existing structure of cyber-physical systems and the trust relationships in cyber-physical systems to balance between the amount of trust individuals place in these systems and their actual trustworthiness. We look at where and how trustworthiness should be integrated into a cyber-physical system. Second, to demonstrate how trustworthiness indications can be integrated into software systems and applications. The ultimate goal is to create a cyber-physical system that is in conformance with respect to the end-user's trust preferences, creating a personalized user-experience. The term "personalized user-experience" here means, the software provides functionalities and qualities which are useful to the end-user.

1.1 Problem Statement

The major problem arising when building trustworthiness into cyber-physical systems is the question of how to transform the complex social concept of trust into an easy-to-use technical property that targets the basic principles of trust.

Trust in cyber-physical systems is an emergent and necessary property. Trust always was one of the drivers that led to a self-reinforcing process of facilitating distribution, sharing and collaboration in society. But, the situation is different today due to communication technologies. There are major concerns on trust in handling sensitive data and valuable assets. People are hesitant in adopting new technologies when confronted with the question whether their sensitive data and assets are treated properly. These concerns are ever-increasing because of following issues:

- A growing number of criminal activities that harm more citizens. Reports about security and privacy incidents gain the attention of public media. Some groups are deliberately seeking to raise awareness about insecurity and lack of trust on the Internet[1] [2] [3].

- Business models are becoming less transparent. There are even *hidden* business roles (e.g. information aggregators and brokers (Siegel et al., 2001)), profilers and networks (Keanini et al., 2007), and delegations to third-parties (Kagal et al., 2001).

- There is a huge imbalance in terms of information and control between end-users and services and their providers.

---

[1]https://www.khanacademy.org/partner-content/nova/cybersecurity/cyber/v/cybersecurity-101 (accessed on 11 October 2018)

[2]https://oit.colorado.edu/it-security/security-awareness/email-web-security (accessed on 11 October 2018)

[3]https://www.internet-sicherheit.de/live-hacking/#live-hackingtermine (accessed on 11 October 2018)

- Because of advances in technologies used by service providers to collect more information about their users, maintaining privacy and protecting data are becoming increasingly difficult for end-users. Users' awareness about the risks is necessary. However, raising awareness alone is not sufficient. For example, toward using cookies by service providers, the end-users gained awareness and they learned how to delete the browser cookies or restrict them. Upon this reaction of end-users, new technologies such as super-cookies[4] and data aggregation has grown. These were responses from the service providers to restrictive policies taken by the users for administering their data access in social networks. These new technologies (e.g. super-cookies, location-sensitive services, data aggregation, profiling) are even less transparent and cannot be controlled by end-users.

- As users become aware of control mechanisms (e.g. deletion of cookies), service providers resort to other types of strategies to collect users' data (e.g. super-cookies, pre-filtering of search queries Yen et al. (2012); Giles (2011)). However, usage of such strategies by service providers worsens the problem of distrust by users, because they lower the transparency of their processes and therefore the users' distrust increases. The increasing number of open trials in court is an indicator that the trust on online services is in danger. Facebook's new data scandal[5] [6] [7] and the new EU Regulation 2016/679 – General Data Protection Regulation[8] – are examples of such indicators. The predominant reason causing this effect is an imbalance between the level of trust placed into a system and its actual trustworthiness, rather than a general lack of trust Solhaug and Stølen (2007); Cho et al. (2011). In other words, the level of trust may be higher or lower compared to the actual trustworthiness of the system, leading to end-users' disappointments of the adopted system and unfulfilled expectations. Hence, imbalance is a barrier to trust in the system:

  - Optimistic attitude toward the system: The case when users place an unreasonable amount of trust in the system. This means that users believe in the systems

---

[4]Super-cookies or forever cookies are a kind of tracking cookies. While many browsers allow their users to delete a regular stored browser cookie, super-cookies are harder to erase due to certain features which make them more persistent. Some websites use different types of local storage for storing the super-cookies.

[5]http://money.cnn.com/2018/04/11/technology/facebook-questions-data-privacy/index.html (accessed on 11 October 2018)

[6]https://www.theguardian.com/news/2018/mar/17/cambridge-analytica-facebook-influence-us-election (accessed on 11 October 2018)

[7]http://fortune.com/2018/03/23/facebook-data-scandal-carolyn-everson/ (accessed on 11 October 2018)

[8]https://gdpr-info.eu (accessed on 14 September 2018)

to be trustworthy more than it actually is. In this case, users are exposing themselves to risks and may suffer harm, which can also reduce their level of trust in any system in the future.

- Pessimistic attitude toward the system: The case when users place a feeble amount of trust in the system. This means that users consider the system as less trustworthy than it actually is. In this case, users are failing to benefit from using the system in high-value applications.

Therefore, a critical contribution towards higher trust in cyber-physical systems is accomplished by the support of balance between the level of trust and the level of trustworthiness of services and applications. Cyber-physical systems execute in diverse risky environments, which is acceptable as long as an adequate level of trust can be perceived in a respective context and situation. The explicit exposure of trustworthiness and the ability to analyze trustworthiness is a key factor to trigger adequate trust perceptions allowing the end-user to make risk-aware and informed decisions when interacting with a system in a given situation.

1.2 Scope

To mitigate the problems mentioned in the earlier Section 1.1, an appropriate balance between the trustworthiness level of the systems and the end-users trust thresholds is needed. Another critical point is to provide means to increase trustworthiness, in terms of methodology, functionality and evaluation.

In this book, we propose a framework that provides requirements engineering and design methods for considering trustworthiness of cyber-physical systems during design-time. In fact, providing these methods does not account for the emergence of trust. It is also necessary to understand how the methods should be used in order to provide and operate a trustworthy system. Furthermore, it is also crucial to understand how trustworthiness will be evident to the end-users in increasing their confidence and hence their level of trust. Trustworthiness spans software, services, infrastructure, and the business processes as well as technical aspects. The indications for trustworthiness of systems must be explicit and comprehensible to the end-users, so that end-users can better assess to which degree they can trust the system for specific requirements (how much and on what). Hence, we also need to investigate what are trust expectation/concerns of end-users in first place. This will help to increase the level of trustworthiness in a way that exposure to risks and hence the frequency of bad experience (disappointments) by the end-users can be reduced.

In summary, the scope of this book is the investigation of different aspects of trust, trustworthiness and their relation. We identify the characteristics of a system that contribute to trustworthiness and thereby influence trust in a positive way. Furthermore, we provide design-time solutions for building a trustworthy cyber-physical system.

1.3 Research Goals and Questions

The overall goal of this book is to deliver requirements engineering methods, design processes (process models), guidelines and tools to design trustworthy cyber-physical systems, which are distributed and connected via the Internet, and to assure their trustworthiness. To this end, the following three **Research Goals (RG)** will be pursued:

RG1 *Identifying key concepts to model trustworthiness*: This research goal is about how to specify a trustworthy system. It includes identifying key characteristics that contribute to trustworthiness. As example of such characteristics, we can consider security, privacy, non-repudiation, resilience, etc.

RG2 *Defining a design process*: This process must allow a constructive, transparent, traceable trustworthiness establishment *("trustworthiness-by-design")*. It includes the analysis of end-users' trust concerns, of means for ensuring privacy and other characteristics that contribute to trustworthiness and address identified trust concerns of end-users, of threats to trustworthiness, and the enforcement of staying trustworthy during run-time.

RG3 *Developing evaluation techniques for the analytical assessment of trustworthiness*: This research goal includes the means to collect evidence for trustworthiness. For instance, evidence of security mechanisms and performed privacy impact assessments are already available. There are different types of evidence. Some of them are intended for end-users, whereas other types are intended for certification authorities.

The research questions in this book are organized along the above goals[9]. Each of the research goals will be addressed with some research questions. Answers to these questions will guide the achievement of each research goal and consequently shape the contribution of this book. The relation between research goals and research questions is shown in Table 1.1.

Here the goals are refined to form the following **Research Questions (RQ)**, which are answered within this book:

---

[9]These research goals are also motivated by the OPTET project.

Table 1.1: Identified research questions to be answered in this book to satisfy the research goals

	Research Goals	Research Questions
RG1	Identifying key concepts to model trustworthiness	RQ1 RQ3
RG2	Defining a design process	RQ2 RQ3 RQ6
RG3	Developing evaluation techniques for the analytical assessment of trustworthiness	RQ4 RQ5

RQ1: What are the contributing characteristics that can foster trustworthiness in cyber-physical systems? Is there any classification of these characteristics in the state of the art?

RQ2: Are the existing development processes appropriate in addressing trust and trustworthiness in the system under development? What are the gaps in these development processes and how can they be addressed?

RQ3: How to elicit the end-users' trust concerns? How can trustworthiness requirements analysis be performed in a way that is uniform and in conformance with the trust concerns of the end-users?

RQ4: Which evaluation methods can be used and extended so that they support the developers in the evaluation of the achieved trustworthiness?

RQ5: Do design-time activities suffice in guaranteeing trustworthiness? If not, which activities for run-time preparation are necessary?

RQ6: How can we generate and document evidence for the trustworthiness of the system under development throughout its lifecycle (design-time and run-time) in a systematic way and in alignment with the documentation demands of certification processes?

1.4 Contribution

To answer the previously introduced research questions, this book contains four main contributions. First, we put an effort in understanding which characteristics of cyber-physical system contribute to trustworthiness. Second, we investigate how the trust expectations of end-users can be dealt with. The trustworthiness characteristics should be built into the system in conformance to the trust expectations of end-users. Third, we analyze specific methodologies, models and tools that cover design-time activities and preparation for the run-time maintenance of trustworthiness, in order to provide trustworthiness evidence at design-time and at run-time. Table 1.2 shows the relation among research goals, questions, and the corresponding contribution. The following list summarises the major four **Contributions (C)** of this book:

C1 Trustworthiness Modelling: We identify key concepts and abstractions to model trustworthiness in cyber-physical systems. This will lead to defined metrics for trustworthiness. Thus, enabling the designers to understand how to address trustworthiness requirements. Specifically, we identify which software character- istics measurably contribute to trustworthiness. These characteristics may include security, privacy, reliability, etc., depending on the application domain and the end-users' trust concerns. These models can be linked with risk analysis models of the system assets, in order to provide appropriate countermeasures. Based on these models, the designers can analyze how trust and trustworthiness should be balanced in the context of potentially adverse system behaviours. Additionally, the designers can deduce what assurances an end-user can be provided with when making a decision whether to trust the system or not. The details of C1 are presented in Chapters 4, 7 and 8.

C2 Trustworthiness-By-Design Process: We develop a design process, namely Trust**W**orthiness-**by**-**D**esign (**TWbyD**). We define an engineering process and patterns that allow building cyber-physical systems, while providing and docu- menting evidence about their trustworthiness. To this end, existing engineering processes are analyzed to identify key design patterns and process chunks that should be followed to achieve "*trustworthiness-by-design*" (e.g. ensuring privacy, reliability). Complementary, development processes that support related kinds of characteristics, such as safety and reliability, are examined to exploit knowledge obtained in related disciplines. The resulting TWbyD process is described by means of a **S**oftware **P**rocess **E**ngineering **M**eta-model[10] (**OMG's SPEM**). We also provide tool support, using the **E**clipse **P**rocess **F**ramework[11] (**EPF**). Thereby, a process handbook can be generated. The handbook as guideline is a key outcome of this contribution. The handbook helps the development team in understanding the ways to document the software engineering process used when developing the

---

[10]SPEM is used to define software and systems development processes and their components. http://www.omg.org/spec/SPEM/2.0/ (accessed on 17 August 2018)

[11]Eclipse Foundation: Eclipse Process Framework, https://www.eclipse.org/epf/ (ac- cessed on 23 July 2018)

systems. In this way, the end-users and other stakeholders of those systems gain insight and transparency in the undertaken design steps. Thus, they can see evidence and gain confidence. Furthermore, elements of processes may accompany the descriptions of applications and services to the marketplaces. Additionally, the development process provides process chunks that define how to design and implement monitoring and adaptation mechanisms to observe, govern and enforce trustworthiness during run-time. The details of C2 are further discussed in Chapter 6.

Table 1.2: The relation among research goal, questions and contribution of this book

Research Goals		Research Questions	Contributions
RG1	Identifying key concepts to model trustworthiness	**RQ1**	**C1** *TrustworthinessModelling*
		RQ3	
RG2 Defining a design process		**RQ2**	**C2** *Trustworthiness-by-design*
		RQ3	**C1** *Trustworthiness Modelling &* **C2** *Trustworthiness-by-design*
		RQ6	**C2** *Trustworthiness-by-design*
			C4 *Preparation for Certification and Run-time*
RG3	Developing evaluation techniques for the analytical assessment of trustworthiness	**RQ4**	**C3** *Trustworthiness Evaluation*
		RQ5	**C4** *Preparation for Certification and Run-time*

C3 Trustworthiness Evaluation: Another contribution of this book is the end-to-end trustworthiness evaluation of the developed services and applications. We develop a method with tool support to evaluate and analytically ensure trustworthiness. This contribution complements the "*trustworthiness-by-design*" process. The evaluation approach considers the requirements of different stakeholders and their relationships, the identified dependencies between measurable characteristics and their contribution to the overall trustworthiness of a system. Our approach and tool support complement and extend existing computational and risk assessment approaches with ways to analyze trustworthiness. For the end-to-end trustworthiness assessment during design-time, we provide a research prototype to demonstrate the tool support. The details of C3 are further discussed in Chapters 11 and 10.

C4 Preparation for Certification and Run-time: The development process of a trustworthy system, and the evaluation phase are producing evidence. The availability and accessibility of the produced evidence, and then monitoring of the trustworthiness status during run-time is also a critical issue. We introduce a structure for "*trustworthiness cases*" to document evidence in a systematic and structured way. The monitoring can be done by observing indicators derived from the evidence and providing the means to react to critical situations. We also provide a support for preparing the monitoring and maintenance system. The full coverage of the design- and run-time is essential to allow consumers to make informed decisions. The details of C4 are further discussed in Chapters 12 and 13.

All above-mentioned contributions are enclosed in the proposed **TrustWorthiness Man**agement (**TW-Man**) framework. The framework is designed to facilitate the management of trustworthiness. It is a collection of methods and patterns for specification, analysis and management of trustworthiness with their corresponding tool support. An overview of the TW-Man framework is presented in Chapter 3.

1.5 Structure of the Book

This book addresses the problems and solutions outlined above. The following chapters present a deeper discussion of the framework and methodologies developed here. Figure 1.2 gives an overview of the structure of the book.

Part I

Chapter 2 presents central concepts and background information on trust and trustworthiness. Current definitions of trust and their implications are discussed. A review of the trust and trustworthiness relationships is given. Furthermore, our definitions of these two concepts is presented.

Chapter 3 presents the overall structure of the TW-Man framework. It starts by providing a definition and a discussion of trust and trustworthiness as it applies to cyber-physical systems. Then, some requirements for the framework are highlighted, and a detailed overview of the TW-Man model is given. Furthermore, we

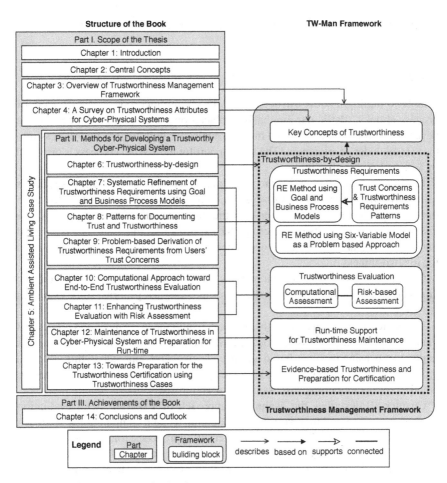

Figure 1.2: The structure of this book

present a description of the ways in which the framework can be used. A general discussion on the possible uses is presented, with examples for clarity.

Chapter 4 provides a comprehensive survey of the contemporary trustworthiness goals and categories in recent trust literature. The end result is a deeper understanding of trustworthiness.

Chapter 5 is devoted to the case study used to illustrate the ideas presented in this book. The selected domain for the case study is **Ambient Assisted Living** (**AAL**). This book uses AAL use case as a running example to validate its approach in selected domain where trustworthiness is seen as a key factor to engage consumers and providers.

Part II

Chapter 6 highlights how trustworthiness-by-design incorporates the concept of process chunks. Particular emphasis is placed on generating guidelines for the developer to follow the proposed methodologies for building trustworthiness into the system under development. The tool support for the TWbyD process is provided by EPF as Eclipse plug-ins.

In Chapter 7, the issue of how to perform trustworthiness requirements analysis using TW-Man is presented. A discussion on how to specify and analyze trustworthiness requirements in accordance with the trust concerns of the end-users is also given. Our requirements engineering (RE) approach to this issue is a combined method using goal and business process modelling enhanced with a specific notation for trustworthiness.

Chapter 8 provides requirement patterns for eliciting and documenting trustworthiness requirements. To illustrate the use of the designed patterns, some examples are given.

In Chapter 9, an alternative trustworthiness requirements analysis and refinement method is presented. A discussion on how to analyze and refine trustworthiness requirements using problem-based approach is give. Our approach to this issue is a problem-based method using six-variable approach enhanced with some specific notation for documenting trust assumptions and trustworthiness requirements.

Chapter 10 describes the evaluation approach of TW-Man. Our evaluation method for end-to-end trustworthiness evaluation using a computational approach is presented. A brief discussion of different approaches for the evaluation of trustworthiness is provided. The basics of the computational approach toward evaluation and analytical approaches are also provided. Then, we present our evaluation method for end-to-end trustworthiness evaluation using a computational approach. A basic architecture of a prototype is also presented.

Chapter 11 describes our extension to the approach from Chapter 10. We present how our method uses a complementary way on the topic of the evaluation of trustworthiness.

In Chapter 12, the necessary components and design-decisions for a solution in order to maintain trustworthiness during run-time is provided.

Chapter 13 shows our approach towards documenting the evidence generated during the design-time in the form of "trustworthiness cases". The structure of the trustworthiness cases is also discussed in this chapter.

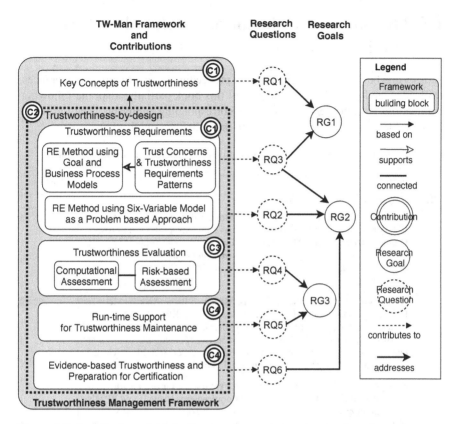

Figure 1.3: Contributions of this book, research questions and research goals

Part III

A discussion on the framework is provided in Chapter 14. Finally, we conclude our work and suggest directions for the future work.

Figure 1.3 illustrates how the contribution of this book as TW-Man Framework contributes to research questions and addresses research goals.

1.6 Overview of Publications Related to this Book

Parts of this book have been published in proceedings of international conferences, workshops and journals. The chapters of this book partially adapt the following publications with the permissions of the corresponding publishers. The following table (Table 1.3) matches the chapters to the individual publications.

Table 1.3: Publications on which the contributions and chapters of this book are based

No.	Publication	Chapters
Trustworthiness Modelling (Contribution 1)		
1	Nazila Gol Mohammadi, Sachar Paulus, Mohamed Bishr, Andreas Metzger, Holger Könnecke, Sandro Hartenstein, Klaus Pohl: **An Analysis of Software Quality Attributes and Their Contribution to Trustworthiness.** *Proceedings of the 3rd International Conference on Cloud Computing and Services Science*, (CloudSecGov 2013): pp. 542-552. © 2013 SCITEPRESS (Science and Technology Publications, Lda.)	4
2	Nazila Gol Mohammadi, Sachar Paulus, Mohamed Bishr, Andreas Metzger, Holger Könnecke, Sandro Hartenstein, Thorsten Weyer, Klaus Pohl: **Trustworthiness Attributes and Metrics for Engineering Trusted Internet-Based Software Systems.** *Cloud Computing and Services Science, the series Communications in Computer and Information Science, CLOSER 2013*, Selected Papers: pp. 19-35. © Springer International Publishing Switzerland 2014	4
3	Nazila Gol Mohammadi, Maritta Heisel: **A Framework for Systematic Analysis and Modelling of Trustworthiness Requirements Using i* and BPMN.** *Proceedings of 13th International Conference on Trust, Privacy and Security in Digital Business (TrustBus 2016)*: pp. 3-18. © Springer International Publishing Switzerland 2016	7
4	Nazila Gol Mohammadi, Maritta Heisel: **Enhancing Business Process Models with Trustworthiness Requirements.** *10th IFIP WG 11.11 International Conference Trust: Management X (IFIPTM 2016)*: pp. 33-51. © IFIP International Federation for Information Processing 2016	7
5	Nazila Gol Mohammadi, Maritta Heisel: **A Framework for Systematic Refinement of Trustworthiness Requirements.** In *Information 2017, 8(2), 46*	7
6	Nazila Gol Mohammadi, Maritta Heisel: **Patterns for Identification of Trust Concerns and Specifications of Trustworthiness Requirements.** *21st European Conference on Pattern Languages of Programs (EuroPLoP 2016)*. © 2016 ACM	8

No.	Publication	Chapters
Trustworthiness-By-Design (Contribution 2)		
7	Nazila Gol Mohammadi, Nelufar Ulfat-Bunyadi, Maritta Heisel: **Problem-based Derivation of Trustworthiness Requirements from Users' Trust Concerns**. *16th Annual Conference on Privacy, Security and Trust (PST 2018)*: pp. 1-10. © 2018 IEEE	9
8	Nazila Gol Mohammadi, Torsten Bandyszak, Sachar Paulus, Per Håkon Meland, Thorsten Weyer, Klaus Pohl: **Extending Software Development Methodologies to Support Trustworthiness-by-Design**. *Proceedings of the CAiSE Forum at the 27th International Conference on Advanced Information Systems Engineering (CAiSE Forum 2015)*: pp. 213-220	6
9	Nazila Gol Mohammadi, Torsten Bandyszak, Sachar Paulus, Per Håkon Meland, Thorsten Weyer, Klaus Pohl: **Extending Development Methodologies with Trustworthiness-By-Design for Socio-Technical Systems**. *7th International Conference Trust and Trustworthy Computing, TRUST 2014, (Extended Abstract)*: pp. 206-207. © Springer International Publishing Switzerland 2014	6
10	Sachar Paulus, Nazila Gol Mohammadi, Thorsten Weyer: **Trustworthy Software Development**. *Communications and Multimedia Security, CMS 2013*: pp. 233-24. © IFIP International Federation for Information Processing 2013	6
Trustworthiness Evaluation (Contribution 3)		
11	Nazila Gol Mohammadi, Torsten Bandyszak, Costas Kalogiros, Michalis Kanakakis, Thorsten Weyer: **A Framework for Evaluating the End-to-End Trustworthiness**. *14th IEEE International Conference on Trust, Security and Privacy in Computing and Communications (TrustCom/BigDataSE/ISPA 2015)*: pp. 638-645. © 2015 IEEE	10
12	Nazila Gol Mohammadi, Torsten Bandyszak, Abigail Goldsteen, Costas Kalogiros, Thorsten Weyer, Micha Moffie, Bassem I. Nasser, Mike Surridge: **Combining Risk-Management and Computational Approaches for Trustworthiness Evaluation of Socio-Technical Systems**. *Proceedings of the CAiSE Forum at the 27th International Conference on Advanced Information Systems Engineering (CAiSE Forum 2015)*: pp. 237-244	11
Preparation for Certification and Run-time (Contribution 4)		
13	Nazila Gol Mohammadi, Torsten Bandyszak, Micha Moffie, Xiaoyu Chen, Thorsten Weyer, Costas Kalogiros, Bassem I. Nasser, Mike Surridge: **Maintaining Trustworthiness of Socio-Technical Systems at Run-Time**. *In Proceedings of 11th International Conference on Trust, Privacy and Security in Digital Business (TrustBus 2014)*: pp. 1-12. © Springer International Publishing Switzerland 2014	12
14	Azadeh Alebrahim, Nazila Gol Mohammadi, Maritta Heisel: **Challenges in Rendering and Maintaining Trustworthiness for Long-Living Software Systems**. *Collaborative Workshop on Evolution and Maintenance of Long-Living-Systems (EMLS). Software Engineering 2014*: pp. 103-105	12

No.	Publication	Chapters
15	Torsten Bandyszak, Nazila Gol Mohammadi, Mohamed Bishr, Abigail Goldsteen, Micha Moffie, Bassem I. Nasser, Sandro Hartenstein, Symeon Meichanetzoglou: **Cyber-Physical Systems Design for Run-time Trustworthiness Maintenance Supported by Tools**. *REFSQ Workshops, International Workshop on Requirements Engineering for Self-Adaptive and Cyber-Physical Systems (RESACS 2015)*: pp. 148-155	**12**
16	Abigail Goldsteen, Micha Moffie, Torsten Bandyszak, Nazila Gol Mohammadi, Xiaoyu Chen, Symeon Meichanetzoglou, Sotiris Ioannidis, Panos Chatziadam: **A Tool for Monitoring and Maintaining System Trustworthiness at Run-time**. *REFSQ Workshops, International Workshop on Requirements Engineering for Self-Adaptive and Cyber-Physical Systems (RESACS 2015)*: pp. 142-147	**12**
17	Francesco Di Cerbo, Pascal Bisson, Alan Hartman, Sebastien Keller, PerHåkon Meland, Micha Moffie, Nazila Gol Mohammadi, Sachar Paulus, Stuart Short: **Towards Trustworthiness Assurance in the Cloud**. *Cyber Security and Privacy (CSP Forum 2013)*: pp. 3-15. © Springer-Verlag Berlin Heidelberg 2013	**13**
18	Francesco Di Cerbo, Nazila Gol Mohammadi, Sachar Paulus: **Evidence-Based Trustworthiness of Internet-Based Services Through Controlled Software Development**. *Cyber Security and Privacy - 4th Cyber Security and Privacy Innovation Forum, (CSP 2015)*: pp. 91-102. © Springer International Publishing Switzerland 2015	**13**
19	Nazila Gol Mohammadi, Nelufar Ulfat-Bunyadi, Maritta Heisel: **Trustworthiness Cases – Toward Preparation for the Trustworthiness Certification**. *In Proceedings of 15th International Conference on Trust, Privacy and Security in Digital Business (TrustBus 2018)*: pp. 244-259. © Springer Nature Switzerland AG 2018	**13**

We had a major contribution in all of these publications. The lead author of most of these publications is Nazila Gol Mohammadi. In the publication number 10, the lead author is Sachar Paulus. Nazila Gol Mohammadi had major contributions. In the publication number 17 and 18, all the authors contributed equally. In the publication 15 and 16, Torsten Bandyszak and Abigail Goldsteen are the lead authors, respectively. Nazila Gol Mohammadi had major contributions in the both papers. The mathematical foundation and formula composition in publication number 11 were contributed by Costas Kalogiros and Michalis Kanakakis.

Additionally, some of the papers have contributed to the deliverables of the European project *"OPerational Trustworthiness Enabling Technologies[12] (OPTET)"*.

---

[12]The EU-funded project with grant no. 317631 under 7th framework programme https://cordis.europa.eu/project/rcn/105733/factsheet/en (accessed on 15 August 2018), www.optet.eu (accessed on 10 September 2016)

The chapters of this book are based on the papers and not directly on the project deliverables. Table 1.4 matches the contributions of the papers to individual deliverables from the OPTET project.

Table 1.4: Relation of our publications to the OPTET deliverables

No.	Publications	Contribution to Deliverables
1	Nazila Gol Mohammadi, Sachar Paulus, Mohamed Bishr, Andreas Metzger, Holger Könnecke, Sandro Hartenstein, Klaus Pohl: **An Analysis of Software Quality Attributes and Their Contribution to Trustworthiness.** *Proceedings of the 3rd International Conference on Cloud Computing and Services Science, (CLOSER 2013):* pp. 542-552	D3.1 _ Initial Concepts and Abstractions to Model Trustworthiness
2	Nazila Gol Mohammadi, Sachar Paulus, Mohamed Bishr, Andreas Metzger, Holger Könnecke, Sandro Hartenstein, Thorsten Weyer, Klaus Pohl: **Trustworthiness Attributes and Metrics for Engineering Trusted Internet-Based Software Systems.** *Cloud Computing and Services Science, the series Communications in Computer and Information Science, CLOSER 2013,* (Selected Papers): pp. 19-35	
3	Sachar Paulus, Nazila Gol Mohammadi, Thorsten Weyer: **Trustworthy Software Development.** *Communications and Multimedia Security, CMS* 2013: pp. 233-24	
4	Francesco Di Cerbo, Pascal Bisson, Alan Hartman, Sebastien Keller, Per Håkon Meland, Micha Moffie, Nazila Gol Mohammadi, Sachar Paulus, Stuart Short: **Towards Trustworthiness Assurance in the Cloud.** *Cyber Security and Privacy, (CSP Forum 2013):* pp. 3-15	D3.2 _ Initial Trustworthiness-by-Design Process and Tool Support
5	Nazila Gol Mohammadi, Torsten Bandyszak, Sachar Paulus, Per Håkon Meland, Thorsten Weyer, Klaus Pohl: **Extending Development Methodologies with Trustworthiness-By-Design for Socio-Technical Systems.** *7th International Conference Trust and Trustworthy Computing (TRUST 2014):* pp.206-207	
6	Nazila Gol Mohammadi, Torsten Bandyszak, Sachar Paulus, Per Håkon Meland, Thorsten Weyer, Klaus Pohl: **Extending Software Development Methodologies to Support Trustworthiness-by-Design.** *Proceedings of the CAiSE Forum at the 27th International Conference on Advanced Information Systems Engineering, 2015:* pp. 213-220	

No.	Publications	Contribution to Deliverables
7	Nazila Gol Mohammadi, Torsten Bandyszak, Costas Kalogiros, Michalis Kanakakis, Thorsten Weyer: **A Framework for Evaluating the End-to-End Trustworthiness**. *14th IEEE International Conference on Trust, Security and Privacy in Computing and Communications (TrustCom/BigDataSE/ISPA 2015)*: pp. 638-645	D3.3 _ Trustworthiness Evaluation Techniques and Prototypes
8	Nazila Gol Mohammadi, Torsten Bandyszak, Abigail Goldsteen, Costas Kalogiros, Thorsten Weyer, Micha Moffie, Bassem I. Nasser, Mike Surridge: **Combining Risk-Management and Computational Approaches for Trustworthiness Evaluation of Socio-Technical Systems.** *Proceedings of the CAiSE Forum at the 27th International Conference on Advanced Information Systems Engineering, (CAiSE Forum 2015)*: pp. 237-244	
9	Nazila Gol Mohammadi, Torsten Bandyszak, Micha Moffie, Xiaoyu Chen, Thorsten Weyer, Costas Kalogiros, Bassem I. Nasser, Mike Surridge: **Maintaining Trustworthiness of Socio-Technical Systems at Run-Time.** *In Proceedings of 11th International Conference on Trust, Privacy and Security in Digital Business (TrustBus 2014)*: pp. 1-12	D6.1 _ Catalogue of Trust and Trustworthiness Events and Mitigation Actions
10	Abigail Goldsteen, Micha Moffie, Torsten Bandyszak, Nazila Gol Mohammadi, Xiaoyu Chen, Symeon Meichanetzoglou, Sotiris Ioannidis, Panos Chatziadam: **A Tool for Monitoring and Maintaining System Trustworthiness at Run-time.** *REFSQ Workshops, International Workshop on Requirements Engineering for Self-Adaptive and Cyber-Physical Systems, (RESACS 2015)*: pp. 142-147	D6.4.1 _ Measurement and Management Tools
11	Torsten Bandyszak, Nazila Gol Mohammadi, Mohamed Bishr, Abigail Goldsteen, Micha Moffie, Bassem I. Nasser, Sandro Hartenstein, Symeon Meichanetzoglou: **Cyber-Physical Systems Design for Run-time Trustworthiness Maintenance Supported by Tools**. *REFSQ Workshops, International Workshop on Requirements Engineering for Self-Adaptive and Cyber-Physical Systems (RESACS 2015)*: pp. 148-155	

2 Central Concepts

This chapter introduces the concept of trust from different perspectives and moves on to define the meaning of trustworthiness as thought of in this book. We then identify the relation between trust and trustworthiness. Finally, we discuss how they relate to cyber-physical systems.

2.1 Trust

Trust is an important aspect of our daily life in society. Luhmann (1979) consider trust as a basic need of human life. Without a foundation of trust, our society may suffer the inevitable collapse (Bok, 1999). Bok stated it clearly that anyone benefits by living in a world in which trust exists. Trust builds the foundation for interpersonal relationships and cooperation, and contributes to stability in society. Many literature sources have aimed to provide insights into various aspects of understanding the nature of trust.

However, there is no systematic classification of who and how people trust (Shapiro, 1987), since different disciplines focus on different aspects of trust. Psychologists are interested on how personality influences trust, while economists emphasize the rational choice, and sociologists focus on social structures (Luhmann, 1979).

In the Oxford dictionary the word *"trust"* is defined as *"a firm belief in the reliability, truth, or ability of someone or something"*. Understanding why people trust and how trust shapes social relations, has been a central interest in various research domains. In social conceptualizations, trust tends to be associated with terms such as honesty, integrity and reliability, which further describes the concept of how people use the term *"to have faith in others"*.

A trust relationship is established between two actors. The actors in trust relationships are referred to as trustor (the trusting actor) and trustee (the trusted actor). The trustor embodies the subject that places trust on another entity/actor. Figure 2.1 shows the trust establishment structure.

Trust is required in situations in which there is some level of uncertainty or risk regarding the outcome, especially in the case that the outcome has some value to the trustor (Luhmann, 1979).

© Springer Fachmedien Wiesbaden GmbH, part of Springer Nature 2019
N. Gol Mohammadi, *Trustworthy Cyber-Physical Systems*,
https://doi.org/10.1007/978-3-658-27488-7_2

Figure 2.1: Overview of the trust relation

Investigations of trust aspects in the context of **I**nformation and **C**ommunication **T**echnology (ICT) play an important role in order to influence the adoption of new technologies. Trust research in ICT has received major attention recently. This book aims to better understand people and their trust perceptions towards new ICT, particularly cyber-physical systems. Therefore, in this chapter, we present various aspects of trust research, including trust constructs and risks associated with ICT.

One of the problems occurring when studying a notion like trust is that everyone experiences trust, and hence has a predefined personal view on what trust means (Golembiewski and McConkie, 1975). This is the first intuitive explanation of why trust has multiple and varying definitions. A second explanation is the fact that there are multiple definitions of trust simply because there are that many types of trust (Deutsch, 1962; Shapiro, 1987). In the following, we present some of frequently cited definitions in the field and provide our understanding of trust.

Definitions of Trust

The following definition, provided by Gambetta (1988), has been adopted by many researchers, e.g. Jøsang et al. (2007); Abdul-Rahman and Hailes (2000):
Definition 1: *"Trust is a particular level of the subjective probability with which an agent (trustor) assesses that another agent or group of agents (trustee) will perform a particular action".*

In the moment of placing trust, the trustor cannot monitor the performance of the trustee. It may even be the case that the trustor has no capability or ability to ever monitor the trustee and to what extent it affects the actions of the trustor.

The most important components taken from this definition are the subjectivity of trust, and the trustor's expectation on the trustee. Trust is tied to the performance of the trustee which affects the actions of the trusting agent (trustor).

Jøsang differentiates between reliability trust and decision trust.

Reliability, also referred to as evaluation trust (Jøsang et al., 2007; Jøsang, 2016), is defined as:
Definition 2: *"Trust is the subjective probability by which an individual, trustor, expects that another individual, trustee, performs a given action on which its welfare depends."*

Decision trust (Jøsang et al., 2007; Jøsang, 2016) is defined as:

Definition 3: *"Trust is the extent to which a given party, trustor, is willing to depend on something or somebody, trustee, in a given situation with a feeling of relative security, even though negative consequences are possible."*

The definition of reliability trust is close to the definition of trust provided by Gambetta. The definition of decision trust extends the previous definition of trust by introducing the notion of risk (Luhmann, 1979). Furthermore, it states that trust is situation-dependent.

Assuming that the context of trust describes the context or the application domain in which one entity assesses the trustworthiness of another one, e.g. splinting a fracture or providing a service for health care, situation dependence is a step beyond context-dependence. For instance, a person might not trust their ear, nose and throat doctor to splint a fracture (context), but make an exception in the situation of an emergency.

Mui et al. (2001) extend the definition provided by Gambetta (Definition 1 by adding the information about how trust is established.

Definition 4: *"Trust is a subjective expectation an agent has about another's future behavior based on the history of their encounters."*

This definition clearly states the idea that trust is a subjective concept, and depends on the expectations of the trustor.

Sztompka (2000) defines trust as:

Definition 5: *"A bet about the future contingent actions of others".*

The components of this definition are belief and commitment. There is a belief or confidence that placing trust in a person will lead to an expected outcome.

Figure 2.2 shows the trust relation between trustor and trustee. Based on the above mentioned definitions the notion of trust decision as well as trust expectation and agreement is assigned to the relation of trust. The trust relation is established when the trustor decides to trust the trustee and thus makes the trust decision. The trust decision depends on the trust expectations of the trustor. After the trust decision is made (commitment to rely on trustee), a trust agreement is established. This agreement is either explicit when it is documented, otherwise it is implicit.

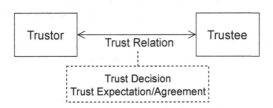

Figure 2.2: Extended overview of the trust relation

In this book, the definition provided by Sztompka will also serve as basis for the definition of trust in cyber-physical systems. In the following, trust is defined as a "bet" about the future contingent actions of a system. Trust is the user's belief that a system behaves like expected, even in extraordinary situations.

We broaden the scope of the definition provided by Sztompka in order to include software-intensive, cyber-physical systems as potential trustees. Because of the delegation of tasks to cyber-physical systems, it can be said that the trustworthiness of such systems is a key concern that needs to be fostered and even engineered into these systems to maintain high levels of trust within society.

Our Definition of Trust

We define trust as:

> **Definition 6:** A *"bet" about the future contingent actions of a cyber-physical system. There is a belief or confidence of a user that placing trust in the system will lead to an expected outcome.*

The components of this definition also include belief and commitment. There is a belief that placing trust in a software or a system will lead to a good outcome. The belief results in a commitment to actually place trust and take an action to use the system under consideration.

This means, when a user decides to use a service, e.g. a health care service on the web, then she/he is confident that it will meet her/his expectations.

Rather than focusing on trust in individuals, this book focuses on the cyber-physical systems as well as its software systems as the trustee.

Properties of Trust

In this section, we briefly mention the identified properties of trust that are relevant when transferring the concept to cyber-physical systems. The following properties are usually assigned to trust (Abdul-Rahman and Hailes, 2000; Marsh, 1994):

- Trust is subjective, i.e. the trust of a trustor "Alice" in trustee "Bob" does not need to be the same as the trust of any other trustor "Christian" in the same trustee "Bob".

- Trust is asymmetric, i.e. one cannot expect the trust of "Alice" towards "Bob" to be the same as the trust of "Bob" towards "Alice".

- Trust is context-dependent and situation-dependent. If "Alice" trusts "Bob" in the context of providing medical service, it does not include that "Alice" trusts "Bob" also in providing secure online bank transfers. Hence, there is a difference in trusting a trustee in different contexts or application domains.

- Trust is dynamic and non-monotonic, i.e. over time and based on experience, trust can increase as well as decrease.

There are many works on recommendation-based or reputation-based trust. In this book, we focus on evidence-based trust. An establishment of evidence-based trust is necessary particularly in systems with no available recommendations or reputations. In some cases, only little, if any, direct experience is available.

2.2 Trustworthiness

Similar to the previous section for the notion of trust, we describe the general notion of trustworthiness and its meaning in the social context, where the trustee is an individual. Then, we move toward defining trustworthiness under consideration of a cyber-physical system as trustee.

Mcknight and Chervany (1996) define a concept called trusting beliefs. Trusting beliefs means the extent to which the trustor believes and feels that the trustee is trustworthy in the given situation. This corresponds to the definitions of trust introduced earlier. To have trusting beliefs in someone else means that the expectations are focused on the trustworthiness of the trusted person. Mcknight and Chervany mention the following attributes as part of the trustee for being worthy of trust (trustworthy): to be benevolent, honest, competent or/and predictable. Benevolent means that the person is willing to serve another's interest. Honest means proving the willingness to arranging and fulfilling agreements to do so. Competent means that the person is able to serve another's interests. Predictable means that one's willingness and ability to serve another's interests does not vary or change over time. A person with these qualities is considered as trustworthy, and interaction with this person would be expected to have a positive outcome.

Figure 2.3 shows the complete model of trust relation between trustor and trustee. The trust decision is taken by the trustor based on her/his expectation and her/his risk evaluation in involving the trustee. This decision can be influenced by the trustor's properties, e.g. age, cultural background. Once the trustor makes a decision and places trust in the trustee, the trustee should keep the trust relation. This means that the trustee should behave as expected or agreed. If a violation arises, the established trust relation will be harmed. Once the trust relation is harmed or lost, there is often no corrective action possible to regain the trust.

The trustee should be worthy of trust by respecting the trust agreement of meeting the trust expectation of the trustor. For instance, a trustor expects a trustee to provide data storage services. The trustor trusts the trustee on the availability of the critical data. This does not include that the storage provider is also trusted related to the integrity or confidentiality of the stored data.

Trustworthiness is the property of a trustee. Trustworthiness can be supported by the capabilities of a trustee. These capabilities are considered as trustworthiness attributes.

In the next section, we will detail the notion of trustworthiness and expand the relevance of this notion to cyber-physical systems.

Definitions of Trustworthiness

In the previous section, we described the general notion of trustworthiness and its meaning in the social context. Above (cf. Definition 6), the focus was already narrowed down by defining trust under consideration of a cyber-physical system as trustee. In the following, we give definitions of trustworthiness in relevance to the cyber-physical systems as well as discuss the most important aspects of trustworthiness. More specifically, we formulate trustworthiness as a system property with several dimensions, namely a set of measurable properties to be used during assessment.

The term "trustworthiness" is not consistently used in literature. Trustworthiness has been used sometimes as a synonym for security and other times for dependability. However, security is not the only aspect of trustworthiness. Most existing approaches for building trustworthiness into the system assume that one-dimensional properties of services, such as certifications or the implementation of certain technologies and methodologies, lead to trustworthiness of these services.

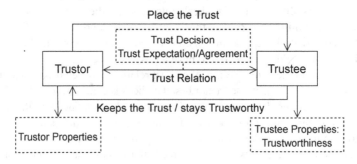

Figure 2.3: Overview of the trust and trustworthiness relation

Gärtner et al. (2014) consider maintaining security for software systems as the only trustworthiness factor. The National Computer Security Center (NCSC) has solely considered security in its promoted standard for Trusted Computer System Evaluation Criteria (TCSEC) (Department of Defense, 1985).

In 1990, some researchers started to use the term "trustworthiness" in a different scope. For instance, Parnas et al. (1990) define trustworthiness as follows:

Definition 7: *"A product (software as product) is trustworthy if we believe that the probability of it having a potentially catastrophic flaw is acceptably low".*

Parnas et al. define trustworthiness as a measure of the probability of a serious flaw remaining after testing and review. In fact, they believe that inspecting and testing can increase trustworthiness.

The essential component of this definition is the "degree" to which software engineering techniques such as enhanced test, reviews, and inspections could be used to reduce the likelihood of errors in the development and maintenance lifecycle. This implies that trustworthiness depends on the development and maintenance lifecycle.

Amoroso et al. (1994) define trustworthiness as follows:

Definition 8: *"The trustworthiness of software is the degree of confidence that exists that it meets a set of requirements".*

Relevant here is the phrase "degree of confidence". This definition leads to the conclusion that trustworthiness depends on decisions made by individuals or groups of individuals evaluating software. Furthermore, the definition provided by Amoroso et al. highlights that the result of the evaluation refers to a set of requirements. Hence, trustworthiness is dependent upon the selected set of requirements.

Similarly, Li et al. (2009) define trustworthiness of software as worthy of being trusted to fulfill requirements which may be needed for a particular software component, application, or system.

Finally, Avizienis et al. (2004) define trustworthiness as follows:

Definition 9: *"Trustworthiness is an assurance that the system will perform as expected".*

Here, truthworthiness is defined similar to dependability, both concepts being equivalent in their goals and addressing comparable threats.

Our Definition of Trustworthiness

The above-mentioned definitions of trustworthiness are not contradictory, and they extend the dimension of trustworthiness from being only a concern of security. We base our understanding of trustworthiness on these definitions.

We can consider cyber-physical systems to be worthy of users' trust if they permit confidence in satisfying a set of relevant requirements or expectations (cf. Definition 8 by Amoroso et al.).

We define trustworthiness as:

> **Definition 10:** *A quality of the cyber-physical system that potentially influences the trust in the system in a positive way.*

Cyber-physical systems are to be made trustworthy in order to gain the users' trust. Based on the definition provided by Avizienis et al. (cf. Definition 9), trustworthiness of a cyber-physical system in general can be defined as the assurance that the system will perform as expected, or meets certain requirements. These certain requirements express the expectations of the users in order to place their trust in the system. Their trust expectations can be manifested as trustworthiness requirements. Trustworthiness is a property of a cyber-physical system that reduces the probability of unexpected outcomes.

As we mentioned earlier, trust is subjective, i.e. two different users may have different levels of trust for the same system depending on social factors such as age, gender, cultural background, or the level of experience with cyber-physical systems. Furthermore, the individual needs define the concept of trust for each user differently. As an example, business organizations require confidence about their business-critical data, whereas an elderly person using a health care service (end-users) may be more concerned about usability.

Likewise, trustworthiness is domain and application dependent. For instance, in a home monitoring system, an insurance company requires confidence about its business-critical data, and usability plays an important role for the end-users of the system. Whereas, in safety-critical domains (e.g. automotive and avionics), safety and failure tolerance of a system might be of a higher priority than its usability.

Hence, software systems and services need to be made trustworthy to mitigate the risks in using systems and address trust concerns of their users.

Based on the definition of trustworthiness by Avizienis et al. (2004) (cf. Definitions 9), we extend our definition of trustworthiness (cf. Definition 10) in the following way:

> **Definition 10 (extended)** *Trustworthiness also means that there is an assurance that the cyber-physical system will perform as expected, or meets certain trustworthiness requirements.*

With a focus on trustworthiness of cyber-physical systems, we use our introduced definitions of trustworthiness and provide a collection of trustworthiness attributes (cf. Chapter 4). We analyze quality attributes and their contribution to trustworthiness, and present a comprehensive set of trustworthiness attributes that should be considered in the design of trustworthy cyber-physical systems. A wide range of quality attributes is covered, instead of focusing only on one specific area, e.g. security, availability or reliability. This allows us to measure overall trustworthiness as the degrees to which relevant quality attributes are satisfied (cf. Chapter 10).

Trustworthiness attributes represent qualities of the system that potentially influence trust in a positive way. For objectively measuring these trustworthiness attributes, metrics can be used. Hence, trustworthiness metrics serve the purpose of objectively measuring system properties that characterize and contribute to trustworthiness attributes. Trustworthiness is a potentially crucial aspect of distributed cyber-physical systems. We consider it as a multi-dimensional construct combining specific attributes (cf. Chapters 4 and 9).

Properties of Trustworthiness

We now further analyze in detail some specific properties of trustworthiness that are relevant to this book (based on (Cho et al., 2011; Solhaug and Stølen, 2007; Jøsang et al., 2005; Marsh and Dibben, 2005; Walker et al., 2003)):

• In contrast to trust, trustworthiness is objective. It means that performing the same test many times under the same conditions and applying the same assumptions, it will always yield the same result. Additionally, trustworthiness does not depend on the subjective trust level a particular user requires of a specific system. This is the reason why trustworthiness is the fundamental information needed by trustors in order to make informed decisions on whether to trust the system to provide an acceptable outcome (on which his/her welfare may depend).

• The trustworthiness level of the system can be considered as an increasing function of invested effort to make the system trustworthy. Hence, higher trustworthiness comes with a higher monetary cost, e.g. invested time and resources.

• Trustworthiness is not constant over time, hence developers have to make continuous effort in order to maintain or improve the trustworthiness level of their product at run-time. This property results from the consideration that there are major potential factors at run-time which may negatively affect a system's trustworthiness (threats), and thus decrease its trustworthiness level. Therefore, the developers have to follow a trustworthiness maintenance process.

- It may not always be possible to improve the degree of satisfaction of the application with regard to an attribute, without negatively affecting it with regard to another, both contributing to trustworthiness. A common example of this inherent trade-off arises between access control and usability.

- In the case of a system composed of an arbitrary number of technical and social components, each being characterized by a determined (certified) level of trustworthiness for each attribute, we may define *"end-to-end trustworthiness"* (of the whole system). Its value depends on the trustworthiness of each individual component and on the system structure.

The evaluation of a specific system component is associated with a set of attributes that are relevant to its purpose. Thus, trustworthiness quantifies the degree of satisfaction of a component with respect to each particular relevant trustworthiness attribute, by determining the value of the respective quality metric. Trustworthiness attributes can be clustered into categories according to the general system property to which they are contributing (cf. Chapter 4). For instance, response time is a member of the "performance" category. Based on our definition of trustworthiness, we consider trustworthiness of one component as a vector of all selected trustworthiness attributes. This detailed representation of trustworthiness is aligned with the definition of trust and trustworthiness by other researchers.

Trustworthiness is relative. Trustworthiness depends on the considered attributes, e.g. even if a system is trustworthy in respect to some quality of service like performance, it is not necessarily trustworthy in being secure.

When studying attributes conducive to trustworthiness, it is important to identify two types of attributes:

- Trustworthiness attributes that have the potential to give the trustor a perception of the system's trustworthiness prior to consenting to use the system. We call these "perceptive trustworthiness attributes".

- Trustworthiness attributes that ensure the trusted individual or system will act according to well defined criteria as expected by the trustor. We call these "operational trustworthiness attributes".

Trustworthiness can then be defined as the combination of perceptive and operational trustworthiness attributes so that a system always gives trustworthiness cues to the trustor and then reinforces these cues by honouring the placed trust.

Note that in this book, we strictly adhere to the perspective of a to-be-constructed system. Therefore, we will ignore potential trustworthiness (or trust) attributes like reputation or similar issues representing other users' feedback since they will only be available when the system is in use.

2.3 Cyber-Physical Systems and their Trustworthiness

Cyber-Physical Systems (CPS) comprise humans as well as software and hardware components. Additionally, they are distributed and connected via the Internet, and are able to dynamically adapt to context changes (Broy et al., 2012). Cyber-physical systems include humans, organizations, and their information systems that are used to achieve certain goals (Sommerville, 2016). These software-intensive systems often perform critical tasks, and the consequences of software failures become tangible in terms of threats to the physical environment. For instance, security vulnerabilities that may be exploited by malicious attacks are severe threats to cyber-physical systems that control critical infrastructures such as vehicle-to-vehicle communication systems (Zalewski et al., 2013).

In cyber-physical systems, people or organizations communicate and collaborate with other people and organizations by means of technology rather than face-to-face communication or collaboration (Whitworth, 2009). The delegation of tasks to such cyber-physical systems and relying on them by individuals or organizations entails establishing some level of trust in such systems. Hence, decisions to trust these systems heavily depend on their trustworthiness, which is especially crucial for software components. We consider trustworthiness as an objective system property that can be measured in terms of several software quality attributes and corresponding metrics.

The relation between trust and trustworthiness concepts always depends on decision-making processes which have to be performed by users of the system explicitly or implicitly considering the risk and possible consequences. There could be an imbalance between the level of trust in the system and its trustworthiness with the possibility of two extreme cases. A typical situation can be described by a highly conservative user missing out on a potential benefit of the system due to her/his lack of trust. Another typical situation can demonstrate the opposite point, when a highly optimistic user takes ill-advised risk by using the system (data misuse (Harris and Goode, 2004), etc.).

Targeting the balance between trust and trustworthiness is an important task during development. The balance between trust and trustworthiness is a core issue for cyber-physical systems development because any imbalance (over-cautiousness or misplaced trust) could lead to severe consequences for example, by preventing legitimate interactions with the cyber-physical system. To bridge the gap resulting from the asymmetry between trust and trustworthiness, it is necessary to make the trustworthiness of a system evident to stakeholders of these systems.

Hence, there are major concerns about the trustworthiness of cyber-physical systems, since the underestimation of side-effects of untrustworthy systems and mismanagement of the vital and critical trust requirements has led to cyber-crime, e-frauds, cyber-terrorism, and sabotage. Reports show an increased number of citizens that have fallen victim to these crimes. All of these issues occur because of either lack of trustworthiness or the awareness thereof. Therefore, trustworthiness has recently gained increasing attention in public discussion. There is an identified gap in research in building a well-accepted cyber-physical system for supporting socio-economic systems in the real world. The cyber-physical systems lack expected (demonstrated) characteristics. Thus, the first step in closing this gap is the identification of trustworthiness attributes that may contribute to trust of socio-economic entities. Then, cyber-physical systems should be made capable of presenting trustworthiness attributes.

There are, though, some inconsistencies between expected trustworthiness properties defined by the users and promised trustworthiness from the software service providers in general. To mitigate these deficiencies and to bridge the gap resulting from the asymmetry between trust and trustworthiness, we will investigate which trustworthiness attributes a system can possess (with which mechanism and/or technologies), and whether these attributes are capable of contributing to trustworthiness addressing the trust expectations expressed by users.

Trustworthiness in the literature has addressed the confidentiality of sensitive information, the integrity of valuable information, the prevention of unauthorized use of information, guaranteed quality of service, the availability of critical data, reliability and integrity of infrastructure, the prevention of unauthorised use of infrastructure, etc. In order to prove being trustworthy, software applications could promise to cover a set of various quality attributes (Mei et al., 2012) depending on their domain and target users.

The stakeholders (e.g. system designers, users or other depending parties) should be able to decide when to expect a system to be trustworthy based on trustworthiness criteria. For example, trustworthiness may be evaluated with respect to the availability, confidentiality, integrity of stored information, the response time, and accuracy of outputs (Avizienis et al., 2004; Mei et al., 2012; Li et al., 2009; Gómez et al., 2007; Yolum and Singh, 2005; Yan and Prehofer, 2007).

2.4 Contribution and Summary of this Chapter

The contribution of this chapter consists in the discussion of existing definitions of trust and trustworthiness and the derivation of our definitions of these concepts with respect to CPS.

In this book, we stick to the earlier mentioned definition of trust provided by Sztompka (2000), while extending it to include cyber-physical systems: "a bet about the future contingent actions of others, be they individuals or groups of individuals, or entire cyber-physical systems". Trustworthiness on the other hand has been used sometimes as a synonym for security and sometimes for dependability. Trustworthiness in general is a broad-spectrum term with notions including reliability, security, performance, and user experience as parts of trustworthiness (Mei et al., 2012). Given our chosen definition of trust we argue that while trust is an act carried out by a person, trustworthiness is a quality of the system that has the potential to influence the trust this person has in the system in a positive way.

We focus on how cyber-physical systems should be made capable to exhibit trustworthiness attributes. Therefore, we ignore potential trustworthiness (or trust) indicators like reputation or similar measures representing user's feedback, since they will only be available when the system is in use, and are based on aggregated subjective values. In other words, a trustworthiness attribute is a property of the system that indicates its capability to prevent potential threats to cause an unexpected and undesired outcome.

The definitions of other concepts related to trust and trustworthiness will be provided in Chapter 3, together with the definition of the other elements of our proposed framework.

3 Overview of the Trustworthiness Management Framework

Enabling trustworthiness in cyber-physical systems is a challenging task, because of heterogeneous and distributed components and very diverse participants and activities. To ease and support the design and development activities, we propose trustworthiness-by-design methods and patterns in this book. Our methods and patterns are gathered in the TrustWorthiness Management (**TW-Man**) framework. A good theoretical framework provides a scientific research base. Our conceptual framework is a blueprint for this book. It provides an outline of how we contribute to the research in the field of trustworthiness and address the conducted research questions defined in Chapter 1. We also position our work within the other research performed in this field.

3.1 The Need for a Trustworthiness Management Framework

We categorize the key factors in the notion of trust and trustworthiness into four nodes shown in Figure 3.1: trust of end-users', trustworthiness-enabling technologies and regulations, application and domain of the system and system characteristics. These nodes have an impact on each other.

As defined in Chapter 2, *trust* is subjective and different from user to user. For instance, in a home monitoring system, an insurance company requires confidentiality regarding its business-critical data, whereas an elderly person using the system might be more concerned about usability. The subjectivity of trust causes that all end-users have different trust concerns and a different perception of the trustworthiness of a system. Furthermore, each end-user has personal responsibilities with regard to trust. For example, when a user receives a credential for using a system, it is his/her personal responsibility to keep these credentials secret. However, the users' personal responsibilities towards trust must be made clear by system developers (e.g. to keep the password secret and to choose strong passwords).

© Springer Fachmedien Wiesbaden GmbH, part of Springer Nature 2019
N. Gol Mohammadi, *Trustworthy Cyber-Physical Systems*,
https://doi.org/10.1007/978-3-658-27488-7_3

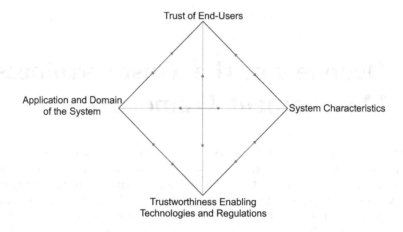

Figure 3.1: The key concepts and their interdependencies

Once subjective trust concerns of users are elicited during a requirements engineering process, they manifest themselves as trustworthiness requirements which describe so-called trustworthiness properties the system must possess (*system characteristics*). These are qualities of the system that potentially influence trust in a positive way.

The trustworthiness requirements are also dependent on *the application and the domain* of the system. In healthcare applications, for example, the following system characteristics influence trust of users in a positive way (cf. Chapter 4): availability, confidentiality, integrity, maintainability, reliability, safety, performance, and timeliness. Whereas, in safety-critical domains the failure tolerance of a system might be prioritized higher than its usability. Thus, trustworthiness requirements will refer to these characteristics.

Trust can be addressed via *trustworthiness-enabling technologies and regulations*. For instance, rules and regulations of the society where the end-users live may enforce trustworthiness of the system by requiring certain characteristics which contribute positively to end-users' trust, e.g. General Data Protection Regulation[1] (GDPR) compliance in European countries. To realize these characteristics, trustworthiness enabling technologies may be used (e.g. usage of enclaves, privacy-enabling technologies).

These bidirectional dependencies and interdependencies among the key concepts make addressing trustworthiness in designing a CPS (cyber-physical system) a

---

[1] https://gdpr-info.eu (accessed on 14 September 2018)

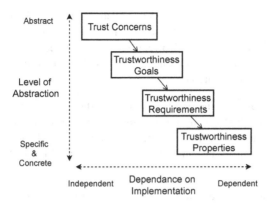

Figure 3.2: The relation between different concepts from trust concern to trustworthiness properties based on (Gol Mohammadi and Heisel, 2016c)

challenging task. Developers need support in addressing trustworthiness during design-time in a systematic way.

To address this need, we suggest starting with the trust of the end-users and eliciting their *trust concerns* as shown in Figure 3.2. These trust concerns can be mapped to the *trustworthiness goals* that a system must satisfy. Trustworthiness goals can be addressed through *trustworthiness requirements* specified for the system. Trustworthiness requirements can be refined to the required *trustworthiness properties* that the system must exhibit to be trustworthy. Figure 3.2 illustrates the relation of these concepts and their granularity. Our framework comprises methods which support the systematic creation and documentation of these concepts/artefacts.

3.2 The Trustworthiness Management Framework

In this section, we provide an overview of our proposed framework for the systematic consideration of trustworthiness in the whole development lifecycle. Based on the research goals and research questions that this book addresses (cf. Chapter 1), we first identify the requirements that such a framework need to address. Then, we describe how our framework supports the development of a trustworthy CPS. When developing a trustworthiness management framework, there are a number of issues that must be addressed. We identified these requirements based on an analysis of the state of the art and based on previous research in the field. Since to date there is no existent trustworthiness management framework that could be used as a reference, we elaborated on these requirements with our industrial partners from the OPTET[2] project. We also reported on these needs in a research paper (Di Cerbo et al., 2013). The requirements are based on the research questions and research goals defined in Chapter 1.

REQ1 A well-structured method is required for the management of the development process of a trustworthy CPS. This method should allow a constructive, transparent, and traceable trustworthiness establishment. It should include best practices and patterns for building trustworthiness into CPS. The details are further discussed in Chapter 6.

REQ2 A clear and well-defined method is required for specifying trustworthiness requirements, i.e. a trustworthiness requirements elicitation and modelling approach. This modelling should also be expressive enough to allow the documentation of trustworthiness that requires a diverse combination of trustworthiness goals. These trustworthiness goals help later on to evaluate whether the required trustworthiness properties are obtained. The details are further discussed in Chapters 7 and 9.

REQ3 An approach should be provided that supports the design-time evaluation of the achieved trustworthiness. The TW-Man framework should provide facilities for assessing trustworthiness properties of systems under development. The trustworthiness evaluation approach should provide the means to collect evidence for trustworthiness (e.g. information on implemented security mechanisms and performed privacy impact assessments). The details are further discussed in Chapters 10 and 11.

REQ4 A method for considering the trustworthiness during run-time is required. This approach should support integrating some run-time trustworthiness maintenance capabilities into CPS, i.e. designing a supplementary monitoring and control system that updates the current state of trustworthiness properties to maintain the overall trustworthiness of the system. The trustworthiness evaluation approach should support discovering and eliminating unwanted situations that may happen during run-time. The details are further discussed in Chapter 12.

REQ5 A systematic method is needed for generating and documenting evidence for trustworthiness of the system under development. The collection of evidence

---

[2]The EU-funded project with grant no. 317631 under 7th framework programme https:// cordis.europa.eu/project/rcn/105733/factsheet/en (accessed on 15 August 2018), www.optet.eu (accessed on 10 September 2016)

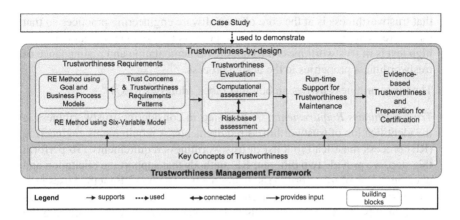

Figure 3.3: The Trustworthiness Management Framework

should take place throughout the whole development lifecycle in alignment with the documentation needs of certification processes. The details are further discussed in Chapter 13.

Figure 3.3 presents the building blocks of our framework. Each of these building blocks addresses one of the above-mentioned requirements for the TW-Man framework.

- *Key Concepts of Trustworthiness*: We provide a collection of trustworthiness attributes (cf. Chapter 4) as *key concepts of trustworthiness*. As described in Chapter 2, trustworthiness attributes support understanding what characteristics of a CPS make it trustworthy and which attributes generally play an important role in the trustworthiness of a CPS. Therefore, the collection of trustworthiness attributes as generic concept is the foundation of trustworthiness-by-design methodologies in our framework. The TW-Man framework can be applied in the sequential order of described methods. However, each of these methods can be used independently. Using the generic concept of trustworthiness attributes supports the application of each method without performing other methods in earlier phases.

- *Trustworthiness-by-design*: This building block of the TW-Man framework is our approach for developing trustworthiness enabling methodologies (cf. Chapter 6). The trustworthiness-by-design is a collection of methodologies, patterns, and practices which can be applied in order to achieve that the system under design is trustworthy. These trustworthiness-by-design methodologies ensure that trustworthiness is at the core of the software engineering practices so that the entire system and its individual components (standalone or chained) have high levels of trustworthiness through the implementation and maintenance of trustworthiness properties in the design process.

The trustworthiness-by-design building block addresses REQ1.

- *Trustworthiness Requirements*: A first step in considering trustworthiness is the identification of trustworthiness requirements. A requirements engineering (RE) process must lead to a list of trustworthiness requirements. To perform this step, we provide two different RE methods that support the elicitation and documentation of trustworthiness requirements. The first RE method uses goal and business process models for elicitation and refinement of trustworthiness requirements (cf. Chapter 7). This process is concerned with identifying the participants and initial context information. The goal model captures the major intentions of the involved participants/stakeholders. Trust concerns of end-users and their dependencies on other participants in the business are identified. Based on trust concerns, the goal model is refined with the trustworthiness goals and their relations to the other goals (conflicts or positive influences). The trustworthiness goals include the purpose of building trustworthiness properties into the system under development. Then, business process models are set up that include trustworthiness properties which fulfill the trustworthiness goals from the goal model. Furthermore, we provide two patterns for capturing trust concern and documenting trustworthiness requirements (cf. Chapter 8). Our second method, which can be used alternatively or complementary to the first one, is a problem-based approach for identification of trust concerns and elicitation and refinement of trustworthiness requirements (cf. Chapter 9). It uses Six-Variable Model that is based on problem diagrams (Jackson, 2001).

  This building block of the TW-Man framework addresses REQ2.

- *Trustworthiness Evaluation*: System design must lead to a system model. The system model must address the trustworthiness requirements (resulting from the RE phase). Any design process can be selected to build the system model of the CPS. We recommend using a model-based method, since such a method will result in a system model. A further benefit of a model-based method is that model-based risk assessment approaches towards trustworthiness can then be used as well. The TW-Man framework provides a method for trustworthiness evaluation of the designed system model. Trustworthiness evaluation must lead to an evaluation result that includes measured values of the trustworthiness properties for the CPS. Our method (cf. Chapters 10 and 11) evaluates objectively the trustworthiness of a whole system based on the evaluation of each of its components. This method is based on computational methods (i.e. trustworthiness metrics) and aggregates trustworthiness measurements for the combined functionality of the components making up a system. In that method, we consider a trustworthiness vector for the whole CPS, whose values depend on the corresponding trustworthiness properties of its components. It is important to emphasize that our trustworthiness evaluation depends on the trustworthiness vector and also on the system structure, i.e. the way the components' functionalities interact. This latter factor is a complementary way to prevent threats becoming active by avoiding architectures that allow for groups of related components to be jointly affected by certain types of threats. Such structural issues should be captured in the design process and should be considered as a major parameter affecting the trustworthiness of the CPS.

Since risk plays a significant role in the trustworthiness decision-making process, risk analysis is an important part of the trustworthiness evaluation building block (cf. Chapter 11). The level of trustworthiness could be related to the level of risk, i.e. high risk results in less trustworthy. Thus, we complement our trust-worthiness evaluation with a risk-based approach. To this end, it includes a risk management component to integrate a component which will perform this evaluation. Our trustworthiness evaluation method allows for comparing alternative system models. Such alternative system models may result from risk reduction practices which may have been performed in the design phase. For instance, designers may include a control to block a specific threat to trustworthiness. The resulting modified system model represents an alternative to the previous system model. In this scenario, our trustworthiness evaluation method helps the designer to perform trustworthiness-related design decisions.

This building block of the TW-Man framework addresses REQ3.

- *Run-time Support for Trustworthiness Maintenance*: Because of the dynamic nature of trustworthiness of a CPS (i.e. it changes over time), trustworthiness properties need to be continuously re-evaluated to ascertain whether the CPS is still trustworthy. It becomes obvious that in order have an effective decision-making support for maintenance of trustworthiness during run-time, CPS should contain a facility for monitoring and evaluating information pertinent to trustworthiness maintenance. In CPS, sub-optimal or incorrect functioning of the system may have detrimental effects. In addition to designing systems with trustworthiness in mind, maintaining trustworthiness at run-time is a critical task in order to identify issues that could negatively affect the trustworthiness of the CPS. To this end, monitoring and mitigation capabilities for the CPS must be provided. Including these capabilities and interfaces for monitoring and adaptation might change the system model. This building block of TW-Man framework provides business processes for monitoring, measuring, and managing trustworthiness, as well as mitigating trustworthiness issues at run-time (cf. Chapter 12). Furthermore, we provide a reference architecture for trustworthiness maintenance systems. When this reference architecture is realized, trustworthiness maintenance capabilities for monitoring and managing the CPS's trustworthiness properties in order to preserve the overall established trustworthiness during run-time exist.

This building block of the TW-Man framework addresses REQ4.

- *Evidence-based Trustworthiness and Preparation for Certification*: Collection of trustworthiness-related information throughout the whole development life-cycle helps in preparation for certification and in providing justification that the developed system is trustworthy. To this end, we provide an approach for documenting the evidence in the form of trustworthiness cases (cf. Chapter 13). This information will also help in determining the basis for trustworthiness establishment and maintenance during run-time.

This building block of the TW-Man framework addresses REQ5.

- A use case study from the ambient assisted living domain illustrates the application of the methods provided in our framework as running example of this book.

3.3 Conceptual Model of the Trustworthiness Management Framework

Different concepts are underlying the methods and techniques in our framework. These concepts and their relationships to each other are shown in Figure 3.4 as a Unified Modeling Language (UML) class diagram.

A *trustworthiness goal* is a special *goal* that addresses the trust concerns of users. A trustworthiness goal is satisfied by *trustworthiness requirements*, which can be realized by more concrete *trustworthiness properties* (cf. Figure 3.2).

Actors have goals that can be satisfied in a *business process*. A business process consists of *business process elements*. Business process elements based on BPMN (Business Process Model and Notation) are: a set of activities, events, and involved resources. An actor performs an *activity*. An activity is supported by resources. For instance, an activity consumes data objects (information resource) as input, or it produces output. We use the term *business process element* to distinguish between generic types of BPMN and concrete *trustworthiness elements* (our extension of BPMN, cf. Chapter 7). We defined *trustworthiness elements* to

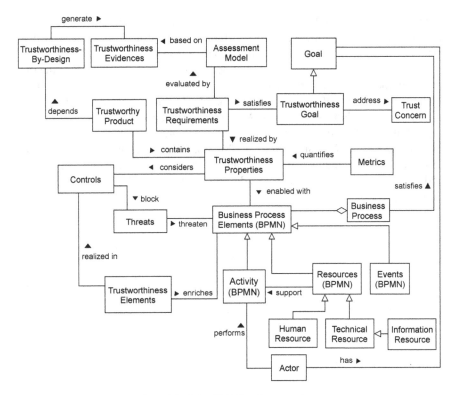

Figure 3.4: The conceptual model of the TW-Man framework

enrich *business process elements*. The precise specification and requirements on the BPMN extension are described in Chapter 7.

In order to incorporate the notion of *trustworthiness-by-design* into development methodologies, we consider and extend the Software Process Engineering Meta-model (SPEM) (Object Management Group: SPEM, 2008). We use the concept of a *Trustworthy Product* (i.e. work product, development artefact) as a product (from SPEM, cf. Chapter 6) that contains a range of trustworthiness properties for realizing its trustworthiness requirements.

A properly applied trustworthiness-by-design process will create a trustworthy product that exhibits certain trustworthiness properties to meet its trustworthiness requirements. Trustworthiness requirements specify requirements that a trustworthy product should fulfill. An *Assessment Model* verifies whether the trustworthiness requirements have been met. A *Trustworthiness Evidence* is some kind of evidence/proof that shows that a trustworthiness-by-design process has been followed. Though this will not guarantee trustworthiness, it is at least an indication that planned measures have been taken into account to ensure it.

A *threat* is a situation or event that, if active at run-time, could undermine the trustworthiness of a system by altering the behavior of involved resources or services in the process. *Controls* aim at blocking threats. *Metrics* are used as functions to quantify trustworthiness properties. A metric is a standard way for measuring and quantifying certain trustworthiness properties as more concrete quality properties of an element (Gol Mohammadi et al., 2013b), (Gol Mohammadi et al., 2015a). Trustworthiness elements realize the control in terms of defining elements which address the trustworthiness, e.g. an additional activity can be defined to block a threat to privacy.

4 A Survey on Trustworthiness Attributes for Cyber-Physical Systems

This chapter[1] provides our attempt to identify software qualities, which contribute to trustworthiness. Based on a survey of the literature, we provide a structured overview on qualities that contribute to trustworthiness. Our aim is to provide a collection of trustworthiness attributes that potentially contribute to trustworthiness, hence influence trust in positive way. We also identify potential gaps with respect to characteristics whose relationship to trustworthiness is understudied. Further, we observe that most of the literature studies trustworthiness from a security perspective while there are limited contributions in studying the social aspects of trustworthiness in computing. We expect this chapter to contribute to a better understanding of which characteristics of a software system should be considered to build trustworthy systems.

4.1 Motivation

The question this chapter deals with is about the software system characteristics (in terms of qualities and characteristics) that can foster trustworthiness in cyber-physical systems mediated through online networks. CPS are increasingly part of our daily life in the form of applications, Internet-based services, etc. Though, the people involved in online businesses have generally limited information about each other and about the cyber-physical systems supporting their online and offline transactions. Individuals and organizations are concerned about trusting and placing confidence on current cyber-physical systems and show interest in how assets are handled, e.g. their business critical data. This issue occurs either due to lack of trustworthiness or due to a lack of awareness thereof. We identified a gap in research in building well-accepted cyber-physical systems for supporting socio-economic

---

[1]This chapter partially adapts Gol Mohammadi et al. (2013a) © 2013 SCITEPRESS (Science and Technology Publications, Lda.), and Gol Mohammadi et al. (2013b) © Springer International Publishing Switzerland 2014, with the permission of the publishers.

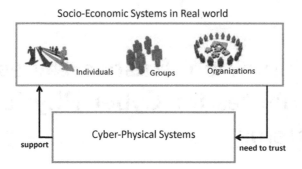

Figure 4.1: The relation between socio-economic systems and cyber-physical systems

systems in the real world. Figure 4.1 illustrates the relation of socio-economic systems in the real world to CPS. Figure 4.1 is inspired from Whitworth (2009). CPS should exhibit trustworthiness characteristics to reflect the needs of individuals, groups and organizations. However, there is no common understanding of what the characteristics are that can foster trustworthiness in CPS. The first step in closing this gap is thus the identification of trustworthiness attributes that may contribute to trust of individuals, groups and organizations. Then, cyber-physical systems should be made capable to exhibit and present these characteristics. Consequently, trustworthiness of a software, application, service or infrastructure becomes a key factor for their wider use and adoption by organizations and end-users.

Understanding which software qualities and characteristics foster trustworthiness is thus increasingly important for successful trustworthy software and system development. There are limited contributions that approach the trust and trustworthiness issues described above from angles other than security. However, security is not the only aspect of trustworthiness. Most existing approaches have assumed that one-dimensional properties of services lead to trustworthiness of such services and even to trust in it by users such as a certification (e.g. Common Criteria (ISO/IEC 15408-1, 2009)), the presence of certain technologies (encryption), or the use of certain methodologies like **S**ystems **S**ecurity **E**ngineering **C**apability **M**aturity **M**odel (**SSE-CMM**) (Pazos-Revilla and Siraj, 2008; Software Engineering Institute, 2002; Huang et al., 2008).

In this book, we assume that such a one-dimensional approach will not work, and instead consider a multitude of characteristics. With a literature review (presented in this chapter), we attempt to identify and capture the characteristics so far known as contributing to trustworthiness. We provide a structured and comprehensive overview of trustworthiness attributes. We classify the identified characteristics into major quality categories that we call *"trustworthiness attributes"* from now on. A collection of trustworthiness attributes guides the CPS designer in building a trustworthy CPS and evaluating it.

The remainder of this chapter is structured as follows: Section 4.2 presents the applied process for conducting the literature review. Section 4.3 describes the classification of trustworthiness attributes. The grouping of the qualities under a category is achieved according to the observed common underlying concepts. Section 4.4 summarizes the lessons learned and the contribution of this chapter.

4.2 The Process of Performing a Comprehensive Literature Review

To identify trustworthiness attributes, we conducted a literature review. We collected and categorized the characteristics and qualities of a software system that contribute to trustworthiness. In this section, we describe how we performed the literature review. Then, we present the results of this review.

Research Method

The aim of the literature study was to identify existing characteristics of a software system that are claimed to be contributing to trustworthiness. This process is based on the systematic literature review Kitchenham (2004); Kitchenham et al. (2009); Kitchenham et al. (2010); Brereton et al. (2007). In the following, we describe our process (shown in Figure 4.2) comprising the three phases planning, conducting, and reporting in detail.

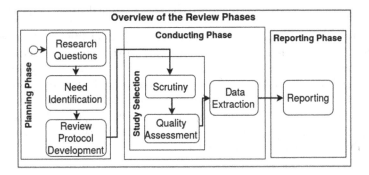

Figure 4.2: Overview of review phases and steps

Planning Phase of the Review

The process of literature review (see Figure 4.2) started with the planning phase consisting of three tasks: 1) research questions specification, 2) need identification, and 3) review protocol development. In the first task, we defined research questions according to one of our research goals (RG2 in Section 1.3). In the second task, we searched secondary studies such as surveys, reviews, and mapping studies to find out whether there is already a review that provides an extensive overview of software qualities that contribute to trustworthiness. As we found no studies that directly address the topic in question as desired, we decided to perform a literature review. Hence, we defined in the third task a protocol that describes the review process. In the following, we describe each task in more detail.

Research Questions Specification

We aimed at reviewing the existing literature for identifying characteristics that cyber-physical systems must exhibit for being trustworthy. To this end, we defined one main research goal and refined it with several research questions. The research goal and its related research questions addressed by this study are:

RG Identifying key concepts to model trustworthiness: It includes identifying key characteristics that contribute to trustworthiness.

   RQ1 What are the contributing characteristics that can foster trustworthiness in cyber-physical systems?

   RQ1.1 Which qualities have been claimed or considered as contributing to trustworthiness in the research community?

   RQ1.2 Is there any classification of these characteristics in the state of the art?

   RQ1.3 How to classify the identified characteristics in the state of the art?

The main research question aims at identifying the qualities in the research field that have been claimed as contributors to trustworthiness. Furthermore, research questions aim at a taxonomy or classification for collected characteristics. The research questions serve as specific criteria for evaluation of the reported characteristics, and whether these characteristic are relevant to trustworthiness of cyber-physical systems. The research questions may be mapped to the trustworthiness goals for cyber-physical systems that we consider to be enabled and managed by the TW-Man framework (see Chapter 3).

Need Identification

The aim of this step was to find related secondary literature such as surveys and reviews, which might have been relevant. In case we would have found such systematic surveys that could answer our research questions, there was no need for conducting a systematic review any more. Then, we could base our further research on the taxonomy presented in the state of the art. Since, we did not find any systematic literature review on the characteristic and qualities of cyber-physical systems for being trustworthy, we confirmed the need for conducting a literature review in this field. We used Scopus[2] as search engine for an automatic search of relevant literature reviews. Scopus is well accepted in the research community, covers most peer-reviewed literature, and only lists peer-reviewed literature[3] [4].

We considered following search terms for finding relevant literature reviews on trustworthiness attributes:

- "literature review" OR survey OR "state of the art analysis"

- trust OR trustworthiness

- categories OR taxonomies OR classifications OR attributes OR qualities OR characteristics

To further limit the search results, we limited the subject area to computer science. The conference reviews and editorials from the search results were excluded, because these should not propose themselves (scientific) contributions. Furthermore, we limited the document language to English.

The search was conducted on 12 November 2012 and the results were updated on 18 February 2013. This search resulted in 251 documents. To limit the number of documents that had to be assessed manually, we limited the search to documents that were published in last 10 years. We read the title and abstract of these documents to decide whether they were really concerned with trustworthiness attributes. In this way, we obtained 54 documents that could not be excluded without a reasonable doubt. We read the full text and we confirmed the need for conducting a literature review to identify trustworthiness attributes based on a state of the art analysis.

---

[2]https://www.scopus.com (last access on 4 June 2018)
[3]https://en.wikipedia.org/wiki/List_of_academic_databases_and_search_engines (last access on 4 June 2018)
[4]https://www.elsevier.com/solutions/scopus (last access on 4 June 2018)

Review Protocol Development

The aim of this step was to define a protocol that describes the review process which is carried out in the conducting phase. The protocol was written before conducting the review itself. The review protocol included the following points:

- The review goal and the research questions

- The search strategy including:

  - The scope and restrictions applied to the literature review
  - The sources that were of interest for the review in the search of primary papers
  - The identification of keywords
  - The generation of search queries

- The inclusion and exclusion criteria and how they apply for the selection of the papers

- The evaluation of the primary studies

- The data extraction process and how it is summarized

The review protocol must be evaluated to assure that the planning was viable (Kitchenham et al., 2009). To this end, in our literature review, we consulted with at least three other researchers in the planning phase. Several other researchers (from our colleagues and project partners in the OPTET[5] project) reviewed the protocol made by us. The literature review protocol includes a data extraction template that we prepared to be filled in the conducting phase. The results of the conducting phase have been published in Gol Mohammadi et al. (2013a); Gol Mohammadi et al. (2013b). The co-authors of that papers were involved in the role of external reviewers of the protocol, the data extraction template, and resulting reports that were created by the main author.

As this literature review has been performed by only one researcher, we prepared an excel sheet that was used as the data extraction template. The Excel sheet was convenient for this purpose instead of preparing a data extraction form which is usually used by literature reviews conducted by several researchers. Preparing such templates requires more effort. Hence, we decided to store the data in an Excel file. The target of the search process was conferences, symposiums, workshop proceedings and journal papers. The papers were initially retrieved from electronic

---

[5]The EU-funded project with grant no. 317631 under 7th framework programme https://cordis.europa.eu/project/rcn/105733/factsheet/en (accessed on 15 August 2018), www.optet.eu (accessed on 10 September 2016)

Table 4.1: The search space

Electronic databases	IEEE Xplore
	SpringerLink
	ISI Web of Knowledge
	ScienceDirect
	Scopus
Searched items	Journal
	Conference
	Workshop
Search applied on	Full text
Language	English

databases (cf. Table 4.1) and then analyzed to identify other meaningful papers through snowballing. Additionally, we also consulted the related publications of the authors of the papers identified in the Digital Bibliography & Library Project[6] (DBLP) database. This supplementary strategy aimed to add any potential works that might have been left out. Table 4.1 shows the source and restrictions applied in the search space.

The search strategies used in this study consisted of search terms, search sources and an applied search process. The following steps were followed based on (Kitchenham et al., 2009) to build the search queries:

1. Define the major terms from the research questions.

2. Identify alternatives and synonyms for major terms.

3. Identify of keywords in relevant papers.

4. Use the Boolean OR to incorporate synonyms.

5. Use the Boolean AND to link the major terms.

We considered the search terms as follows:

- trust OR trustworthiness

- categories OR taxonomies OR classifications OR attributes OR qualities OR characteristics

- cyber-physical system OR CPS OR software OR application OR software system OR internet-based application OR distributed systems

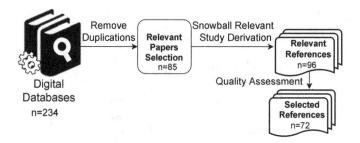

Figure 4.3: Overview of the paper selection process

We identified 234 papers by this search process (see Figure 4.3), where some of the papers were an extended version of another paper by the same authors. Hence, we considered such papers as one paper. The papers that had been identified as potentially relevant papers were reviewed once again and inclusion and exclusion criteria were applied to the relevant papers. There were some potentially relevant papers that were excluded as a result of a quality assessment of study. In the quality assessment of the relevant papers, we assessed whether the papers exhibit a certain quality to be qualified for the data extraction. At the end, 72 relevant papers were identified.

Inclusion and exclusion criteria

To determine whether a paper should be included, the following inclusion and exclusion criteria were used:

- Inclusion criteria:
  1. The paper is a peer-reviewed publication.
  2. The paper is in English.
  3. It is relevant to the search terms defined in search criteria.
  4. It is a research paper, an experience report, or workshop paper.
  5. The paper was published between 1998 and 2013. The earliest published paper that addressed at least one of the research questions after scrutiny was in 1998. The year 2013 is the starting point of the research performed in this book.

---

[6]The dblp computer science bibliography: This service provides open bibliographic information on major computer science journals and proceedings. https://dblp.org (accessed on 26 September 2018)

- Exclusion criteria:

1. Papers that do not focus explicitly on cyber-physical systems, or do not refer to Internet-based applications or distributed systems connected via the Internet.

2. Papers that do not discuss trust or trustworthiness.

3. Papers that do not meet the inclusion criteria.

4. Opinions, viewpoints, discussions, editorials, comments, prefaces, and anecdote papers and presentations in slide formats without any associated papers.

4.3 Findings of the Review

In this section, we present the results of our literature review for identifying characteristics of a CPS that can foster trustworthiness.

To answer RQ1.1, we performed the literature review. After analyzing 72 relevant papers (cf. Table 4.2), we listed all trustworthiness attributes that were considered in these papers. A flat list of trustworthiness attributes was not a well-structured option for presenting the results of our literature review. To answer RQ1.2, we performed the search for the "Need Identification". We did not find any classification of trustworthiness attributes, neither within the papers for the "Need Identification" nor within the 72 relevant papers of the literature review. To address RQ1.3, we classified the identified trustworthiness attributes. Our aim was to provide a well-structured collection of these attributes.

We built our structured collection of trustworthiness attributes based on the software quality reference model defined by S-Cube (2008). We chose the software quality reference model as a basis for our classification, because the S-Cube model is extensive and has considered several other models such as: Boehm et al. (1976); Adrion et al. (1982); McCall et al. (1977); ISO/IEC 9126-1 (2001). The software quality reference model focuses on service-based systems. We use it since, a CPS can be considered as a composition of distributed services connected via the Internet, where we have technical services like software services as well as physical services provided by human actors. Therefore, some of the trustworthiness attributes refer to services, while others refer to the system as whole.

From the software quality reference model, we excluded two types of software qualities defined by S-Cube (2008) from our analysis. Firstly, some of the qualities were not identified in our literature review as contributing to trustworthiness. Hence, they were excluded. Secondly, some qualities, e.g. integrity, can be achieved, among other ways, through cryptography. In this case we included the high-level quality category (integrity) as a contributor to trustworthiness but did not include

Table 4.2: The indices of the surveyed papers

Nr.	Paper Reference	Nr.	Paper Reference
1	Song and Wang (2010)	37	Aßmann et al. (2006)
2	Jøsang et al. (2007)	38	Aikebaier et al. (2012)
3	Grandison and Sloman (2000)	39	Hasselbring and Reussner (2006)
4	Mei et al. (2012)	40	Ying and Jiang (2010)
5	S-Cube (2008)	41	Qureshi et al. (2012)
6	Zuo-Wen et al. (2010)	42	Irvine and Levitt (2007)
7	Homeland Security (2009)	43	Patil and Shyamasundar (2005)
8	Sterbenz et al. (2010)	44	Verberne et al. (2012)
9	Elshaafi et al. (2012)	45	Harris and Goode (2004)
10	Corritore et al. (2003)	46	Luarn and Lin (2003)
11	Wang and Emurian (2005)	47	Jing et al. (2008)
12	Scheffelmaier and Vinsonhaler (2003)	48	Shi et al. (2012)
13	Belanger et al. (2002)	49	Ding et al. (2012)
14	McKnight et al. (2002)	50	Gómez et al. (2007)
15	Lenzini et al. (2010)	51	Yolum and Singh (2005)
16	Chopra et al. (2011)	52	Yan and Prehofer (2007)
17	Castelfranchi and Tan (2002)	53	Kuz et al. (2012)
18	Lipner (2004)	54	Avizienis et al. (2004)
19	Koufaris and Hampton-Sosa (2004)	55	Rao et al. (2009)
20	Zheng et al. (2009)	56	Dai et al. (2012)
21	ISO/IEC 15408-1 (2009)	57	Li et al. (2009)
22	Zhang and Zhang (2005)	58	Dewsbury et al. (2003)
23	Neumann (2004)	59	Paja et al. (2013)
24	Liang et al. (2007)	60	Ba (2001)
25	Hussain et al. (2006)	61	Teler and Cristea (2012)
26	Limam and Boutaba (2010)	62	Sommerville and Dewsbury (2007)
27	Meng et al. (2012)	63	Fred B. Schneider (1999)
28	Cassell and Bickmore (2000)	64	Hall and McQuay (2011)
29	San-Martín and Camarero (2012)	65	Barber (1998)
30	Chen et al. (2009)	66	He et al. (2009)
31	Pavlidis et al. (2012)	67	Yang (2006)
32	Cofta et al. (2010)	68	Gefen (2002)
33	Reith et al. (2007)	69	Hussain et al. (2007)
34	Xin-zhi et al. (2011)	70	Yu et al. (2010)
35	Neto and Vieira (2009)	71	Ray and Chakraborty (2004)
36	Waluyo et al. (2012)	72	Yuan et al. (2012)

cryptography on its own because it is encompassed by the higher-level attribute. Both cases are further discussed in Section 4.3.1.

Additionally, we have included qualities and characteristics that have been studied in the literature in terms of trustworthiness but they were not part of the quality reference model presented by S-Cube (2008). These characteristics are marked with an asterisk "*" in Figure 4.4. Figure 4.4 outlines the result of this literature

Figure 4.4: Overview of identified trustworthiness attributes (Gol Mohammadi et al., 2013a) in the state of the art and their classification

review and our classification of trustworthiness attributes. Figure 4.5 presents the distribution of the analyzed papers in different classified quality categories. In the following, we explain our classification in more detail.

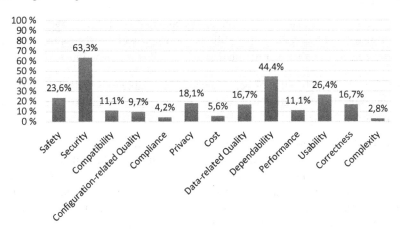

Figure 4.5: The distribution of the quality categories of trustworthiness attributes based on (Gol Mohammadi et al., 2013b)

4.3.1 Trustworthiness Attributes

Contributing characteristics of software systems to trustworthiness are captured as trustworthiness attributes. These characteristics and belonging quality category are discussed in the following sub-sections. Trustworthiness attributes that were named in the surveyed papers as contributing characteristics to trustworthiness are listed in Tables 4.3 to 4.15 with an indication of the respective papers (with the indices from Table 4.2).

Safety

The ability to operate without risk of injury or harm to users and the system's environment. It can be achieved by absence of consequences on the users and the environment. Table 4.3 presents the cite map for the safety quality category as trustworthiness attribute.

Table 4.3: Safety category and its cite map

Quality Category	Citing
Safety	1, 6, 8, 20, 22, 23, 39, 48, 49, 53, 54, 57, 58, 62, 63, 64, 70

Security

Security covers the capability of a software system to protect entities against attacks and misuse despite certain vulnerabilities and to protect the access to resources. The sub-category of the security quality are the following (listed in Table 4.4):

- Accountability: The state of being accountable, liable to be called on to render an account, the obligation to bear the consequences for failure to perform as expected.

- Auditability/Traceability: Capability of the service to be monitored and to generate in a reliable and secure way events producing an audit trail. Based on this audit a sequence of events can be reconstructed and examined. Security events could include authentication events, policy enforcement decisions, and others. The resulting audit trail may be used to detect attacks, confirm compliance with policy, deter abuse, or other purposes.

- Confidentiality: The ability to limit access to the system and its data only to authorised agents. It is defined as the absence of unauthorized disclosure of information.

- Integrity: The ability to ensure that the system and its data are not corrupted, improper system state alterations either accidental or malicious alternation or removal of information are prohibited.

- Non-Repudiation: The ability to prove to the data sender that data has been delivered, and to prove the sender's identity to the recipient, so that neither the sender nor the recipient can deny operations of sending and receiving data.

Table 4.4: Security category and its contributing sub-categories to trustworthiness

Quality Category	Sub-categories	Citing
Security		1, 2, 3, 6, 8, 9, 11, 18, 19, 20, 22, 23, 24, 27, 29, 30, 31, 32, 33, 34, 35, 38, 39, 40, 41, 42, 43, 49, 52, 53, 55, 56, 57, 63, 64, 66, 67, 70, 71, 72
	Accountability	43, 65
	Auditability/ Traceability	8, 20, 43
	Confidentiality	8, 9, 17, 38, 43, 53, 54, 58, 62, 63, 64
	Integrity	1, 8, 13, 20, 30, 34, 38, 41, 43, 46, 53, 54, 56, 58, 61, 62, 63, 64
	Non-Repudiation	8, 43, 56

Compatibility

Compatibility/Interoperability (cf. Table 4.5) has been defined as the ability of diverse services to work constructively with each other. Actually, different services can coexist without side effects, without even knowing each other. Compatibility amounts to the necessity of two interacting parties to fulfil each other's constraints and, therefore, to correctly interact. The following sub-categories belong to the compatibility quality category:

- Openness means the system is designed in such a way that it is transparent how it works and how to connect to the system. This relates to other qualities like interoperability, transparency and extensibility (McKnight et al., 2002; Patil and Shyamasundar, 2005). In most cases more transparent systems are considered more trustworthy than less transparent ones.

- Reusability can be defined on two levels, namely, a syntactic level and an operational level. A reusable system needs a simple and intuitive design (Neumann, 2004). This reduces the complexity of the system. For example, functions of components are well-defined, their inputs and outputs and effects are well-defined. The name of a function reflects its purpose. The structure, role and interfaces of components are simple. This makes the system more trustworthy. During operation, a system that is designed to be reusable may intentionally duplicate some components to achieve other trustworthiness attributes e.g. performance, reliability. Therefore, reusability contributes positively to trustworthiness.

Table 4.5: Compatibility or Interoperability category and its cite map

Quality Category	Sub-categories	Citing
Compatibility/ Interoperability	22, 23, 67, 72	
	Openness*	8, 14, 20, 43, 72
	Reusability*	22, 23, 67, 72

Configuration-related Quality

This quality category contains qualities that influence the way a service is configured to function or that characterize whether the promised functional and quality level has been actually delivered during the service's lifetime period e.g. completeness, change cycle. The following sub-categories belong to configuration-related quality category (listed in Table 4.10):

- Change Cycle: Possibility of making changes related to the service in terms of its interface and/or implementation/recomposition. A change may be crucial, for example, when the regulation or requirements evolve. This can be the case also with trustworthiness requirements. Systems that have the ability of making changes with respect to new trustworthiness requirements are considered more trustworthy.

- Completeness: A measure of the difference between the specified set of features (e.g. functions) and the implemented set of features. Completeness can apply to trustworthiness requirements as well. Hence, it contributes positively to trustworthiness.

Table 4.6: Configuration-related quality category and its contributing sub-categories to trustworthiness

Quality Category	Sub-categories	Citing
Configuration-related Quality	35, 72	
	Change Cycle	1, 9, 57, 72
	Completeness	6, 64, 72

Compliance

The service should comply with standards (e.g. industry specific standards) and/or regulations (e.g. the European Union's General Data Protection Regulation (GDPR)). This can affect a number of other qualities such as the security, privacy, portability and interoperability of the service. In general, behaviour of a service should always meet the user's expectation. Additionally, systems that provide the users with the means to have confidence that the system is compliant to the standards and regulations will be more trustworthy systems. For instance, a system that guarantees a user that it is compliant to GDPR is more trustworthy than a system that provides no such indication. The cite map for this category is shown in Table 4.7.

Table 4.7: Compliance category and its cite map

Quality Category	Citing
Compliance	6, 3, 60

Privacy

In internet connected systems, privacy (cf. Table 4.8) is viewed as the system's ability and functionality that allows users to take control of the usage of their private information or personal data[7]. From this system perspective, privacy is a strong contributor to trustworthiness of the system. Systems that provide the users with the means to have visibility and control on how the users' private information is used will be more trustworthy systems. For instance, a system that guarantees a user that no third parties can access or use their private information is more trustworthy than a system that provides no such control or guarantees.

Moreover, in most countries (e.g. in the European countries) privacy is a human right and strict privacy laws must be respected. Consequently, when designing systems the designers must ensure through their design process that the way in which the system will handle private information is in compliance with the applicable legislation in order to render these systems trustworthy.

Table 4.8: Privacy category and its cite map

Quality Category	Citing
Privacy*	1, 13, 29, 31, 39, 43, 49, 58, 60, 61, 63, 64, 65

Cost

Cost (cf. Table 4.9) is a (composite) quality consisting of three (atomic) service characteristics: cost model, fixed costs and variable costs. Actually, cost can be computed either from all atomic cost characteristics or only from the fixed costs characteristics. A system can be considered as more trustworthy when the invested

---

[7]The European term that is also used in the regulation is "personal data".

effort to make the system trustworthy is high. Hence, higher trustworthiness comes with a higher monetary cost, e.g. invested time and resources. Note that by cost we mean the development cost of the system, not the final price for buying this system or service as a user.

Table 4.9: Cost category and its cite map

Quality Category	Citing
Cost	9, 26, 50

Data-related Quality

Data-related quality (information and data quality) characterize input/output data by qualities that traditionally have been used in the information and data quality domains, e.g. accuracy and timeliness. The way that this information is provided (sensed or derived), delivery time, and the level of detail affects the quality of context information. These attributes are important factors that contribute to trustworthiness. These factors also have an impact on other trustworthiness attributes like adaptability. They should be designed and executed considering the quality of context that is delivered in the way that will be able to make rational and realistic decisions when and how to adapt. The following sub-attributes belong to the data-related quality category (listed in Table 4.10):

- Data Integrity: Data integrity means that the data is accurate, consistent and valid during its whole life-time. The data should not be altered by unauthorized parties. Data integrity can be compromised by human errors, malicious attacks, intentional data modification, transmission errors, system/software bugs or viruses, or hardware malfunctions.

- Data Reliability: Correctness of the sensed data used by the system. It depends on the sub-systems used as well as on the provenance of the data.

- Data Timeliness: The property of information being able to arrive early or at the right time.

- Data Validity: The data values satisfy acceptance requirements of validation criteria or fall within the respective domain of acceptable values. Validity criteria are often based on "expert opinion" and are generally viewed as "rules of thumb" although some validity criteria may be based on established theory or scientific fact.

Table 4.10: Data-related quality category and its cite map

Quality Category	Sub-categories	Citing
Data-related Quality	14, 20, 49, 57, 61	
	Data Integrity	14, 20, 56, 57
	Data Reliability	5, 14, 36, 68
	Data Timeliness	49, 67, 70
	Data Validity	56, 64, 68

Dependability

Dependability of a computing system is the property/ability that reliance can justifiably be placed on the service it delivers. It also has been defined as a correct and predictable execution and ensured that, when executed, it functions as intended. Avizienis et al. (2004) consider dependability and trustworthiness to have the same goals while both suffer from the same threats (faults, errors, and failures). The sub-categories belonging to this quality category are the following (cf. Table 4.11):

• Accuracy: Definition of the error rate produced by the service calculated on the basis of the expected results.

• Availability: The ability to deliver services whenever it is required.

• Fault Tolerance: The ability of a service to provide its functionality to clients in case of faults. In general, it is the capability of a service to handle faults. The circumstances of service faults and how a service will react to faults are described.

• Flexibility/Robustness: It refers to the capability of the service to behave in an acceptable way in anomalous or unexpected situations or when the context changes. Adaptability, reparability, self-healability, recoverability, predictability and survivability are grouped under this category.

  – Adaptability and controllability refer to the capability of the service to dynamically modify its state and behaviour according to the context, e.g. user preferences, device and network characteristics, available user peripherals, user location and status, natural environment characteristics, and service and content descriptions and can be expressed in parameters that are time and space dependent.

  – Predictability is the expected behaviour of a non-deterministic system.

  – Reparability is the ability of a system and its repair actions to cope with any unexpected situation.

Table 4.11: Dependability quality category and its cite map

Quality Category	Sub-categories		Citing	
Dependability	8, 14, 54, 58, 59, 71			
	Accuracy		49	
	Availability		1, 8, 6, 9, 20, 22, 23, 39, 47, 49, 52, 53, 54, 58, 62, 64	
	Fault Tolerance		8, 20, 49, 6, 22, 23, 70	
	Flexibility/ Robustness	8, 20, 30		
		Adaptability/ Controllability	1,6, 20, 22, 31, 50, 53, 54, 55, 58, 62	
		Predictability*	9, 6, 14, 20, 23, 50	
		Reparability	6, 53, 54	
		Self-healability	49	
		Recoverability/ Survivability	8, 6, 9, 20, 22, 23, 24, 55, 62, 63, 64, 66, 67, 70	
			Resistance Recognition/ Observability/ Diagnosability/ Monitorability	6, 9, 20, 24, 31, 57
	Reliability		1,6,8,9,14,20,22,27,36,39,45,48,49, 52, 53, 54, 58, 62, 63, 64, 67, 68, 70, 71	
	Scalability		49, 22, 72	
	Maintainability*		1, 8, 53, 54, 58, 62, 67	
			Testability	22, 23

- Self-healability is the property that enables a system to perceive that it is not operating correctly and, without human intervention, make the necessary adjustments to restore itself to normality.

- Recoverability and survivability allows the service to continue to fulfil its mission even if there are attacks, failures, or accidents. The system should be able to restore essential services during attacks and to recover to full service after attack. Resistance and recognition are grouped under recoverability/survivability. Resistance is the ability of the service to repel attacks. Recognition, observability, diagnosability, and monitorability have been used interchangeably. They refer to the capability of a system and its monitors to exhibit different observables for different anticipated faulty situations. It is a prerequisite for performing run-time checks on a system.

- Reliability: The ability of a service to perform its required functions under stated conditions for a specified period of time (failure-free operation capability in specified circumstances and for a specified period of time).

- Scalability: The capability of increasing the computing capacity of the service providers' computer system and the ability of the system to process more operations or transactions in a given period.

- Maintainability is the ability of a system to undergo evolution with the corollary that the system should be designed so that evolution is not likely to introduce new faults into the system (Sommerville and Dewsbury, 2007). Maintainability has been defined as the process of making engineering changes to the system by involving the system designers and installers. Testability is the possibility of validating software upon modification.

Performance

This quality category contains quality characteristics that characterize how well a service performs. The following sub-categories belong to the performance quality category (listed in Table 4.12):

- Transaction Time: Time elapsed while a service is processing a transaction.

- Throughput: It refers to the number of event responses handled during an interval. It can be further distinguished into input-data-throughput (arrival rate of user data in the input channel), communication throughput (user data output to a channel) and processing throughput (amount of data processed).

- Response Time: The time that passes while the service is completing one complete transaction. Latency, as sub-category of response time, is the time passed from the arrival of the service request until the end of its execution/service. Latency itself has been constructed with execution time and delay time in queue. The former is the time taken by a service to process its sequence of activities. The latter is the time it takes for a service request to actually be executed.

Table 4.12: Performance quality category and its cite map

Quality Category	Sub-categories	Citing
Performance		8, 9, 22, 23, 39, 47, 49, 72
	Throughput	39
	Response Time	39, 47

Usability

Usability collects all those quality characteristics that can be measured subjectively according to user feedback. It refers to the ease with which a user can learn to operate, prepare input for, and interpret the output of the service. The characteristics belonging to the usability quality category are described below (listed in Table 4.13):

- Satisfaction: Freedom from discomfort and positive attitudes towards the use of the service. Attractiveness as a sub-category is the capability of the service to attract the user and their trust (e.g. having contact information and pictures of staff).

- Learnability: Capability of the service to enable the user to learn how to apply/use it.

  Comprehensibility is the capability of the service to enable the user to understand whether its functionality is suitable, and how it can be used for particular tasks and under particular conditions of use.

  Perceivable content makes the service useable and understandable to users, unambiguous or difficult.

- Effectiveness: Accuracy and completeness with which users achieve specified goals.

- Efficiency of Use: Resources expended in relation to the accuracy and completeness with which users achieve their goals.

Table 4.13: Usability quality category and its cite map

Quality Category	Sub-categories	Citing		
Usability	9, 10, 11, 12, 15, 16, 19, 29, 30, 67, 72			
	Satisfaction	1, 28, 45		
		Attractiveness	11, 12, 14, 15, 28, 69	
	Learnability	11, 13, 67, 72		
		Comprehensibility	11	
			Content Perceivability	11, 13
	Effectiveness	1, 20, 22		
	Efficiency of Use	29, 67		

Correctness

Correctness (cf. Table 4.14) deals with the system behaviour conformed to the formal specification (accordance to expected behaviour and the absence of improper system states). Correctness can address whether behaviour of a system is in accordance to the user's requirements including the trust expectations of users' and trustworthiness requirements. Therefore, correctness has a positive contribution to trustworthiness of a system.

Table 4.14: Correctness and its cite map

Quality Category	Citing
Correctness*	1, 9, 6, 20, 24, 25, 37, 53, 63, 64, 68, 72

Complexity

Complexity (cf. Table 4.15) deals with highly fragmented composite services which in most cases would be considered less trustworthy than a more atomic one. Composability has been defined as the ability to create systems and applications with predictably satisfactory behaviour from components, subsystems, and other systems.

Table 4.15: Complexity and its cite map

Quality Category	Sub-categories	Citing
Complexity*	9, 67	
	Composability*	9

4.3.2 Discussion of the Results

Based on the state of the art analysis, we consider trustworthiness as a context and application-dependent property of a system. We discuss the domain-, context- and application- dependence of trustworthiness by looking at a few examples:

- Ambient Assisted Living (AAL) application and health care domain: For AAL systems, the set of characteristics which have primarily been considered in the state of the art consists of: availability, confidentiality, integrity, maintainability, reliability and safety, but also performance and timeliness.

- For the area of critical infrastructures: The major trustworthiness attributes considered in the state of the art are: integrity, timeliness, correctness, fault tolerance, and availability.

- For safety critical systems: Safety and dependability are the major trustworthiness attributes that are considered in the state of the art.

We define trustworthiness as a vector of trustworthiness attributes. The trustworthiness attributes can be chosen dependent on the context and the application from the collection of trustworthiness attributes given in this chapter. The systematic identification of relevant trustworthiness attributes and the building of a trustworthiness vector can be performed using requirements engineering approaches. In Chapters 7 and 9, we present our two alternative approaches for trustworthiness requirements elicitation and refinement.

Furthermore, based on our analysis of quality reference models S-Cube (2008); Boehm et al. (1976); Adrion et al. (1982); McCall et al. (1977); ISO/IEC 9126-1 (2001) in our literature review, we found some qualities from which we believe that they have an impact on trustworthiness but are understudied. These qualities are the following ones:

- **Provability**: The service performs provably as expected, respectively as defined. This is more a property of the engineering process rather than of the delivered system, but should be taken into account as well. This quality addresses gaining confidence and providing evidence for trustworthiness. Hence, this quality is an important trustworthiness attribute which affects the development process.

- **Predictability**: In general, the service performs in such a way that the user can predict its behaviour, either according to past experience (= best practices), or just due to logic inference of activities. Unpredictable systems are considered as less trustworthy.

- **Flexible continuity**: In case the service does not perform as expected or fails, there is a process to not only fix the issue in adequate time, but also to inform the user, give her/him the chance to be involved, and to re-use the service as soon as possible. This relates to recoverability and flexibility but specifically applies to situations with failure potential.

- **Level of Service** is defined as the type of QoS (quality of service) commitment given to the application or user. It is often part of contractual agreements and therefore is often expressed in measurable terms. Although less well treated in literature related to trustworthiness, it constitutes an important trustworthiness component in most business applications. This quality should be part of the "performance" category.

- **Accessibility** defines whether the service is capable of serving requests, specifically to clients with limited capabilities. While many services are ready to use, they might not be accessible to specific clients. For instance, the connection between the service and the client is problematic or the service requests the clients to be able to read. This quality should be part of the "usability" category.

- **Content Accessibility** is ensuring that the content of the service can be navigated and read by everyone, regardless of location, experience, or the type of computer technology used. It is also part of the "usability" category.

- **Data Accuracy** is defined as correctness of a data value or set of values as source in view of an expected level of exact computing. It should be part of the "data-related qualities" category.

- **Data Completeness** is defined as the availability of all required data. Completeness can refer to both the temporal and spatial aspect of data quality.

- **Data Consistency** means that when a service fails and then restarts, or is evoked to different points in time, the data returned by the service should be still valid, it should respectively be responding with the same result.

- **Resolution** denotes the granularity of information treated, and although being of good value for decision making, it does not reflect a characteristic of the system in general.

4.4 Contribution and Summary of this Chapter

Cyber-physical systems lie at the intersection of the social aspects of people, society and organizations with the technical aspects and information systems used by and underlying such social structures.

Trust can be viewed as a mechanism to reduce complexity in society and trustworthiness can be viewed as a driver for building trusting relationships. Hence, determining the system characteristics that foster trustworthiness contributes to building and optimizing CPS such that higher trust can be achieved in such systems.

To identify the qualities that foster trustworthiness, we have performed an extensive literature survey. The result of the literature review has been structured and classified based on the quality reference of the S-Cube project, which has been established based on ISO/IEC 9126-1 (2001).

While passing through this survey, we also identified some software qualities that either have ambiguous definitions or their relationships to trust have not been well studied. This study highlights several interesting issues about the subject of trustworthiness with respect to cyber-physical systems:

- The concept of trustworthiness needs rigorous specification and definition in the context of CPS.

- To be able to work operationally and objectively with trustworthiness, trustworthiness attributes are necessary. By creating a trustworthiness vector of these trustworthiness attributes for each CPS (dependent on its context and application), the designers of CPS will be able to set targets and identify the best possible practices.

- Much like trust, trustworthiness in the context of cyber-physical systems includes some subjective component, and always will to some extent. To limit the subjective nature of trust, the trustworthiness attributes bring an objective view on trustworthiness of a CPS with objectively building trustworthiness attributes into a system and evaluating them.

The main ideas and findings were investigated in the European project OPTET[8]. In the next chapters, we focus on three important questions:

- Investigate existing development methodologies (cf. Chapter 6) and show how they can be enhanced to enable taking trustworthiness attributes into account, in a comparable way.

- Understand how to define a trustworthiness vector for a specific CPS (cf. Chapters 7 and 9). We need to understand how to identify interdependencies between different trustworthiness attributes, and how to define a "profile" (= set of trustworthiness requirements) for a certain application area.

- Evaluate the trustworthiness of a designed CPS based on its relevant trustworthiness attributes or trustworthiness requirements during design-time (cf. Chapters 10 and 11) and during run-time (cf. Chapter 12).

- Investigate current certification and attestation programs to assess how they could benefit from taking a wider range of characteristics into account than just those related to security, as it is mostly the case today (cf. Chapter 13).

---

[8]The EU-funded project with grant no. 317631 under 7th framework programme https:// cordis.europa.eu/project/rcn/105733/factsheet/en (accessed on 15 August 2018), www.optet.eu (accessed on 10 September 2016)

5 Ambient Assisted Living Case Study

The health-care sector is an application domain profiting a lot from the development of new ICT applications (Avancha et al., 2012; Gritzalis, 2004). Ambient assisted living (AAL) represents technologies that may extend the time people can live in their own home or any preferred place by boosting their independence, autonomy, self-confidence and mobility (AAL Joint Programme, 2013).

In this chapter, we provide an overview of the context of typical AAL systems, discuss the relevance of trustworthiness for AAL systems, and elaborate on the AAL system considered in the OPTET[1] project (cf. OPTET Consortium (2013c)).

5.1 Context Analysis

In Figure 5.1, we illustrate the high-level view of involved entities in an AAL system. Such AAL systems are distributed and connected via Internet in order to support the realization of their business processes. The entities consist of hospital information systems, general practitioners, social centers, insurance companies, patients, their relatives, etc. Some indicative examples of electronic medical transactions are:

- Home monitoring including (but not limited to) alarms and fall notifications,

- Emergency consultation with a physician,

- Electronic notification of laboratory examination results,

- Access to the electronic medical records of patients by general practitioners, and

- Insurance claims.

Developing AAL technologies to be deployed for a beneficial use is a long and costly activity that involves cooperation among various stakeholders. In Figure 5.1,

---

[1]The EU-funded project with grant no. 317631 under 7th framework programme https://cordis.europa.eu/project/rcn/105733/factsheet/en (accessed on 15 August 2018), www.optet.eu (accessed on 10 September 2016)

© Springer Fachmedien Wiesbaden GmbH, part of Springer Nature 2019
N. Gol Mohammadi, *Trustworthy Cyber-Physical Systems*,
https://doi.org/10.1007/978-3-658-27488-7_5

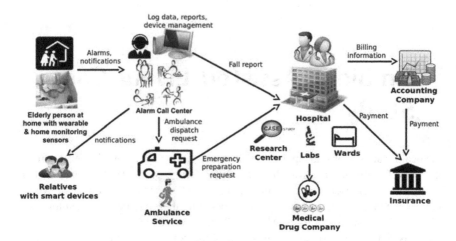

Figure 5.1: The context of an AAL system and involved parties and actors in the scenario (Gol Mohammadi and Heisel, 2016c)

we illustrate the context of an AAL system as well as the high-level view of its involved entities and stakeholders.

The initially identified stakeholders in this scenario are based on (Van den Broek et al., 2010; Gritzalis, 2004; OPTET Consortium, 2013c):

- End-users: The end-users are the service recipients of AAL services, also known under the term "primary users". The end-users are the main beneficiary of the provided value. They are the people with special care needs due to, for example, physical or cognitive impairments. The majority of this group is represented by the elderly people. AAL services are offered primarily for them. By using these services, they are able to overcome limitations of physical, cognitive, social or other nature. AAL services also influence the lives of caregivers, including family, close friends, and staff who are in daily contact with the care service recipient. In this book, only elderly people are considered as end-users since they represent the individuals consuming the offered service. The main concern of these end-users is related to the usability and utility of the AAL services, especially with respect to independent living in their own home (Memon et al., 2014).

- Care service providers: These are the secondary users of the AAL systems. These stakeholders represent physical service providers as for example health-care providers, health-care authorities, health-care centers, clinics and hospitals. They are instances of organizations that together compose a larger group of public or private institutions offering AAL solutions as care services. The quality of the provided physical care services pertains to the responsibility of the care service provider, who have signed a formal agreement to offer a care service to assist people in exchange for money or other value. In many European countries, AAL care service providers are mostly public bodies such as municipalities, state-owned hospitals and nursing homes. Recently, there are also a growing number of private companies entering the European AAL market. We also consider service providers (e.g. housekeeping, personal care and transportation services), financial service providers (e.g. pension and insurance companies paying for AAL services) and housing providers as members of this group (non-ICT service providers). These service providers wish to provide their service to as many people as possible, their main interest is to maintain the agreed quality with the most efficient usage of their available resources.

- Technology providers: Technology providers include software developers of home monitoring systems, fall detection systems or infrastructure providers like telecommunication providers, internet service providers, etc. They are institutions that develop technologies for realizing AAL solutions. These technologies can be both, hardware and software. The main concern of this group is to develop their technology in a most cost-effective way - meaning to reduce production costs while increasing sales revenue in the same time.

- The authorities: Since the AAL solutions are integrated into the daily life of the end-users and other involved people (e.g. their relatives), they are especially vulnerable to, for example, loss of privacy, freedom and control over their lives. For this reason, regulations (e.g. GDPR) are put in place in the European countries. In many other countries, there also exists local regulation for health-care services (e.g. health insurance portability and accountability act[2] (HIPAA) in United States). In addition, many AAL solutions function in the borderline of health-care services, where ethical issues are already a major concern. The role of the authorities in the AAL ecosystem is to create new laws and to monitor compliance with existing laws.

Any successful implementation of AAL services needs to involve and consider all relevant stakeholders.

---

[2]https://www.cms.gov/Outreach-and-Education/Medicare-Learning
-Network-MLN/MLNProducts/Downloads/HIPAAPrivacyandSecurity.pdf (accessed on 22 October 2018)

5.2 Relevance of Trustworthiness in AAL Systems

In Chapters 2 and 3, we explained different factors that impact the trust properties of the trustors. For example, trust in general depends on different factors including age, culture, and health conditions (Harrefors et al., 2010). Considering the trustworthiness of the trustee (here, the AAL system), privacy and integrity of collected data from medical devices are two major trust concerns in AAL systems (cf. Chapter 4). Ziefle et al. (2011) investigate user attitudes towards health-care services at home. Ziefle et al. demonstrate that regardless of age of users if the personal data protection is unclear to them, then users are sceptical about accepting health-care services. Users are also concerned about the data loss or corruption related to technical problems (Ziefle et al., 2011). Another major concern being stated by elderly people using sensors is the reliability and usability (Steinke et al., 2012; Rashidi and Mihailidis, 2013; Steinke et al., 2013). Similar results are found by Rahimpour et al. (2008) who discovered usability and unawareness concerns about system functionality as important trust issues. As further trust issues, Dahl and Holbø (2012) reveal that privacy and accountability as concerns when using location-tracking health-care services for dementia patients. Based on the state of the art analysis, it can be concluded that trustworthiness is an emergent property of AAL systems for the following reasons (OPTET Consortium, 2013c):

- A large amount of personal data is collected by AAL systems from their end-users. AAL systems are also capable of collecting and processing sensitive information due to their ambient nature. Trustworthiness is hence an important and strong business success factor from which AAL service providers can benefit.

- Business processes of an AAL systems involve multiple participants and are distributed. As an example, a service for detection and management of incidents of elderly people collects and shares their movement data with alarm and ambulatory service providers. Therefore, trustworthiness of such an AAL system must be assured and demonstrated.

- In the application domain of an AAL system, advanced privacy settings set by the users of the health-care service are unrealistic. Therefore, AAL services need to be made trustworthy. A trustworthy service requires less reliance on advanced user knowledge since it is developed in a way that a misuse of user data is blocked.

- Strict requirements on end-to-end system reliability and data delivery (from the sensors, e.g. challenges related to radio frequency communication when the end-user moves around his/her home) are imposed by AAL services.

As regards the trustworthiness of health-care services, we consider a vector of trustworthiness attributes, which either address the fulfillment of the mission or the privacy perspective. Reliability, safety, and availability of the system, when the elderly person needs help, are some examples of trustworthiness attributes that address fulfillment of the mission.

5.3 AAL Use Case in the OPTET Project

In this section, we describe the real-life use case study of the OPTET project. This use case serves as running example to demonstrate the applicability of the developed methods in this book. While the next chapters are based on different scenarios described in the respective chapter, this chapter discusses the general context of the AAL use case.

Alarm Call Center. The AAL use case in OPTET was developed in collaboration with the municipality of Trondheim, Norway striving for the goal to create a realistic scenario to be implemented in close collaboration with end-users and stakeholders (OPTET Consortium, 2013c).

So-called coordination reform ("Samhandlingsreformen") (Hanssen, 2008), which got effective in January 2012 by the Norwegian government[3] (Monkerud and Tjerbo, 2016; Heimly and Hygen, 2011), triggered Trondheim Municipality (TM) to set up an advanced alarm call center for unplanned health-care and welfare services. The coordination reform intends to transform the Norwegian health-care system into a more distributed one. This requires strengthening of the local forces in the primary care services. Therefore, the Norwegian municipalities require structural changes to cope with early discharged patients and with new responsibilities transferred from hospitals to primary care service providers (Heimly and Hygen, 2011). The establishment of an advanced alarm call center is one of the means to handle the increased number of unplanned enquiries. Additionally, the alarm call center is planned to be the coordinator for future AAL services being introduced in the region of Trondheim (OPTET Consortium, 2013c). Its main responsibilities are: (i) 24/7/365[4] reception of unplanned and emergency visits related to health-care and assisted living, (ii) decisions on further treatment, hospitalization, etc., (iii)

---

[3]https://www.regjeringen.no/en/id4/ (accessed on 7 August 2018)
[4]An health-care service that is available any time and every day.

ambulant emergency units and follow up procedures, and (iv) operation of AAL technologies approved as services to the public.

Alarm Service in the Alarm Call Center. Another required enhancement for alarm centers with implemented AAL services is the so-called safety alarm service. It includes a home-based alarm device known as Personal Emergency Response Systems (PERS) allowing the end-users to call for help in an emergency situation. Generally, PERS consists of three components: (i) a wearable alarm device powered by battery that includes a radio transmitter and a pushbutton, (ii) a base station including loudspeaker and microphone, which is connected to an in-house telephone, and iii) the alarm call center that monitors all incoming requests. A wireless communication protocol is usually used between the wearable alarm device and the base station. The base station sends an emergency message to an alarm call center, where the staff is available to handle the situation and take an appropriate action (e.g. dispatching medical aid to the elderly person needing help, cf. Figure 5.1).

PERS help to reduce the consequences of incidents in the elderly people's homes by shortening the time between the incident and the arrival of medical care (Roush et al., 1995). However, first generation PERS have some restrictions in home nursing. For instance, the elderly person can not trigger the alarm by pushing a button if she/he is unconscious due to, for example, a fall (Gurley et al., 1996). Some further limitations of mobile safety alarm systems are identified (Svagård et al., 2014; Svagård and Boysen, 2016; Porter, 2005; OPTET Consortium, 2013c). The ones interesting for us are as follows: (i) The alarm does not work when the end-users are outside the range of the base station, e.g. when they are in the basement or outside their home; (ii) The alarm does not work if the end-users are not able to press the button; (iii) The alarm devices are sometimes inconvenient for the end-users while they are sleeping and are, hence, not always worn. This becomes critical, when the end-user gets out of bed during the night and she/he is not wearing the alarm device. The effect of a "mobile push button safety alarm" on outdoor walks, fear of falling, and quality of life was tested in a randomized controlled trial by Scheffer et al. (2012). Results indicated that the outdoor alarm had no added value over the usual home-based alarm. The most common reason for not using the outdoor mobile alarm device was that the alarm device was considered too heavy to carry, or the alarm was not perceived as user-friendly. Those who used the additional outdoor mobile alarm device had more outdoors walks at baseline than those who did not use it. Elderly people feel barriers to the use of new technologies, which is why technology for elderly people should be based on the users' perspective and that they should be engaged in all parts of the development process (Scheffer et al., 2012; Tacken et al., 2005).

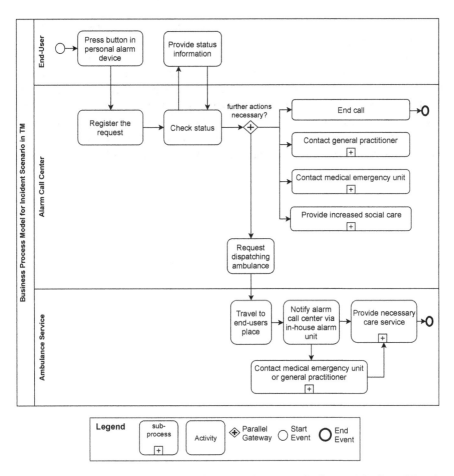

Figure 5.2: An exemplary usage scenario of an AAL system in the municipality of Trondheim based on (OPTET Consortium, 2013c)

Figure 5.2 describes a usage scenario of the municipality of Trondheim: the
end-user has a fall incident in her/his home. This event is not observable as long as
the end-user does not activate her/his alarm device, which however is supported
by the mobile safety alarm device and the in-house alarm unit. The request is
then received, registered and responded to by the alarm call center. Based on
the information provided by the end-user, the alarm call center decides on an
appropriate action. Such an action may include dispatching ambulatory staff from

the ambulance service (cf. Figure 5.1) to the end-user's home, and possibly offering medical assistance.

The goal in this book is to find out how existing AAL systems can be made trustworthy and how new ones can be developed trustworthy right from the beginning. Furthermore, the AAL system can be enhanced by using the methods presented in this book. However, the presented methods in this book can be applied to any CPS. The need for these methods has been motivated by the real-life case study from the OPTET project. In the next chapters, the proposed methods will be illustrated using a part of the AAL system with its supporting tools and applications.

Part II

Methods for Developing a Trustworthy Cyber-Physical System

6 Trustworthiness-by-design

Software development projects have to address trustworthiness requirements from the very early stages of development using 1) constructive methods to enable trustworthiness-by-design and 2) analytical methods for quality assurance. However, applying trustworthiness-by-design methods alone does not guarantee trustworthiness by itself. There should be evidence that indicates the trustworthiness of software so that the stakeholders can make informed decisions. In this chapter[1], we first analyze existing engineering methods and discuss whether they address trustworthiness as an important step in the development process or if it is only thought of as an optional add-on. Then, we propose a generic mechanism as an extension to existing methods to enable trustworthiness-by-design. More precisely, we provide process chunks that can be incorporated into the methods, thus leading to a higher value of trustworthiness. The extension mechanism is illustrated by means of an application example.

6.1 Motivation

As mentioned in Chapter 1, organizations and individuals are not readily able to understand who processes their data, for which purpose it is being used, and whether or not the use complies with security rules and privacy laws in a given country. Thus, CPS need to be trustworthy to mitigate the risks and trust concerns of their users. A major reason for these vulnerabilities, defects, and non-transparencies are failures and flaws in the development processes of software systems (Broy et al., 2012; Broy and Schmidt, 2014; Khaitan and McCalley, 2015). We believe that bringing transparency to the processes will help users in making conscious decisions and remove their uncertainty in the developed software. Understanding how to address trustworthiness in early design has become increasingly important for successful trustworthy software and system development. The design methodologies and mechanisms should address the different challenges of building trustworthy software as well as evaluating its trustworthiness. In this chapter, we aim at enabling a

---

[1]This chapter partially adapts Gol Mohammadi et al. (2015c), Paulus et al. (2013) © IFIP International Federation for Information Processing 2013, and Gol Mohammadi et al. (2014b) © Springer International Publishing Switzerland 2014, with the permission of the publishers.

© Springer Fachmedien Wiesbaden GmbH, part of Springer Nature 2019
N. Gol Mohammadi, *Trustworthy Cyber-Physical Systems*,
https://doi.org/10.1007/978-3-658-27488-7_6

trustworthiness-by-design process to increase the trustworthiness of the developed systems.

There are limited contributions that approach trust and trustworthiness issues other than those related to security. Most existing approaches have assumed that one-dimensional properties of services lead to trustworthiness of such services, and even to trust in them by users, such as a certification (e.g. Common Criteria (ISO/IEC 15408-1, 2009)), the presence of certain technologies (e.g. encryption), or the use of certain methodologies (e.g. Systems Security Engineering - Capability Maturity Model (ISO/IEC 21827, 2008)). In this work, we relax the assumption of a one-dimensional approach and instead consider a multitude of quality attributes. Important software qualities and their impact on system trustworthiness have been analyzed in Chapter 4. This allows us to propose a general approach for designing trustworthy CPS, even though the relevance of the attributes might differ across several domains. Trustworthiness of the software is a major factor that should be considered in the whole lifecycle of a CPS. Trustworthiness must be considered in all development phases and should be carefully woven into the core of the system rather than bolted on as an afterthought. Existing engineering processes are not successful in considering trustworthiness as a multifaceted concept. Therefore, in order to address this gap in the development of trustworthy software, we believe that appropriate methods and developer guidance should be defined, preferably as generic and reusable process building blocks that can be added to existing software engineering methodologies.

Defining reusable process chunks instead of defining yet another development process model brings flexibility and reduces the complexity in adapting trustworthy software processes. The contribution of this chapter is twofold. First, we review and analyze a set of common development methodologies. We discuss which character-istics of these methodologies are promising to build trustworthy systems, and which ones indicate improvement potential. Second, we provide a generic mechanism for enhancing software development methodologies to enable trustworthiness-by-design. To this end, we use the results of our performed literature review. Based on our findings, we propose an extension of the Software Process Engineering Meta-model (SPEM)[2] (Object Management Group: SPEM, 2008), which allows for tailoring certain "trustworthy" process chunks into the development methodologies. In particular, we define trustworthiness capability patterns, which provide guidance for developing trustworthy systems. We show the applicability of our approach by exemplarily extending an existing software development methodology, namely User-Centered Design, to involve threat analysis and trustworthiness measurement.

---

[2]SPEM is used to define software and systems development processes and their components. The SPEM 2.0 Meta-Model is a MOF-based model that reuses other OMG specifications. http://www.omg.org/spec/SPEM/2.0/ (accessed on 17 August 2018)

Furthermore, we illustrate how to facilitate this extension mechanism by means of an initial Computer-Aided Software Engineering (CASE) tool support.

The remainder of this chapter is structured as follows. In Section 6.2, we present the analysis results of a comparative study on existing engineering processes, with regard to the question whether they address trustworthiness. Section 6.3 presents our solution and the contribution of this chapter. In particular, we introduce the general mechanism to extend existing engineering methodologies in order to cover trustworthiness attributes. Section 6.4 illustrates the application of our approach by showing how a well-known engineering methodology can be extended to support trustworthiness-by-design. Section 6.5 provides a summary of this chapter and lessons learned.

6.2 Analysis of Software Development Methodologies

Based on the following distinction of development process categories (cf. Section 6.2.1), we report on our findings from the analysis of well-established development methodologies with respect to their suitability to enable trustworthiness-by-design (cf. Section 6.2.2).

6.2.1 Categories of Development Methodologies

Before analyzing development methodologies regarding their support for designing trustworthy systems, it is useful to consider general categories of software development in order to narrow the scope of the analysis. One may distinguish the following three main categories of development methodologies (Dahrendorf, 2005; Paulus et al., 2013) with respect to the consideration of trustworthiness:

- Uncontrolled: The applications are developed without any special considerations of trustworthiness. This approach is very risky regarding the effort (and costs) required for reconstructing, measuring and documenting the elements of trustworthiness of the development process.

- Controlled: Trustworthiness is considered along some or even all phases of the development process. It does not necessarily mean that the developed application is trustworthy (or not) but only that trustworthiness has been considered with a specific attention.

- Constrained: The application is developed in a special way and with a specific language, assuring that the design principles result in measurable elements enabling trustworthiness and are de facto applied.

Although they may in principle all lead to trustworthy systems in the end, it is more likely that this will be the case using a controlled or constrained rather than an uncontrolled methodology. However, it may not be feasible to apply a constrained methodology to all development projects. A major reason for not using controlled or constrained development methodologies in practice is that they require a relatively high initial investment and effort, and only "pay back" at a relatively late point in the development process (Paulus et al., 2013). Depending on the development goals, it might be sufficient to create a system that is "trustworthy enough" for its purpose. In contrast to the controlled and constrained methodologies (e.g. using automated reasoning and model-driven engineering (Schmidt, 2006), or Common Criteria (ISO/IEC 15408-1, 2009)), industry has widely picked up many of the methodologies that we have identified to be uncontrolled, such as the trustworthy computing security development lifecycle (SDL) (Lipner, 2004), or BSIMM[3].

A number of standards and other activities that address security in the software development process fall into the controlled methodologies category. Security is, in that sense, primarily a set of quality requirements that need to be specified in the first place, and assured along the remaining development and operational activities. With this in mind, addressing trustworthiness within the development lifecycle could very much benefit from the activities that are meant to address security since they in general encompass practices for the assurance of specific (security) properties. However, these methodologies still show potential for improvements with regard to trustworthiness. Our focus is on extending development processes, ideally by defining standards-based additional activities (process chunks) that particularly allow for considering trustworthiness requirements and characteristics.

6.2.2 Review of Development Models and Practices

During the analysis process, a significant number of other methodologies and approaches have been investigated, among others, plan-driven process (Royce, 1987) or incremental development (Sommerville, 2016). The Waterfall model is a well-known example of plan-driven development. We dropped these here since they either replicate some of the features of other software development processes or because their contribution to trustworthiness showed to be rather very small.

---

[3]BSIMM is not a development methodology. It's a model for measuring how well a software development methodology or practice performs, in terms of security. We consider it here since it helps quantifying and improving the practices and methodology.

The comprehensive set of trustworthiness attributes presented in Chapter 4 was a starting point and basis for selecting and studying existing methodologies. For example, when considering usability as a trustworthiness attribute, i.e. in oder to build intuitively usable systems, user-centered approaches have been analyzed. The list of analyzed software development methodologies contains either well-known and widely used methodologies in the state of the art or methodologies that were used by the industrial project partners of the OPTET[4] project.

In the following, we briefly describe which elements of the development approaches actually increase or inhibit trustworthiness, and how the approaches could be used for enabling trustworthiness.

Reuse-Oriented Methodologies

Very few systems today are created completely from scratch; in most cases there is some sort of reuse of design or code from other sources within or outside the organization (cf. Sommerville (2016)). Existing code can typically be used as-is, modified as needed or wrapped with an interface. Reuse is of particular relevance for service-oriented systems where services are mixed and matched in order to create larger systems. Reuse-oriented methodologies (Hardung et al., 2004; Pohl et al., 2005; Brugali et al., 2012) can be very ad-hoc, and often there are no means to assure trustworthiness.

Pros with regard to Trustworthiness:

- The system can be based on existing parts that are known to be trustworthy. This does, however, not mean that the composition is just as trustworthy as the sum of its parts.

Cons with regard to Trustworthiness:

- Re-use of components that are "not-invented-here" leads to uncertainty.

- Increased complexity due to heterogeneous component assembly.

- The use of existing components in a different context than originally targeted may under certain circumstances (e.g. not monitored re-use of in-house developed components) jeopardize an existing security or trustworthiness property.

This approach has both pros and cons regarding trustworthiness modelling. On the positive side, already existing, trustworthy and trusted components may lead

---

[4]The EU-funded project with grant no. 317631 under 7th framework programme https://cordis.europa.eu/project/rcn/105733/factsheet/en (accessed on 15 August 2018)

to easier, trustworthiness modelling for the overall solution. Adequate software assurance, e.g. a security certification, or source code availability may help in improving trustworthiness of re-used "foreign" components. The drawback is that there is a risk that the trustworthiness of the combined system may decrease due to the combination with less trustworthy components.

Model-Driven Methodologies

Model-Driven Engineering (MDE) (Schmidt, 2006; Weigert and Weil, 2006) (encompassing the OMG term Model-Driven Architecture (MDA) and others) refers to the process of creating domain models to represent application structure, behavior and requirements within particular domains, and the use of transformations that can analyze certain aspects of these models and then create artifacts such as code and simulators. A lot of the development effort is put into the application design, and the reuse of patterns and best practices is central during modelling. Model-driven development typically belongs to the uncontrolled category, but can turn in a controlled or a constrained methodology when there are measures in place for ensuring trustworthiness.

Pros with regard to Trustworthiness:

- Coding practices that are deemed insecure or unreliable can be eliminated through the use of formal reasoning of the models.

- Coding policies related to trustworthiness, reliability and security could be systematically added to the generated code.

- Problems that lead to trustworthiness concerns can, at least theoretically, be detected early during model analysis and simulation.

- Separation of concerns allows trust issues to be independent of the platform, and results also in less complicated models and a better combination of different expertise.

Cons with regard to Trustworthiness:

- Systems developed with such methods tends to be expensive to maintain, and may therefore suffer from a lack of updates.

- Requires significant training and tool support, which might become outdated.

- A structured, model-driven approach does not prevent forgetting security and trustworthiness requirements.

- Later changes during development need to review and potentially change the model.

- The (time and space) complexity of the formal verification of especially non-functional properties may lead to omitting certain necessary computations when the project is under time and resource pressure.

With a model-driven approach, it is possible to eliminate deemed insecure or unreliable design and coding practices. An early model analysis and simulation with respect to trustworthiness is possible and of high value. In addition, model-driven security tests could improve the trustworthiness. However, in general, there are no specific trustworthiness related modelling properties, the methodology is just model-driven. The major drawback is that the computational complexity for verifying non-functional properties is very high.

Test-Driven Development Methodologies

Test-driven development (Beck, 2003; Astels, 2003) is considered to be part of agile development practices. In test-driven development, developers first implement test code that is able to test corresponding requirements, and only after that the actual code of a module, a function, a class is implemented. The main purpose for test-driven development is to increase the test coverage, thereby allowing for a higher quality assurance and thus requirements coverage, specifically related to non-functional aspects. The drawback of test-driven approaches consists in the fact that, due to the necessary micro-iterations, the design of the software is subject to on-going changes. This makes e.g. the combination of model-driven and test-driven approaches impossible.

Pros with regard to Trustworthiness:

- The high degree of test coverage (that could be up to 100%) assures the implementation of trustworthiness related requirements.

Cons with regard to Trustworthiness:

- The programming technique cannot be combined with (formal) assurance methodologies, e.g. using model-driven approaches, Common Criteria, or formal verification.

Test-driven development is well suited for assuring the presence of well-described trustworthiness requirements. Moreover, this approach can be successfully used to address changes of the threat landscape. A major drawback, though, is that it cannot easily be combined with modelling techniques that are used for formal assurance methodologies

User-Centered Design

In software engineering there is a drive to better integrate user-centered approaches and software engineering (Sutcliffe, 2005). Generally speaking, user-centered design processes consist of the following general steps; 1) Knowledge elicitation and attempt at understanding the context of use; 2) defining user requirements; 3) prototyping the system and 4) evaluation, which provides input for the refinement of the design. This model is generally used iteratively and by going through the process multiple times developers converge on a user-friendly system. These systems have also been proposed for the development of e-Services (Velsen et al., 2009).

Pros with regard to Trustworthiness:

• New and evolving requirements for trustworthiness may be incorporated as part of an iterative process.

• The end-users will have a good sense of ownership and understanding of the product after participating in the development process.

• User-centered design is a specialisation of incremental development and therefore shares trustworthiness characteristics of those as well (see Table 6.2).

• By using an incremental user-centered process, it is possible that throughout the design process the design is validated to establish whether the trustworthiness attributes designed into the system appropriately address any concerns with respect to trust that the system end-users might have.

Cons with regard to Trustworthiness:

• Possible mismatch between organisational procedures/policies and a more informal or agile process.

• Little documentation, increasing complexity and long-lifetime systems may result in security flaws. Especially, documentation on non-functional aspects that are cross-cutting among different software feature implementations could be not well documented.

• Security and trustworthiness can be difficult to test and evaluate, specifically by the user, and may therefore lose focus on the development.

The user centred design processes are unrelated to trustworthiness modelling. Only the use of modelling techniques in general for a user-centred design will allow for also modelling trustworthiness requirements. The incremental nature of user-centerd design allows new and evolving requirements for trustworthiness to be incorporated as part of an iterative process. After participating in the development process, the end-users will have a good sense of ownership and understanding of the product. Iterative processes allow for modelling of properties, but changes to the model that reflect changed or more detailed end-user expectations, will in turn require changing the design and code, eventually in another iteration. Additionally, there are no specific trustworthiness modelling capabilities.

Common Criteria – ISO 15408

The Common Criteria[5] (CC) (ISO/IEC 15408-1, 2009) is a standardized approach to evaluate security properties of (information) systems (Avizienis et al., 2004). A "Target of Evaluation" is tested against so-called "Security Targets" that are composed of given Functional Security Requirements and Security Assurance Requirements (both addressing development and operations) and are selected based on a protection requirement evaluation. Furthermore, the evaluation can be performed at different strengths called "Evaluation Assurance Level".

On the downside, there are some disadvantages: the development model is quite stiff, and does not easily allow for an adjustment to specific environments. Furthermore, Common Criteria is an "all-or-nothing" approach, one can limit the Target of Evaluation or the Evaluation Assurance Level, but it is then rather difficult to express the overall security or trustworthiness of a system with metrics related to CC.

Pros with regard to Trustworthiness:

- Evaluations related to security and assurance indicates to what level the target application can be trusted.

- CC evaluations are performed by (trusted) third parties.

- There are security profiles for various types of application domains.

Cons with regard to Trustworthiness:

- Protection profiles are not tailored for cloud services.

---

[5]Strictly speaking, Common Criteria is not a development model. However, the necessary documents for this standard are created along the development process. It is one of major international standards for security certification. Therefore, we consider it here as well.

- A CC certification can be misunderstood to prove the security or trustworthiness of a system, but it actually does only provide evidence for a very specific property of a small portion of the system[6].

The Common Criteria approach is unrelated to modelling in general, although the higher evaluation assurance levels would benefit from modelling. The functional security requirements may serve well as input for a (security-related) trustworthiness modelling, whereas the security assurance requirements, as the properties of the development process itself, shall be used for a modelling of the developing organization. Note that these constitute two different modelling approaches.

A drawback is a) that not many organizations use CC and b) that the development process is relatively stiff and time consuming. CC belongs to the controlled development category though it is mainly designed for evaluation.

ISO 21827 Systems Security Engineering - Capability Maturity Model

The Systems Security Engineering - Capability Maturity Model (SSE-CMM) is a specialization of the more generic Capability Maturity Model (CMM) developed by the Software Engineering Institute at the Carnegie Mellon University. Originally, in 1996, SSE-CCM was an initiative of the NSA, but was given over later to the International Systems Security Engineering Association, that published it as ISO/IEC 21827 (2008). In contrast to the previous examples, SSE-CMM targets the developing organization and not the product or service to be developed. There are a number of so-called "base practices" (11 security base practices and 11 project and organizational base practices) that can be fulfilled to different levels of maturity. The maturity levels are identical to CMM.

Pros with regard to Trustworthiness:

- The developing organization gains more and more experience in developing secure and generically good quality software.

- The use of a quality-related maturity model infers that user-centric non-functional requirements such as security and trustworthiness will be taken into account.

Cons with regard to Trustworthiness:

- This is an organizational approach rather than a system-centric approach; hence there is not really any guarantee about the trustworthiness of the developed

---

[6]We are aware that this statement depends on the specified Target of Evaluation (ToE). If the ToE is the complete system then the certification is for the complete system. However, in practice it is infeasible to evaluate a complete system based on CC.

application (which could e.g. be put to use in another way than it was intended for).

This approach focuses on the development of trustworthiness for the developing organization, instead on the to-be developed software, service or system. The security best practices may serve as input for modelling trustworthiness requirements when modelling the development process.

Building Security In Maturity Model and OpenSAMM

The Building Security In Maturity Model (BSIMM)[7] initiative has recognized the caveat of ISO 21827 being oriented towards the developing organization, and has proposed a maturity model that is centralized around the software to be developed (McGraw, 2006). It defines activities in four groups (Governance, Intelligence, Secure Software Development Life Cycle (SSDL) Touchpoints[8], Deployment) that are rated in their maturity according to three levels. The Open Software Assurance Maturity Model (OpenSAMM)[9] [10] is a very similar approach that has the same origin, but was developed slightly differently and is now an Open Web Application Security Project (OWASP)[11].

The BSIMM presents an ideal starting point for developing trustworthiness activities within an organization, since it allows tracking the maturity of the development process in terms of addressing security requirements. This could also be used for trustworthiness.

Pros with regard to Trustworthiness:

- The maturity-oriented approach requires the identification of security (and potentially) trustworthiness properties and assures their existence according to different levels of assurance.

- The probability of producing a secure (and trustworthy) system is high.

Cons with regard to Trustworthiness:

- There is no evidence that the system actually is trustworthy or even secure.

---

[7]https://www.bsimm.com (accessed on 15 August 2018)

[8]https://www.bsimm.com/framework/software-security-development-lifecycle.html (accessed on 17 August 2018)

[9]https://www.owasp.org/index.php/OWASP_SAMM_Project (accessed on 17 August 2018)

[10]http://www.opensamm.org (accessed on 17 August 2018)

[11]https://www.owasp.org/index.php/About_The_Open_Web_Application _Security_Project (accessed on 17 August 2018)

This approach means to develop trustworthiness for the developing organization instead of the to-be developed software, service, or system. The security best practices may serve as input for modelling trustworthiness requirements when modelling the development process.

The Security Development Lifecycle

In 2001, Microsoft[12] has started the security-oriented software engineering process that has probably had the largest impact across the whole software industry. Yet, the "process" was more a collection of individual activities along the software development lifecycle than a real structured approach. Microsoft SDL has been adopted by a large number of organizations in different variants. The focus point of the Microsoft SDL[13] is that every single measure was optimized over time to either have a positive ROI (return on investment) or it was dropped again. This results in a number of industry-proven best practices for enhancing the security of software. Since there is no standardized list of activities, there is no benchmark to map activities against. Consequently, deducing comparable metrics from that approach seems almost impossible. An exception might be found in all cases where Microsoft tools are used since in that case one might measure the use of security-configurations during compilation etc., that are therefore relatively engineering-centric measures.

The use of metrics in this environment seems unlikely to produce comparable and sustainable results; some standardization activities might be necessary, e.g. the number (percentage) of components that have been subject to threat modelling might be necessary, or the "size" of the attack surface identified by threat modelling means.

Pros with regard to Trustworthiness:

- Microsoft, which is the world's largest software manufacturer does use this approach.

- The identified measures have proven to be usable and effective over the course of more than a decade.

Cons with regard to Trustworthiness:

- There is no evidence that the system actually is trustworthy or even secure.

Microsoft SDL is a development-related threat modelling and was Microsoft's major investment to increase the trustworthiness of its products ("Trustworthy

---

[12]https://www.microsoft.com/ (accessed on 15 July 2018)
[13]https://www.microsoft.com/en-us/SDL (accessed on 17 August 2018)

Computing Initiative"). The comparability is only given if more detailed parameters are specified. For the modelling of trustworthiness, this method is only of limited help.

Software Security Touchpoints

Software security touchpoints is not a methodology by itself, but a set of best practices that can be applied (even several times) throughout the software lifecycle. As such, it represents a set of activities that can be "added" to existing development models and practices to enhance an uncontrolled and thus turn it into a controlled one. McGraw has defined the following seven (plus one) touchpoints that are both constructive and destructive activities (McGraw, 2006): 1) Code review, 2) Architectural risk analysis, 3) Penetration testing, 4) Risk-based security tests, 5) Abuse cases, 6) Security requirements, 7) Security operations, and 8) External analysis. All of these touchpoints can reveal measurable results such as a number of software vulnerabilities, critical risks, successful attacks, potential attackers and security requirements, but these numbers will eventually depend on how thorough these practices are performed and what level of expertise the people involved have. They are therefore not good subjects for revealing the trustworthiness of the developed application itself.

Pros with regard to Trustworthiness:

- Proven set of best practices makes it relatively probable that security (and potentially trustworthiness) is addressed right.

- Measurable results provide some indications for revealing how security (and potentially trustworthiness) has been treated.

Cons with regard to Trustworthiness:

- There is no evidence that the system is actually trustworthy or even secure.

Software security touchpoints reveal measurable results, but these are not a good basis to measure or model the trustworthiness of the software, because they are based on individual competencies of the involved people.

OWASP Comprehensive, Lightweight Application Security Process

The OWASP[14] is a non-profit, worldwide initiative that originally centralized its activities on web application security. But, in the meantime, it produces software,

---

[14]https://www.owasp.org/index.php/About_The_Open_Web_Application
_Security_Project (accessed on 17 August 2018)

documentation, methodologies, and tools for almost every software component. The efforts are community-driven, so it may happen that a project might be highly supported in one year, and does not get any attention the year after. There is no common methodology, but a multitude of projects trying to enhance the security of software.

A major contribution in terms of metrics is the OWASP risk rating methodology that helps rating security risks and vulnerabilities of software in a comparable fashion. As such, the OWASP risk rating presents a starting point for further metric investigation.

Pros with regard to Trustworthiness:

- Very advanced risk methodology as the basis of security or trustworthiness decisions.

- Proven set of best practices makes it relatively probable that security (and potentially trustworthiness) is addressed right.

Cons with regard to Trustworthiness:

- There is no evidence that the system actually is trustworthy or even secure.

- There is a risk that the methodology will not be developed further and thus that it may reflect outdated knowledge.

The metrics stemming from the OWASP risk rating are risk-oriented. A modelling of trustworthiness would actually involve first modelling the risks and the actors involved in the OWASP risk rating analysis process.

The SHIELDS approach

Similarly to the software security touchpoints, the SHIELDS[15] approach consists of a set of activities that are process-agnostic, but tied together by a repository of security information and tool artefacts (SHIELDS, 2010). These activities are basically:

- Security modelling: is the first step that identifies threats and causes of vulnerabilities, security inspection process descriptions.

- Security detection: tools and methods that help the developer spot security bugs based on the already identified concerns from the first step.

---

[15]The EU-funded project with grant no. 215995 under FP7-ICT program https://cordis.europa.eu/project/rcn/85431_en.html (accessed on 15 August 2018)

- Security inspection: manual (human) review of design documents and code, but with tool support for guidance and documentation.

- Security testing: active and passive testing tools and techniques that target the identified concerns from the first step.

- Elimination: models that guide the developer on how to remove and avoid vulnerabilities, typical security patterns, and process descriptions.

- Education: activities to help an organisation learn from past mistakes and share that information with others. Typically done by modelling causes and sharing them in the common repository.

Though each activity does not give any good benchmark on the trustworthiness of the target application, the repository itself is able to collect statistics from static analysis tools and testing tools, indicating what kind of vulnerabilities occur more frequently than others.

Pros with regard to Trustworthiness:

- The set of activities is structured around security properties, and yields with high probability a secure system.

- Proven set of best practices makes it relatively probable that security (and potentially trustworthiness) is addressed right.

Cons with regard to Trustworthiness:

- There is no evidence that the system actually is trustworthy or even secure.

- All activities are optional.

The SHIELDS approach collates the results of the activities in the development process to help optimize future developments. The statistics thus obtained can enhance the trustworthiness of the process as common vulnerability types are identified. The measurability as well as the modelling of the trustworthiness of a specific application is not given, it is yet mandated to develop a security modelling that may serve as a starting point. Moreover, the use of this approach in itself may actually enhance the trustworthiness of the developing organization, and the activities mandated in this approach may serve as input for a trustworthiness modelling of the development process.

The Open Group Architecture Framework

The Open Group Architecture Framework (TOGAF)[16] (Andrew Josey, 2009), an open group standard, is a framework and methodology for developing enterprise architecture. An enterprise is defined as any collection of organizations that has a common set of goals, e.g. government agency, a whole corporation, or a single department. TOGAF guides the process of creating enterprise architecture that includes different types of architecture:

- Business Architecture: The business strategy, governance, organization, and key business processes.

- Data Architecture: The structure of an organization's logical and physical data assets and data management resources.

- Application Architecture: A blueprint for the individual applications to be deployed, their interactions, and their relationships to the core business processes of the organization.

- Technology Architecture: The logical software and hardware capabilities that are required to support the deployment of business, data, and application services.

Central to TOGAF is the architecture development method. The method is supported by a number of guidelines and techniques. The process consists of multiple phases that develop the architecture vision, specify the baseline and target architectures, identify the transitions between them, plan, and manage the implementation of the architecture. Central to these phases is the requirements management phase that is always active and used to validate the outputs of the other phases.

TOGAF does not certify the product architecture, i.e. there is no structure in place to validate the system design and implementation. However, the focus is on certifying the architects who will apply the methodology.

Pros with regard to Trustworthiness:

- The architectural approach based on the business strategy leads by "design" to a trustworthy system.

Cons with regard to Trustworthiness:

- There is no evidence that the system is actually trustworthy or even secure.

- No architectural patterns available for better guidance.

---

[16]`http://www.opengroup.org/TOGAF-9.2-Overview` (accessed on 17 August 2018)

From our perspective, TOGAF allows building and managing a system based on stakeholders requirements and shows the different domains of the system that need to be addressed (business, application, data, technology) to this end. It constitutes an approach that would allow the corresponding development of models for business, data, application, and technology (a translation or mapping of the architecture to models would be necessary) and due to the tight integration such an approach would yield potentially trustworthy systems. Nevertheless, formal trustworthiness requirements for such a modelling beyond the integrated approach are not given.

We could benefit from architecture patterns provided by TOGAF. However, TO-GAF architecture patterns are a work-in-progress and they have not been integrated yet into the process. TOGAF (in its current version 9.2) provides information about what types of patterns there are and what the content should be without explicitly listing any.

6.2.3 Summary

We have performed a literature survey and included typical, well-known software development methodologies as well as a few additional approaches typically found in the area of software security. For each methodology, we have identified elements, properties, or characteristics that are either interesting with respect to trustworthiness, or indicating improvement potential, respectively. Thereby, we analyzed to what extent the methodologies already address building trustworthiness attributes into the system, and what needs to be done to extend the respective approaches for achieving the "trustworthiness-by-design" property. Hence, this is useful information for the choice and combination of methodologies to optimize trustworthiness-by-design. Table 6.1 shows our summary of the thirteen methodologies and summarizes the comparative study.

There are many approaches towards constructive quality assurance of software systems, proposing guidelines, principles, and methodologies for developing high-quality software. There are also more generic and well-established development methodologies that can be tuned into more security-aware variants, and there are specialized constrained methodologies that are probably not relevant for most organizations. Sommerville (2016) states that reuse-oriented or test-driven development can, in principle, result in trustworthy systems as well, since continuous user feedback, reuse, and early testing can enhance software quality and mitigate risks. Eliciting end-user requirements is also a key aspect of User-Centered Design (Sutcliffe, 2005), which can be seen as a potential to consider user's trust concerns early in the development.

Table 6.1: Development methodologies and their support for trustworthiness-by-design

Development Methodology	Elements that could contribute to Trustworthiness	Improvement Suggestions with respect to Trustworthiness
Reuse-oriented (Sommerville, 2016)	Re-use of trustworthy components.	1) Trustworthiness certification improves faith in externally created components. 2) Monitoring gives alerts about changes to external components.
Model-driven (Schmidt, 2006), (Weigert and Weil, 2006)	Trustworthiness attributes guaranteed by certain modelled properties.	Trustworthiness models that can be integrated into MDE-tools and directly queried from there.
Test-driven (Sommerville, 2016)	Strong, practice-proven methodology for assuring implementation of requirements.	Enhance requirements (and test cases) with metrics for trustworthiness attributes.
User-centered (Sutcliffe, 2005)	Taking user's expectations into account right from the start by changing perspective.	Identify trustworthiness expectations of end-user and define risk assessments.
ISO 15408 Common Criteria (ISO/IEC 15408-1, 2009)	Certifiability of the security of certain artifacts.	A trustworthy-by-design methodology should ease the identification of artifacts that support certification.
ISO 21827 SSE-CMM (ISO/IEC 21827, 2008)	Development maturity related to security contributing to trustworthiness.	Trustworthiness characteristics related to maturity can be used to indicate maturity level (though SSE-CMM focuses more on the organization).
ISO/IEC 27001:2013 (ISO/IEC 27001, 2013)	Deduce trustworthiness requirements from the use of the Software in an ISO 27001 compliant context.	1) A trustworthy-by-design methodology should ease the identification of artifacts that support certification. 2) Provide concrete tool support and ways of measurements related to security and trustworthiness.
BSIMM/ OpenSAMM	Security best practices during development.	Complement the identification of security and trustworthiness properties.
Microsoft Trustworthy Computing SDL (Lipner, 2004; Microsoft)	Security best practices during development.	Develop metrics and use a development methodology for assuring the trustworthiness attributes.

Development Methodology	Elements that could contribute to Trustworthiness	Improvement Suggestions with respect to Trustworthiness
Software Security Touchpoints (McGraw, 2006)	Security best practices during development.	Develop metrics and use a development methodology for assuring the trustworthiness attributes.
OWASP CLASP (OWASP, 2009)	Security best practices during development.	Use OWASP risk rating as input to trustworthiness requirements modelling.
The SHIELDS approach (SHIELDS, 2010)	Security best practices during development notably refer to security activities found in the SHIELDS repository.	Develop metrics and use a development methodology for assuring the trustworthiness attributes.
TOGAF (Andrew Josey, 2009)	Artifacts that could also support the trustworthiness of the software.	Define formal trustworthiness requirements.

Weigert and Weil (2006) conclude that model-driven engineering (Schmidt, 2006) significantly facilitates the development of trustworthy software. TOGAF (Andrew Josey, 2009) is a comprehensive framework for developing enterprise architectures based on stakeholder requirements.

Some approaches have been standardized and explicitly focus on certain software quality attributes, mostly considering security. ISO/IEC 27001 (2013) considers certification based on the development and operation of Information Security Management Systems, and explicitly addresses requirements for secure software development. Common Criteria (ISO/IEC 15408-1, 2009) aims at evaluating and certifying software systems with respect to security properties, whereas SSE-CMM (ISO/IEC 21827, 2008) proposes a maturity model for developing secure software, mainly covering organizational and process aspects. The Building Security In Maturity Model (BSIMM) initiative also aims at assessing maturity and describing related activities. Process-independent best practices for developing secure software are proposed in Microsoft Security Lifecycle (MSDL)[17] (Lipner, 2004; McGraw, 2006). Furthermore, some projects, such as OWASP (2009) or SHIELDS (2010), provide methods and tools for detecting, assessing, and mitigating security hazards and risks.

In summary, we can state that existing development methodologies for trustworthy systems typically focus on robustness, correctness, and security functionality, while there is a need for a broader view of trustworthiness, taking for instance social and economic aspects into account when designing trustworthy systems. Hence,

---

[17]https://www.microsoft.com/en-us/sdl (accessed on 17 August 2018)

there is potential to enhance and tailor existing development methodologies so that certain aspects of a holistic view on trustworthiness are taken into account.

6.3 Integrating Trustworthiness-by-Design into Development Methodologies

For enhancing and tailoring existing development methodologies, we suggest an initial set of reusable, trustworthiness-enhancing process chunks in the form of so-called trustworthiness capability patterns. The concept of capability patterns stems from SPEM, the Software Process Engineering Metamodel, which allows for tailoring development methodologies. Thus, capability patterns represent the extension mechanism that we use. To ease the use of our extensions, we also provide tool support using EPF[18] (the Eclipse Process Framework).

In this section, we first describe the requirements on a Trustworthiness-by-Design (TWbyD) methodology (Section 6.3.1). Then, we introduce the extension mechanism that we use (Section 6.3.2) as well as the tool that we use to offer tool support (Section 6.3.3). Afterwards, we present our capability patterns (Section 6.3.4). Finally, we discuss related work that can be compared to our approach of extending development methodologies to achieve the development of trustworthy systems (Section 6.3.5).

6.3.1 Requirements on a Trustworthiness-by-Design Methodology

In this section, we emphasise the needs of the trustworthiness value chain in the perspective of the development of artefacts which will leverage classical engineering means in order to ensure the design, development, operation and maintenance of trustworthy applications. The needs shall cover the whole system and software lifecycle of the engineering process. They will be presented across the different chapters of this book.

These requirements on the trustworthiness-by-design methodology have been evaluated using the OPTET project. The TWbyD methodology needs to fulfil a number of requirements (REQ1 from Chapter 3): on the one hand, it should be flexible enough, so that it actually can be used by organizations that apply modern software engineering approaches. This means that the "enrichment" of the development activities must be divided into individual activities. We will use

---

[18]Eclipse Foundation: Eclipse Process Framework, https://www.eclipse.org/epf/ (accessed on 23 July 2018)

the concept of capability patterns to describe them, so that they can be easily combined and used. On the other hand, the TWbyD methodology must allow for a certification to enable a provably ("constrained") trustworthy software development methodology.

Note that, in this book, we do not present a full-scope development process. Rather, we offer individual trustworthiness capability patterns that ideally, when used in an integrated fashion, support a controlled or constrained development methodology. But additional, standard steps need to be carried out, that also impact the trustworthiness of a CPS, for example, the standard requirements engineering activity, the software design and architecture activity, the coding activity, or the deployment activity.

6.3.2 Conceptual Model for Extension Mechanism

In order to incorporate the notion of trustworthiness-by-design into development methodologies, we consider and extend SPEM (Object Management Group: SPEM, 2008) developed by the Object Management Group (OMG)[19]. SPEM provides adequate concepts that allow describing development practices and methods on a fine-granular level, i.e. assigning concrete tasks, responsible roles, guidance, or involved artifacts (Object Management Group: SPEM, 2008). The concepts that we use from SPEM are the following:

- *Delivery processes* represent a complete and/or integrated process model for performing a specific type of project.

- *Capability patterns* are process chunks that represent best development practices for specific disciplines, technologies, or management styles. These building blocks form a toolkit for quick assembly of processes based on project-specific needs. A capability pattern does not relate to any specific phase or iteration of a development lifecycle, and should not imply any. In other words, a capability pattern should be designed in a way so that it is applicable anywhere in a delivery process. However, some capability patterns would be more relevant to a specific phase of a development process. For instance, a capability pattern on requirements elicitation is useful in the phase related for collecting the requirements, and is not much relevant during the software deployment phase. Hence, we will give a guidance on how to integrate our proposed trustworthiness capability patterns into any development process, and make little assumptions on other capability patterns used, whenever possible. On the other side, the concept is so

---

[19]https://www.omg.org (accessed on 17 August 2018)

flexible, that even full-scale development methodologies can be described using capability patterns.

- A *content element* describes what is to be produced, the necessary skills required and the step-by-step explanations describing how specific development goals are achieved. These content element descriptions are independent of a development process.

- *Guidance* can be defined to provide exemplary walkthroughs of a process, for instance checklists, examples, or roadmaps.

- A *role* defines a set of related skills, competencies and responsibilities. Roles are not individuals, perform *tasks* and are responsible for Work Products.

- A *task* defines an assignable unit of work. Tasks have a clear purpose, and provide step-by-step descriptions of the work that needs to be done to achieve the goal. Tasks modify or produce *work products*.

- A *Work Product* represents the tangible things used, modified or produced by a task.

We extend SPEM by specializing the "delivery process" concept so that it subsumes trustworthiness-by-design processes. We also extend the concept of "capability patterns". We define a "trustworthy product" (i.e. work product, development artifact) as a product that holds a range of its trustworthiness attributes for satisfying its trustworthiness requirements. Figure 6.1 shows the corresponding concepts for trustworthiness-by-design processes. This figure details the parts of the overall conceptual model given by the TW-Man framework (cf. Figure 3.4) presented in Chapter 3 that are related to trustworthiness-by-design. The gray colored concepts are our extensions to SPEM concepts.

Our extension to SPEM consist of the following elements:

- The *trustworthiness capability pattern* is a specialization of a capability pattern and contains a set of trustworthiness-related tasks, roles, etc. We define trustworthiness capability patterns that particularly address trustworthiness to improve existing design process models. For describing trustworthiness capability patterns, we provide the necessary content elements, e.g. concrete tasks, responsible roles, guidance, and involved work products.

- The *trustworthiness-by-design* is a specialization of a delivery process and contains a set of trustworthiness capability patterns. Trustworthiness-by-design methodology ensures that trustworthiness is at the core of the software engineering practices so that the entire system and its individual components (standalone

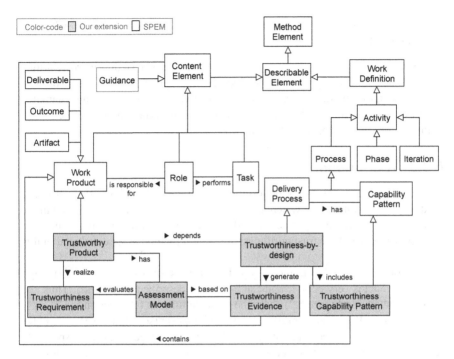

Figure 6.1: Conceptual model for TWbyDesign processes based on Gol Mohammadi et al. (2015c)

or chained) have high levels of trustworthiness through the implementation and maintenance of trustworthiness attributes in the design process.

- The *trustworthy product* depends on the execution of the trustworthiness-by-design methodology. A properly applied trustworthiness-by-design process will create a trustworthy product that exhibits certain trustworthiness attributes to meet its trustworthiness requirements.

- *Trustworthiness requirements* specify which requirements a trustworthy product should fulfill.

- The *assessment model* is a concept that verifies that the trustworthiness requirements have been met. Metrics could be used to evaluate the trustworthiness of products. *Assessment model* includes the assets of the CPS that are relevant for its trustworthiness. The *assessment model* evaluates the satisfaction of the trustworthiness requirements based o the trustworthiness evidence (cf. Chapters 10, 11 and 13).

- *Trustworthiness evidence* consists of *work products* produced during trustworthiness-by-design. There must be some kind of evidence to show that a trustworthiness-by-design methodology has been followed. Even though this will not guarantee trustworthiness, it is at least an indication that planned measures have been taken into account to ensure it (cf. Chapter 13).

6.3.3 Tool Support

In order to provide tool support for designing, tailoring, and sharing a trustworthiness-by-design methodology in a systematic and flexible way, we use EPF. This technique allows us to systematically describe and ease the usage of the trustworthiness capability patterns and the trustworthiness-by-design methodology developed in this book.

EPF concepts have a meta-model based on OMG's SPEM version 2.0[20] (though the meta-model is very generic and can be used to describe any process). Thus, the concepts (shown in Figure 6.2) share the same definitions (cf. Section 6.3.2).

According to Peter Haumer (2007) the EPF Composer (see Figure 6.3) is a tool for process engineers, project leads, project and program managers who are responsible for maintaining and implementing processes for development organizations or individual projects. The main principle behind EPF Composer is that there are libraries of best practices that can be selected and added to existing development processes through a dedicated configuration. The result is a process description, or a handbook for the project team that explains what must be done, when to do it, who should do it, what is required and what is produced. No project is equal to another one and for this reason instead of having generic development processes, the EPF

▥ Method Content	◆ Process
♟ Role	▥ Delivery Process
▢ Task	✿ Capability Pattern
▤ Work Product	▥ Task Descriptor

Figure 6.2: Notation of the EPF concepts

[20]Object Management Group (OMG), "Software & Systems Process Engineering Meta-model Specification (SPEM) Version 2.0" Release Date: April 2008 http://www.omg.org/spec/SPEM/2.0/ (accessed on 20 July 2018)

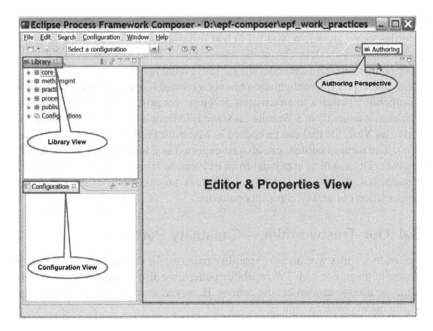

Figure 6.3: Overview of the basic user interface of the EPF Composer

theory is to tailor process descriptions to fit the needs of each project, thereby removing irrelevant activities and the amount of documentation to be read (OPTET Consortium, 2013a). This means one can define or take an existing development process described in EPF, customize it to suit a specific organization or project, and enrich it with our trustworthiness capability patterns. In this way, one can create a trustworthy-by-design process that suits specific needs. Consequently, our approach that is focused on capability patterns for engineering trustworthiness can be realized, represented, and supported by EPF. All our capability patterns are organized in a plugin that can be imported into any EPF project, which, again, can be exported to online process handbooks (OPTET Consortium, 2013a). Tasks define concrete steps on what to do and how to do it, associated roles, input and output artifacts, key considerations, and can be further linked to other guidance documents and tools.

The user interface of the EPF Composer (shown in Figure 6.3) can be divided into four main sections. In the upper left corner, there is a panel showing the libraries that are currently available. Here, a number of method content plugins can be opened and combined to create a "trustworthiness-by-design" process configuration. The configuration view in the lower left side of the screen basically shows which library parts are included in the currently selected configuration. The Editor and Properties views are where you fill in text information through forms, tables, or draw process flow models. One of the advantages of using EPF Composer, is that it is open source and released under the Eclipse Public license.

After a new process configuration has been created (i.e. after adding trustworthiness capability patterns to an existing development process), the EPF Composer can publish it either (i) to a Website (as static HTML or a Java EE Web application) or (ii) to an XML file that can be opened in Microsoft Project (OPTET Consortium, 2013a). The method content can also be exported as a method plugin for the EPF Composer. The installation manual from EPF can be found on the EPF webpage[21].

Figures 6.4, 6.5, 6.6, 6.7, 6.8, and 6.9 show an excerpt from the EPF-based documentation of our TW capability patterns.

6.3.4 Our Trustworthiness Capability Patterns

We provide six trustworthiness capability patterns. In the following, we give an overview of them. For each TW capability pattern, we also define a concrete method that maybe used to implement the pattern. However, the methods are described in the subsequent chapters.

TW Capability Pattern 1: Elicitation and Refinement of Trustworthiness Requirements using Goal and Business Process Models

This TW capability pattern describes the process of eliciting and refining trustworthiness requirements for the CPS that needs to be developed. A more detailed description of the developed method is provided in Chapter 7.

Purpose: The system should fulfill the trustworthiness requirements to address the trust concerns of the end-users. This activity can be done by providing a method for the requirements engineer to elicit and refine the trustworthiness requirements to concrete trustworthiness properties that a CPS should exhibit. This is an important activity, since it "encodes" the trustworthiness expectations for the other activities (in later phases).

Main description: This activity is carried out during the design-time of the system in the requirements engineering phase. The requirements engineer uses this capability to analyze and refine trustworthiness requirements using goal and business process models.

---

[21]Eclipse Foundation, "EPF Composer – Installation, Introduction, Tutorial and Manual", March 2010. `https://www.eclipse.org/epf/general/EPF_Installation_Tutorial_User_Manual.pdf`(accessed on 23 July 2018)

Scope: Requirements engineering phase, design-time

Usage notes: During design-time, the capability must be used to elicit and refine trustworthiness requirements that the CPS under development should satisfy.

Alternatives: Trustworthiness capability pattern for elicitation and refinement of trustworthiness requirements using a problem-based approach.

How to staff: The staff performing this activity must be part of the development team.

Figures 6.4 show an excerpt from the EPF-based documentation of this TW capability patterns.

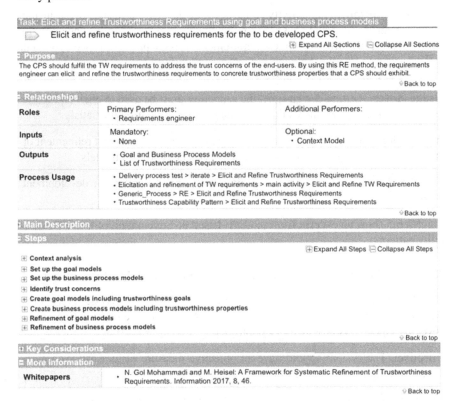

Figure 6.4: EPF excerpt from the TW Capability Pattern "Elicitation and refinement of trustworthiness requirements using goal and business process models"

TW Capability Pattern 2: Derivation of Trustworthiness Requirements from Users' Trust Concerns using Problem-based Approach

Similarly to the previous TW capability pattern, this TW capability pattern describes the process of eliciting and refining requirements for a CPS. A more detailed description of the developed method is provided in Chapter 9.

Purpose: The system should fulfill the trustworthiness requirements to address the trust concerns of the end-users. This activity can be done by providing method for the requirements engineer to elicit and refine the trustworthiness requirements to concrete trustworthiness properties that a CPS should exhibit. This is an important activity, since it "encodes" the trustworthiness expectations for the other activities.

Main description: This activity is carried out during the design-time, in the requirements engineering phase. The requirements engineer uses this capability to analyze and refine trustworthiness requirements using a problem-based approach.

Scope: Requirements engineering phase, design-time

Usage notes: During design-time, the capability must be used to elicit and refine trustworthiness requirements that CPS under development should satisfy.

Alternatives: Trustworthiness capability pattern for elicitation and refinement of trustworthiness requirements using goal and business process models

How to staff: The staff performing this activity must be part of the development team.

Figures 6.5 show an excerpt from the EPF-based documentation of this TW capability patterns.

TW Capability Pattern 3: Evaluation of End-to-End Trustworthiness

This TW capability pattern computes the trustworthiness of a system based on the trustworthiness of its components (assets). A more detailed description of the developed method is provided in Chapter 10.

Purpose: The system should have an objective measure of its trustworthiness, both, at design-time and at run-time.

Main description: This activity is carried out at design-time and at run-time. The system designer/developer can use this TW capability pattern at design-time to evaluate a particular design alternative and assess whether the trustworthiness of a proposed system configuration meets the trustworthiness requirements. At run-

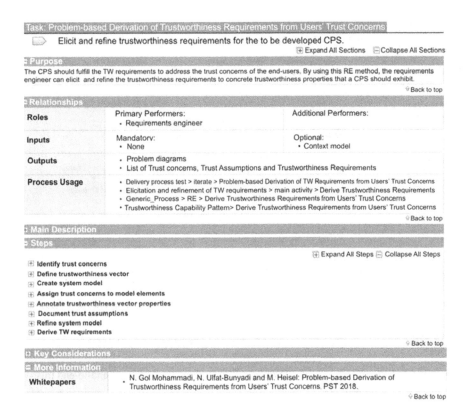

Figure 6.5: EPF excerpt from the TW Capability Pattern "Derivation of trustworthiness requirements from users' trust concerns using problem-based approach"

time, the trustworthiness monitor can re-evaluate the trustworthiness periodically in order to assess the current trustworthiness of the system (on the run-time model of the system) in case of changing circumstances or when a certain threat is active.

Scope: Design-time, run-time

Usage notes: At run-time the implementation should be triggered automatically whenever the system configuration is altered by adding a new asset or in case of a reconfiguration of an existing asset. There should also be a trigger for the emergence of new previously inactive threats to trustworthiness or sudden loss of trust.

Alternatives: None

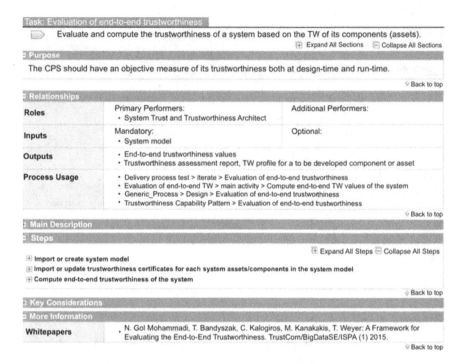

Figure 6.6: EPF excerpt from the TW Capability Pattern "Evaluation of end-to-end trustworthiness"

How to staff: The activity should be performed at design-time by the system trustworthiness architect. At run-time it can be used by the system trustworthiness monitor.

Figures 6.6 show an excerpt from the EPF-based documentation of this TW capability patterns.

TW Capability Pattern 4: Identification of Threats to Trustworthiness and Mitigating Controls

This TW capability pattern supports identification of threats to trustworthiness and the controls that can mitigate these threats. A more detailed description of the developed method is provided in Chapter 11.

Purpose: The design of the CPS should incorporate controls to the threats that may compromise its functions.

Main description: This activity is carried out during the design time of the system. The system designer/developer can use this capability in order to identify the threats to the system assets and choose controls that mitigate these threats. The capability relies on a knowledge base of threats mapped to asset types. The designer/developer should go through the identification process whenever a new threat is included in the knowledge base or an asset is changed (added/removed). The architecture and topology of asset combination is also a trigger for this process. The process can also be carried out after the design of the system during runtime, if the system is dynamic (i.e. new assets are added/removed dynamically). Furthermore, the process should also be followed for auditing and certification purposes, in order to verify that the required controls were implemented.

Scope: Design-time, run-time and audit

Usage notes: During design-time, the capability can be used in many iterations as the system develops. This will make sure that the different control possibilities are investigated and chosen according to feasibility and effectiveness criteria. If new assets, threats, or controls are identified at runtime, this capability is needed to reconfigure the monitoring and management system.

Alternatives: None

How to staff: The staff performing this activity must be integrated into the team.

Figures 6.7 show an excerpt from the EPF-based documentation of this TW capability patterns.

TW Capability Pattern 5: Preparation for Run-time Monitoring and Maintaining of Trustworthiness

This trustworthiness capability pattern supports the design and implementation of the interfaces for run-time monitoring and maintenance of the system's trustworthiness. A more detailed description of the developed method is provided in Chapter 12.

Purpose: The system should facilitate monitoring of trustworthiness by providing methods for a run-time monitor to gather the values of the trustworthiness properties, observe the events in the running system, and activate corresponding controls to deal with threats.

Main description: This activity is carried out during the design and development time of the system. The system designer/developer uses this TW capability pattern to create interfaces which are accessible to the run-time monitoring and

⟹   Identify the system threats and the controls that block or mitigate the threats.

                                              ⊞ Expand All Sections   ⊟ Collapse All Sections
Purpose

Make sure that the system are immune to internal and external threats.

                                                                    ▽ Back to top
Relationships

Roles	Primary Performers: • Risk analyzer	Additional Performers:
Inputs	Mandatory: • None	Optional: • Asset model
Outputs	• System Model • Statement of Trustworthiness threats and controls	
Process Usage	• Delivery process test > iterate > Identify threats and controls • Identification of threats and mitigation controls > main activity > Identify threats to TW & controls • Generic_Process > Design > Identify threats to trustworthiness and controls • Trustworthiness Capability Pattern > Identify threats to trustworthiness and controls	

                                                                    ▽ Back to top
Main Description

Steps

                                              ⊞ Expand All Steps ⊟ Collapse All Steps
⊞ **Identify the system and its scope**
⊞ **Model assets**
⊞ **Identify threats**
⊟ **Select controls**

Controls that block or mitigate threats are also provided in the knowledge base. If the system is automated, the required controls and their types (e.g. preventive or corrective) are provided alongside the identified threats. The analyser can choose the controls to be implemented according to their effectiveness and feasibility.

⊞ **Approve residual risks**

                                                                    ▽ Back to top
Key Considerations

More Information

Whitepapers	• N. Gol Mohammadi, T. Bandyszak, A. Goldsteen, C. Kalogiros, T. Weyer, M. Moffie, B. I. Nasser, M. Surridge: Combining Risk-Management and Computational Approaches for Trustworthiness Evaluation. CAiSE Forum 2015

Figure 6.7: EPF excerpt from the TW Capability Pattern "Identify threats to trustworthiness and controls"

management functions. For each asset, an interface is defined which exposes the values of the trustworthiness properties. For each threat, a set of symptoms is defined, and the designer provides interfaces for the observation of these symptoms. For each control, the designer provides an interface to the maintenance subsystem to invoke the control.

Scope: Design-time

Usage notes: During design-time, this TW capability pattern must be used to enable monitoring and maintenance of trustworthiness. If new assets, threats, or controls are identified at run-time, this TW capability pattern can be used to reconfigure the monitoring and maintenance system.

Alternatives: None

How to staff: The staff performing this activity must be part of the development team.

Figures 6.8 show an excerpt from the EPF-based documentation of this TW capability patterns.

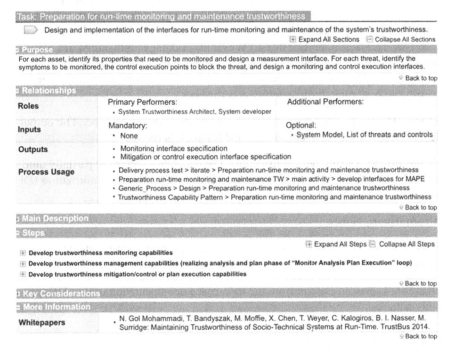

Figure 6.8: EPF excerpt from the TW Capability Pattern "Preparing for run-time monitoring and maintenance of trustworthiness"

TW Capability Pattern 6: Preparation for Trustworthiness Certification

This capability pattern should allow for the assembling of trustworthiness evidence/proof for trustworthiness of a CPS. A more detailed description of the developed method is provided in Chapter 13.

Purpose: The preparation for trustworthiness certification activity deals with providing trustworthiness assurance for a CPS through the whole development lifecycle (and as a basis for run-time evaluations of the CPS) in the form of a well-understandable artifact.

Main description: This activity is carried out at design time with the goal of producing a "trustworthiness case" that documents trustworthiness evidence in two different ways. The first consists of disclosing a system's architecture, its relevant assets, and a threat model and providing controls and practices performed to produce these artefacts. The second is represented by a number of evidences collected during the trustworthiness evaluation process that support the claims about the presence/implementation of trustworthiness attributes, controls and so on. Therefore, it is important that a TWbyD methodology is structured in a way to incorporate trustworthiness from the very beginning of the development phase and to document this process to produce evidence for the creation of a trustworthiness certificate (e.g. digital trustworthiness certificates).

Scope: Preparation for certification should be done in design-time. The output could be used as a basis for run-time and for audit purposes.

Usage notes: During design-time, this TW capability pattern is partially automated to capture and assemble the necessary trustworthiness information (Di Cerbo et al. (2014, 2015)).

Alternatives: None

How to staff: This activity is performed at design-time by the system trustworthiness architect. It provides some input for run-time monitoring.

Figures 6.9 show an excerpt from the EPF-based documentation of this TW capability patterns.

6.3.5 Related Work

To the best of our knowledge, the Trusted Software Methodology (TSM) (U.S. Department of Defense, 2007; Amoroso et al., 1994) is the only comprehensive approach that describes processes and offers guidance for engineering and assessing trustworthy software. It covers multiple qualities, in conformance with our notion of trustworthiness as presented in Chapter 4, and focuses on processes instead of evaluating development artifacts. TSM provides a set of so-called Trust Principles, which describe established development practices or process characteristics that enhance software trustworthiness. A development process can be assessed by means

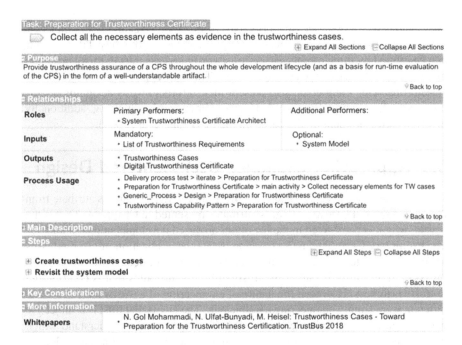

Figure 6.9: EPF excerpt from the TW Capability Pattern "Preparation for trustworthiness certification"

of five different levels of trustworthiness, according to the conformance to the trust principles. This also constitutes the basis for process improvement with respect to trustworthiness. Even though, the principles constitute general best practices, the methodology is assumed to be applied following a military standard for software development (Amoroso et al., 1994).

In contrast, our focus is on enhancing a broad spectrum of general software development methodologies in order to incorporate the consideration of trustworthiness and use them to create trustworthy software.

Yang et al. (2009) review a set of software development methodologies in order to derive a meta-model for trustworthy development processes. They define process trustworthiness as "the degree of confidence that the software process produces expected trustworthy work products that satisfy their requirements" (Yang et al., 2009). The meta-model includes, for example, trustworthy products that depend on a trustworthy process. It also depicts the connection to trustworthiness requirements. For modelling process trustworthiness, they adopt the process area concept from Capability Maturity Model Integration (CMMI) (Software Engineering Institute,

2002) and extend it with the trust principles from Amoroso et al. (1994), then constituting Trustworthy Process Areas (TPAs) (Yang et al., 2009). The TPAs, in turn, can be refined by three categories, i.e. trustworthiness assurance, trustworthiness monitoring, and trustworthiness engineering. Thus, the approach covers the whole system lifecycle. Yang et al. also present their efforts towards designing a comprehensive Trustworthy Process Management Framework, which e.g. additionally involves a measurement model based on metrics (Yang et al., 2009).

6.4 Application Example: User-Centered Design

User-Centered Design (UCD) addresses the usability trustworthiness attribute from the collection of the trustworthiness attributes presented in Chapter 4. That is the reason, why it is considered in the list of our analyzed development methodologies. The exemplary CPS that we use to demonstrate the application of our method is an ambient assisted living system which is described in detail in Chapter 5. In this system, usability is one of the trustworthiness attributes that is contributing to trustworthiness. However, the nature of engineering of a trustworthy system is different from simply engineering a usable one. The key is that trust is a subjective value judgment of stakeholders in a CPS. There is a need to understand which trustworthiness attributes of the system will enhance the trust of a stakeholder in that system and how system design can thus help to circumvent any distrust-related concerns that the stakeholders have about the service. This makes it necessary to not only elicit requirements with respect to the way in which people will use the system (as would be done in a standard UCD process (Sutcliffe, 2005)) but also to draw up a set of requirements describing which trustworthiness attributes will address the potential trust issues that the end-users of the system highlight.

There seems to be a duality between trustworthy and secure systems on the one hand and usability on the other hand (Earl Eugene Schultz, Robert W. Proctor, Mei-Ching Lien, Gavriel Salvendy, 2001). In general, developers try to create a system that for instance is secure, under the assumption that a secure system is also a system that is trustworthy. The methods that are used to create a secure system, if applied with little caution, can burden the user with additional tasks such as entering and remembering unique usernames and passwords, eventually leading to a decrease in the usability of the system perceived by the user. Therefore, some effort is needed for the development team to potentially re-design the software so that usability and security go hand-in-hand. This, however, does not necessarily need to be the case. A design process aimed at developing trustworthy systems needs to find design solutions that are both trustworthy and usable. Based on this, it will be necessary to not merely involve end-users in the design process to elicit their needs and requirements for system design with respect to usability and trustworthiness attributes that can mitigate any potential distrust issues. Thus, a standard user-centered process by itself is not necessarily sufficient to design trustworthy systems (Zurko, 2005). A small number of design processes, specifically aimed at the design of usable, trustworthy, and secure systems have been proposed (Gerd tom Markotten, 2002; Flechais et al., 2003). The Appropriate and Effective Guidance in Information Security (AEGIS) model proposed by Flechais et al. is a design process that involves both the end-user and the security expert perspective. By doing so, it is possible to make well-informed design decisions in terms of the trade-off between risks, mitigations, and user experience of the system. This is an iterative approach, incorporating multiple cycles of design, risk analysis, prototyping, validation, and review. The process proposed by (Gerd tom Markotten, 2002), provides a good understanding of how the two separate disciplines of security and usability engineering can form a concurrent design, development, and testing process. The processes proposed above do not provide detailed descriptions of the activities that take place in the early phases of a user-centered design approach (Knowledge elicitation, trying to understand the context of use, and defining user requirements). In the area of knowledge elicitation, the work of Karvonen (1999); Karvonen et al. (2000) could provide useful input on how to elicit knowledge from end users with respect to trust and trustworthiness design requirements. In the area of defining user requirements and transferring those to systems design the use of trust ontologies (Chang et al., 2007) and trust enabling frameworks (Stephens, 2004) have proven to be useful.

In order to assess the product with respect to the satisfaction of trustworthiness requirements, the overall structure of the UCD approach can remain the same, with the only difference that, beside usability and usefulness, the process specifically addresses trust and trustworthiness.

Table 6.2 briefly sketches the trustworthiness analysis for user-centred design process (based on Section 6.2.2 and Table 6.1). We suggest the following extensions to the four major phases of the User-centered Design methodology:

- In Phase 1, a usability expert elicits from the future end-users their potential trust concerns regarding the planned system.

- In Phase 2, these concerns can then be turned into use case descriptions of situations in which the trust issues become apparent to the user. To this end, TW Capability Pattern 4 (Section 6.3.4) should be incorporated into User-Centered Design. By means of involved analysis tools (cf. Chapters 10 and 11), threats to trustworthiness can be derived. It should also be determined which controls can be applied in the design to mitigate the identified trustworthiness and trust issues.

Table 6.2: Indicative trustworthiness analysis for User-Centered Design

---

Name: User-Centered Design Process

Description: The User-Centered Design process (Sutcliffe, 2005) consists of the following general phases:

1. Specify context of use;

2. Specify user requirements;

3. Produce design solutions, and

4. Evaluate against requirements, which provides input for the refinement of the design.

This process model is generally used iteratively and by going through the process multiple times, developers converge on a user-friendly and usable system.

Elements interesting for trustworthiness:

- The UCD is a specialization of incremental development and therefore shares the same trustworthiness characteristics. In incremental development, initial implementations are presented to the user at regular intervals until the software satisfies the user expectations. A fundamental principle in incremental development is that not all requirements are known completely prior to development. Thus, they are evolving as the software is being developed. Hence, incremental development supports new and evolving requirements for trustworthiness to be incorporated as part of an iterative process. After participating in the development process, the end-users have a good sense of ownership and understanding of the product. Iterative processes allow for modelling of properties, but changes to the model that reflect changed or more detailed customer expectations will in turn require changing the design and code, eventually in another iteration. However, there are no specific trustworthiness modelling capabilities.

- By using an incremental UCD process, it is possible that throughout the design process the design is validated to establish whether the trustworthiness attributes designed into the system appropriately address any concerns with respect to trust that the system users might have.

Improvement potential:

- Documenting trustworthiness requirements and thereafter generating trustworthiness evaluation results for the explicit documentation of trustworthiness evidence in order to support designers when making design decisions. Additionally, these documents bring awareness about the designed system to the end-users.

- Involvement of end-users to derive their trustworthiness expectations and to evaluate the system design towards the satisfaction of those expectations.

Usability for modelling trustworthiness: The UCD processes are unrelated to trustworthiness modelling. Only the use of modelling techniques in general for a UCD will enable to also model trustworthiness requirements.

- Phase 3 should then implement (e.g. in a prototype) the identified trustworthiness requirements.

- TW Capability Pattern 3 (Section 6.3.4) can enhance Phase 4 by providing appropriate metrics and measurement approaches to validate that the system satisfies the required trustworthiness level.

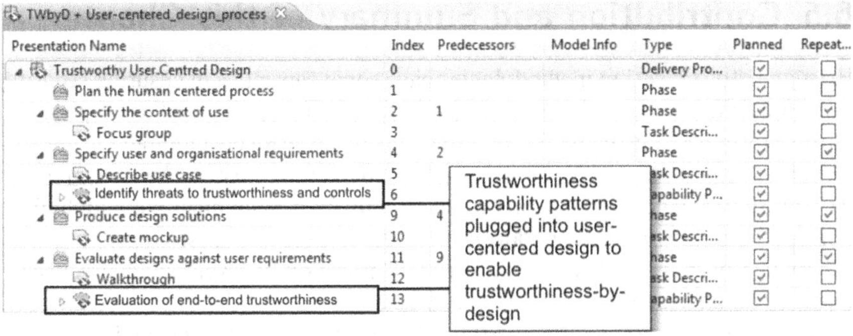

Figure 6.10: Enhancing the UCD methodology with trustworthiness capability patterns (Gol Mohammadi et al., 2015c)

Figure 6.10 illustrates the extensions of UCD by plugging in two of the proposed trustworthiness capability patterns.

As we have already shown above, the extension of the user-centered design process can be supported by using the EPF Composer. Figure 6.10 shows an excerpt from the description of the extended User-centered design methodology as part of a software development process model.

As the excerpt sketches, the corresponding "Trustworthy User-Centered Design" methodology integrates the two additional capability patterns "TW Capability Pattern 3 and 4" into specific phases of the original User-Centered Design process (Figure 6.10, Index number 6 and 13).

This example is just one suggestion of how one could extend UCD by using two of our proposed trustworthiness capability patterns. One could also use all six trustworthiness capability patterns. For instance, two TW capability pattens for RE, "Elicitation and refinement of trustworthiness requirements using goal and business process models" and "Derivation of trustworthiness requirements from users' trust concerns using problem-based approach" can be integrated into Phase 1 and Phase 2 of UCD. TW capability pattern "Preparing for run-time monitoring and maintenance of trustworthiness" can be integrated into Phase 3 of UCD. TW capability pattern "Preparation for trustworthiness certification" can be integrated either into Phase 4 of UCD or into each phase to document the elements necessary for trustworthiness cases (co-development of CPS and its trustworthiness cases).

6.5 Contribution and Summary of this Chapter

Existing software design methodologies have some capacities in ensuring security and a few other trustworthiness attributes. However, the treatment of a complete set of trustworthiness attributes and requirements in software development is not yet well studied. We analyzed development methodologies for trustworthy development. As a result, we concluded that among these thirteen development methodologies, none of them fully assures or addresses the development of trustworthy software. Consequently, individual activities, so-called "trustworthy development practices", must be identified and incorporated into these processes in order to proceed towards systematically developing trustworthy software. We have introduced the concept and an initial set of reusable, trustworthiness-enhancing process chunks and best practices in the form of "Trustworthiness Capability Patterns" together with an application example. The intention is to increase the confidence that the development processes will result in trustworthy CPS by the usage of appropriate trustworthiness capability patterns.

7 Systematic Refinement of Trustworthiness Requirements using Goal and Business Process Models

In order to address users' trust concerns, trustworthiness requirements of software systems must be elicited and satisfied. The aim of this chapter[1] is to address the gap that exists between end-users' trust concerns and the lack of implementation of proper trustworthiness requirements. Trust is subjective; trustworthiness requirements for addressing trust concerns are difficult to elicit, especially if there are different parties involved in the business process. We propose a user-centered trustworthiness requirement analysis and modelling approach. We integrate the subjective trust concerns into goal models and embed them into business process models as objective trustworthiness requirements. We extend Business Process Model and Notation (BPMN) to enable modelling trustworthiness requirements. This chapter focuses on the challenges of elicitation, refinement and modelling trustworthiness requirements. The use case from Chapter 5 is used as application example to demonstrate our approach.

7.1 Motivation

Trustworthiness requirements must be assured, in order to meet users' trust concerns. To support users' confidence (leading to adoption of a CPS), the right mechanisms should be put into place. Trustworthiness requirements should be in accordance with the end-users' trust concerns. Furthermore, business processes and their involved software systems and services need to be made trustworthy to mitigate the risks of engaging those systems.

---

[1]This chapter partially adapts Gol Mohammadi and Heisel (2016b) © Springer International Publishing Switzerland 2016, Gol Mohammadi and Heisel (2016c) © IFIP International Federation for Information Processing 2016, and Gol Mohammadi and Heisel (2017), with the permission of the publishers.

The peculiarity about trust is, first, that it is subjective for different groups of end-users and, second, that it is achieved by satisfying a set of other qualities or properties. Consider, for example, a healthcare system that involves not only the elderly person who is monitored at home, but also the hospital, doctors, ambulance service, insurances, etc. For the elderly person, the system is trustworthy if it provides a certain degree of reliability, availability and usability. For a hospital, in contrast, it is trustworthy if the privacy of sensitive data is guaranteed. Additionally, for the doctors, the system is trustworthy if the correctness of raised alarms is ensured. Therefore, for being trustworthy, business information systems must fulfill a variety of qualities and properties. Software systems that provide support to different stakeholders should fulfill a variety of qualities and properties for being trustworthy, depending on the application and the domain.

Traditional development methodologies do not respect users' trust concerns in dynamic, heterogeneous and distributed settings. Recently, innovative technologies, like trustworthiness-by-design methodologies (cf. Chapter 6) are attracting researchers' attention. Requirements Engineering (RE) is a critical activity in such "by-design" methodologies. However, there is only a small set of well-accepted requirements refinement methods and complementary decision support (supporting design decisions), which can be applied in a systematic way for considering trustworthiness (Haley et al., 2004; Giorgini et al., 2006). Our hypothesis is that trustworthiness of business systems is strongly dependent on their development processes, especially the elaboration of trustworthiness requirements during the requirement engineering phase. Our contribution in this chapter is twofold: to support requirements engineering phase we provide a framework and a corresponding method.

To refine and elaborate trustworthiness requirements along with design artifacts, we propose a framework (cf. Section 7.3). According to this framework, trust concerns are identified and addressed by trustworthiness goals in goal models. Trustworthiness requirements are refined in these goal models iteratively in combination with the business process models defined for satisfying the goals. In this way, it is ensured that trustworthiness requirements will not be violated or ignored, while developing or implementing the activities, resources and data objects involved in the business processes.

In business processes, resources are either human or non-human assets, e.g. software or IT devices (Cabanillas et al., 2015). Non-human assets can provide either fully-automated or semi-automated support to the activity performers. Since end-users rely on these technical resources when performing their activities, trustworthiness properties of these technical resources play a major role in gaining the trust of end-users (e.g. the reliability of the system that deals with monitoring the vital signs of a patient). There are specific conditions that must be defined concerning human resources that contribute as well to trustworthiness, e.g. people's skills and expertise when performing particular tasks. In addition to trustworthiness requirements on resource management, the usage of digital documents and data plays a central role in trustworthiness. For instance, in order to respect privacy regulations, digital documents have to be protected from unauthorized use (e.g. being shared on public networks). This clearly demands the consideration of trustworthiness properties and, hence, the specification of trustworthiness requirements on data objects by defining usage rules, as well as the respective mechanisms for enforcing the usage of such rules. Consequently, trustworthiness should be considered in the management of both human and non-human resources in all stages of the business process lifecycle: design, modelling, implementation, execution, monitoring and analysis.

In addition to the framework, we propose a method for the systematic elicitation, refinement and modelling of trustworthiness requirements in a user-centered manner. The chapter aims at performing trustworthiness requirements analysis with regard to trust concerns and thereafter building trustworthiness properties into underlying systems for performing business processes. Our objectives are to analyze and specify trustworthiness requirements in the business process models to support the process designer and tool developers in fulfilling trustworthiness requirements and a later evaluation of them. We use i* (Yu, 1997) for goal-modelling and the BPMN (Object Management Group, 2011) for modelling business processes. We also focus on specifying trustworthiness requirements starting from the business processes level by providing modelling capabilities to understand and express trustworthiness requirements. The main challenges that we discovered based on an analysis of the state of the art (Gol Mohammadi and Heisel, 2016c) are a lack of concepts relevant for trustworthiness (e.g. delegations) and a lack of inter-model consistency checks between BPMN and i* models. Goal models combined with business process models specify how business processes fulfill the trustworthiness goals.

The remainder of the chapter is structured as follows. In Section 7.2, we explain the fundamentals of our framework. Section 7.3 presents our framework for combining goal models and business process modelling to support eliciting and refinement of trustworthiness requirements and embedding them in business process models. The classification of trustworthiness requirements, which can be expressed in the business process model, is also described. The method for elicitation and refinement of trustworthiness requirements is presented in Section 7.4. We demonstrate the application of our framework using the case study from Chapter 5 (cf. Section 7.5). In Section 7.6, the benefits of applying our method are presented. In Section 7.7, related work is discussed. Finally, we conclude our work in Section 7.8.

7.2 Background and Fundamentals

In this section, we briefly introduce the fundamental techniques and concepts for the framework that is described in Section 7.3.

7.2.1 Business Process Modelling Using BPMN

Business process models are frequently used in software development for understanding the behavior of the users, their requirements and for the assignment of requirements to particular well-defined business process elements. A business process is a specific ordering of activities across time and place, with a start, an end and clearly-defined inputs and outputs. A business process model is the representation of the activities, documents, people and all of the elements involved in a business process, as well as the execution constraints between them (Stroppi et al., 2011a). By using business process modelling, different information can be captured such as organizational, functional, informational, behavioral and context information. The organizational information focuses on the actors and their activities. The functional information describes the process element activity that is being performed during a business process execution. A resource can either be a human resource or a technical resource, such as tools, or a service used in performing an activity, or informational resources, such as data. The business process models also represent how the informational resources are manipulated in a process. The behavioral information includes the time aspects of activities by focusing on when activities are performed and when they are sequenced. We can show control flow and data flow in business process models. BMPN (Object Management Group, 2011) is a standard for modelling business processes, which is broadly extended and used widely in both industry and research. The basic elements of the BPMN notation for business process modelling are shown in Figure 7.1.

7.2.2 Goal Modelling Using i*

In requirements engineering, goal modelling approaches have gained considerable attention in varying contexts. These approaches aim at capturing the rationale of the software system development. A goal model defines organization goals and the tasks necessary to achieve these goals. Thus, goal models relate the high-level goals of an organization to low-level system requirements. Goals can be classified into two different categories: hard goals and soft goals. Soft goals can be achieved at different levels of satisfaction, which means that there is no clear-cut definition for their satisfaction (Yu, 1997); whereas, for hard goals, the condition for judging whether a goal is satisfied is clearly defined.

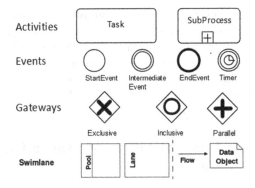

Figure 7.1: The basic elements of the BPMN

Hard goals may refer to the functional properties of the system behavior, whereas soft goals may represent quality preferences. There exists a number of different goal modelling languages used in requirements engineering.

The i* notation was developed with the purpose of modelling and reasoning within an organizational environment and its information systems (Yu, 1997). The basic elements of the i* modelling notation are shown in Figure 7.2. The i* notation

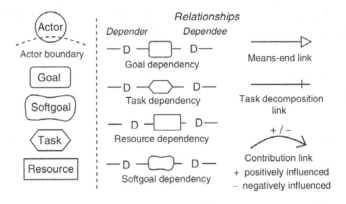

Figure 7.2: Notation of the i* modelling elements

consists of two main models, a Strategic Dependency Model (SDM) and a Strategic Rationale Model (SRM). The SDM is used to express strategic relationships among different actors in an organizational context. The SRM captures both an internal view of each actor and external relations among actors. The main concepts used in i* models are actors, goals, tasks, resources and soft goals. An actor is a role who carries out a task to achieve a certain goal. A resource is an object that is needed to complete a goal or to perform some task. The following dependencies can be defined in i*: goal, soft goal, task or resource dependencies. For the internal view of an actor in an SRM, the links are as follows: means-ends, task decomposition and contribution. Examples of the use of SDM and SRM are provided in Section 7.5 (Figure 7.7 and 7.9, respectively).

7.2.3 Choice of i* and BPMN as Modelling Languages in Our Approach

We analyzed different goal modelling languages with respect to their ability to assist business process models in addressing trustworthiness. It is important that the chosen languages are able to model the concepts given in our conceptual model (that will be presented in Figure 7.5). Every goal modelling language that supports these concepts can be used. For instance, goal modelling languages can be used where goals are assigned to actors (or so-called agents). The same condition, namely that the concepts of our conceptual model can be mapped to it, holds for business process modelling languages.

As a goal modelling language, we have selected i*. However, also other languages, such as Knowledge Acquisition in autOmated Specification (KAOS) (Van Lamsweerde and Letier, 2000; Letier and Lamsweerde, 2002), could be used. i* is applied when business-level analysis is the starting point of the modelling, while KAOS is widely used in goal-oriented requirements engineering for IT systems. One of the major reasons to use i* instead of KAOS is the possibility of analyzing trade-off decisions based on dependency and positive/negative contribution relations. These links clarify the relation between different qualities (e.g. security, privacy, usability, etc.) and their contribution to the overall trustworthiness goal.

As for BPMN, we use it because it is a widely-accepted business process modelling language, and it fits our needs very well. However, any other business process modelling language that supports the needed concepts (shown in Figure 7.5) can be used instead of BPMN.

In summary, we selected BPMN and i* because these two languages fit well with our conceptual model. However, our proposed framework is independent of particular languages. The framework including the conceptual model (Section 7.3) explains why it is beneficial to combine goal and business process modelling in general (without considering specific languages). Our method (Section 7.4) then shows how this combination can look when selecting BPMN and i*.

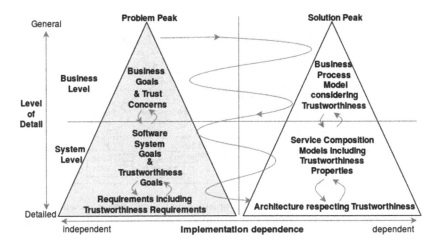

Figure 7.3: Overview of the proposed framework (Gol Mohammadi and Heisel, 2016b)

7.3 Framework for Trustworthiness Requirements Refinement

Our framework is employed to decompose high-level goals into low-level goals. We shape and structure our framework (shown in Figure 7.3) based on the twin peaks model (Nuseibeh, 2001). The cornerstone of embedding the development of business information systems in the twin peaks model is that requirements engineers and designers co-develop a system's requirements and its architecture specification concurrently and iteratively. The same applies to our proposed approach for the analysis of trustworthiness requirements and the integration of them into business models.

The framework captures the progression and refinement from general to detailed understanding and expression of both requirements and design. The problem peak is independent of the technical description related to the implementation of the requirements. The solution peak incrementally introduces technical implementation details. In the problem peak, we see that business goals and trust concerns are refined to system/software goals and trustworthiness goals and finally to requirements including trustworthiness requirements. In the solution peak, the business process model that considers trustworthiness is refined to service composition models, which include trustworthiness properties. These may be further refined into an architecture respecting trustworthiness.

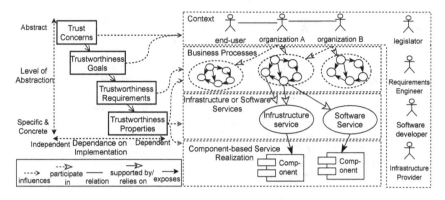

Figure 7.4: Alignment of our RE approach, for enriching business processes with TW requirements, with software development (Gol Mohammadi and Heisel, 2017)

In order to produce the artifacts shown in our framework, we suggest the method that is described in Section 7.4. However, other methods may also be applied to produce them. Our method starts with the problem peak. Yet, one may also start with the solution peak.

The method for eliciting and refining trustworthiness requirements combines goal models (to say WHAT, problem peak) and business process modelling (to show HOW, solution peak). There should be a rationale about where a trustworthiness requirement originates from. To this end, the most appropriate level is considering trust concerns with goals of other actors starting from the business level. Our framework aligns organizational (business) requirements in an adequate way with trustworthiness requirements. The framework supports elicitation and refinement of system-level goals and trustworthiness requirements from business goals and trust concerns at the business level. Furthermore, the framework tackles the problem of high-level and low-level trustworthiness requirements' misalignment between the business/organizational level and the application and software service level. The elaborated business process model in the solution peak satisfies business goals, as well as trustworthiness goals.

Figure 7.4 shows how our proposed framework streamlines trustworthiness to the software development. The left-hand side of Figure 7.4 shows the abstraction level of trustworthiness and its influence on the system on the right-hand side (simplified service-oriented architecture layers (Papazoglou, 2003; Papazoglou et al., 2007)). The participants of a business process are presented on the context layer. In a business process, an end-user has different trust concerns than an organization. The

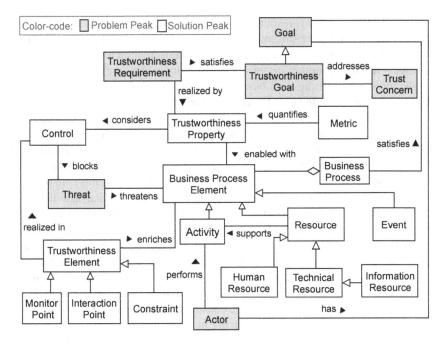

Figure 7.5: Conceptual model of our proposed framework and the RE method (Gol Mo-hammadi and Heisel, 2016b)

business goal of an organization might even be in conflict with the trust concerns of an end-user. The legislator may affect both business goals and trust concerns.

Since our framework suggests to refine trustworthiness requirements by combining goal models and business process models, we have created a conceptual model that supports combining existing goal modelling and business process modelling languages. The conceptual model is given as a Unified Modelling Language (UML) class diagram in Figure 7.5. This figure details the parts of the overall conceptual model of TW-Man framework (cf. Figure 3.4) presented in Chapter 3 that are related to the requirements engineering building block (using goal and business process models).

A *trustworthiness goal* is a special *goal* that addresses the trust concerns of users. A trustworthiness goal is satisfied by *trustworthiness requirements*, which can be realized by more concrete *trustworthiness properties*.

Actors have goals that can be satisfied in a *business process*. A business process consists of *business process elements*: a set of activities, events and involved resources. Here, activity, resource or event are more concrete *business process elements*. An actor performs an *activity*. An activity is supported by resources. For instance, an activity consumes data objects (information resource) as input or technical resources support performing an activity such as software services and applications. We use the term *business process element* to distinguish between the business process element and the *trustworthiness element*. A *trustworthiness element* can pertain to a type of *business process element*.

A *trustworthiness element* enriches a *business process element* by defining either a *monitor point*, an *interaction point* or a *constraint* on a *business process element*. For instance, a trustworthiness element may be a constraint on an activity, which is trustworthiness-related. Enriching an activity with a constraint enhances the refinement of the activity with respect to trustworthiness. We call an activity that is enriched with a constraint a trustworthiness-related activity. In general, a business process element that is enriched with a trustworthiness element is trustworthiness related. A notification for satisfying transparency can be defined as a constraint on an activity. A *monitor point* marks the start and the end point in a business process that shall be monitored during run-time. In a monitor point, we can not only specify which part of the process needs to be monitored during run-time, but also the desired behavior by adding the constraint. An *interaction point* marks the elements of a business process, which are in direct interaction with the end-user. These *enriched relations* enable us to derive trustworthiness requirements in the form of commitments reached among the actors for the achievement of their goals.

A *threat* is a situation or event that, if active at run-time, could undermine the trustworthiness by altering the behavior of involved resources or services in the process. A *control* aims at blocking a threat. A *metric* is used as a function to quantify trustworthiness properties. Trustworthiness elements realize the control in terms of defining elements that address the trustworthiness, e.g. an additional activity can be defined to block a threat to privacy. These additional activities could involve documenting or triggering a notification upon a delegating case of a patient to another authority or an engagement of a new service from a new third party.

In our conceptual model, we use the basic concepts used in goal modelling and show how to align them with process model elements. As mentioned earlier, every goal modelling language that supports these concepts can be used. The same is valid about business process modelling languages.

7.4 Method for Trustworthiness Requirements Refinement

Our method consist of the following eight steps:

Step 1. Context analysis: The first step is concerned with identifying the stakeholders or participants in the business process and the initial context information (cf. Chapter 5.1). The latter can be captured in a context model. The context information provides an overview of the business process, as well.

Step 2. Set up the goal model: This step is concerned with setting up the goal model by capturing the major intentions of the involved stakeholders. The goals are captured either by interviewing involved stakeholders or are based on the expertise of a requirements engineer or business engineer at the business level. We start with high-level goals and then refine them within the problem peak. We model and document the goals in the SDM and SRM models.

Step 3. Set up the business process models: We select a specific goal from the SDM. For satisfying the selected goal, we set up a business process model. To create the business process model, we use information shown in the SDM and SRM. Based on the SDM, the dependency between roles and other goals can be analyzed. SRM models give insight into the resources and activities. The business process model for a specific goal visualizes the control and data flow between identified tasks, used resources and involved actors.

Step 4. Identify trust concerns: Trust concerns of end-users and their dependencies on other participants in the business are identified. Trust concerns can be collected either by interviewing involved end-users or are based on the expertise of a requirements engineer. As a support in this step (especially due to the subjectiveness of trust), the questionnaire provided in Chapter 8 may be used.

Step 5. Refine goal model with including trustworthiness goals: Based on the trust concerns, we refine the goal model with trustworthiness goals and their relation to the other goals (negative or positive influences). The trustworthiness goals include the purpose for incorporating trustworthiness properties into the system under development. As a support in this step, the collection of trustworthiness attributes that contribute to mitigate trust concerns and is provided in Chapter 4 may be used.

Step 6. Create business process model including trustworthiness properties: In this step, we enhance the business process model from Step 3 by adding trustworthiness properties, which fulfill the trustworthiness goals. To support this step, we provide the following new trustworthiness elements shown in Figure 7.5 and described Table 7.1:

- *Monitor points:* We introduce so-called monitoring points with start and end points in the process model for monitoring the trustworthiness properties that must be considered in the defined points of the process as well as the desired/target values for them. Furthermore, metrics can also be provided for quantifying trustworthiness properties that will be under observation at run-time. Monitor points can be used in combination with constraints to express the desired values and metrics for measuring trustworthiness properties at run-time.

- *Interaction points:* These points specify the interfaces where the end-user is involved in the business process, e.g. she/he may interact with the technical resources (e.g. applications, software services) that support her/him in performing her/his tasks. In these interfaces, there are factors that could signal the trustworthiness of the system to the end-user, e.g. reliability, quality of visualization, usability, understandability of represented information, quality of service like availability or response time. For example, if an elderly person uses an app for reviewing his/her medical plan and medication, the visualization of his/her health status and medical plan influences her/his trust about the correctness of those health reports, medications or medical plans. Therefore, the trustworthiness requirements in these points need to be investigated further, and the resources involved in these points should include related trustworthiness properties that satisfy the trustworthiness requirements.

- *Trustworthiness constraints:* In addition to new elements like monitor and interaction points, each BPMN element can be enriched/annotated with the constraints that it should keep for satisfying trustworthiness requirements. The action with trustworthiness requirements and constraints is tagged with "TW" in the business process model, e.g. time constraints on activities or constraints on the resources that are used in performing a specific activity.

The business process model from Step 3 is analyzed by identifying which business process elements are related to the identified trustworthiness goals from Step 5. We select one of the business process models for including trustworthiness requirements satisfying trustworthiness goals. This selection is based on the relation of the trustworthiness goal to the other goals. This step goes through business process elements and control flow and questions whether the element in the business process is trustworthiness-related. The relation of trustworthiness goals in the goal model to the other goals from Step 5 assists this step.

Table 7.1: Extended elements to model TW requirements in BPMN (Gol Mohammadi and Heisel, 2016c)

Defined Trustworthiness Element (Extension)		Definition	Symbols
Monitor Point		Inserting monitor points into the business process defines the start and end point of monitoring at run-time. Monitor points can be used in combination with constraints to express the desired values and metrics for measuring trustworthiness properties at run-time.	
Interaction Point		Interaction points are the places where the end-user interacts with the system. The interaction is normally supported by the apps or software services. Qualities of these apps and software services have an impact on the trust perception of users. Therefore, it should be studied well how to signal their trustworthiness to the end-user. Interaction points can be further detailed in combination with constraints on technical resources (in interaction points), e.g. specifying which quality, to what extent (e.g. 99% availability).	
Constraint	Constraints on Activity	Trustworthiness requirements on a specific activity, e.g. expected duration of an activity.	
	Constraints on Resources	Trustworthiness requirements on a specific resource (either human or non-human), e.g. expertise of the involved human resource.	
	Constraints on Delegations	Trustworthiness requirements on delegation, e.g. if a delegation (e.g. activity delegation) is allowed or delegation to whom or which roles are allowed.	

Step 7. Refinement of goal model (problem peak): During this step, the goals and trustworthiness goals are further refined in order to obtain user-centered trustworthiness requirements on resources and tasks. This refinement is performed within the problem peak. However, based on the output of this step, revisions of business process models can be necessary.

Step 8. Refinement of business process model (solution peak): During this step, the business processes are detailed by including trustworthiness properties on resources, activities, etc., for satisfying trustworthiness requirements. This refinement is performed within the solution peak. However, based on the output of this step, revisions of goal models can be necessary. Refinement of the business process model details business processes by including more concrete trustworthiness properties on business process elements. This step can be performed concurrently to the goal and trustworthiness goal refinements, and both models can develop iteratively.

7.5 Application Example

This section demonstrates our method of eliciting and refining trustworthiness requirements and specifying trustworthiness properties on business process elements. We use the case study from Chapter 5 and the following scenario.

Alice is an elderly person who lives alone in her apartment. She does not feel comfortable after a heart attack. She was unconscious in her home for several hours. Alice has been informed that there are some AAL services available in the marketplace. She considers using one of those services to avoid similar incidents in the future. She desires an AAL service that will suit her specific needs. We illustrate in Figure 7.6 a general approach using supporting tools and provided apps to perform the activities. We assume that some of these software services are to be built by software developers, who will also benefit from the results of our work in developing trustworthy applications, software services, etc.

Step 1. Context analysis: The system-to-be is a Home Monitoring System (HMS) for incident detection and detection of abnormal situations to prevent emergency incidents. The HMS allows elderly people to call for help in case of emergency situations in their homes. Furthermore, the HMS analyzes the elderly person's health status for preventing incidents in the first place. The incidents are reported to an alarm call center that, in turn, reacts, for example, by sending out ambulances or other medical caregivers and notifying the elderly person's relatives. For preventing emergency situations, the vital signs of the elderly person are diagnosed at regular intervals to reduce hospital visits and falls. Figure 7.6 shows an exemplary design-time system model including physical, logical and human resources/assets. Using

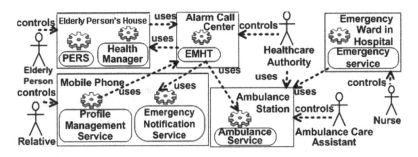

Figure 7.6: Part of the home monitoring system for handling healthcare cases

this system, an elderly person uses a Personal Emergency Response System (PERS) device to call for help, which is then reported to the alarm call center that uses an Emergency Monitoring and Handling Tool (EMHT) to visualize, organize and manage emergency incidents. Furthermore, elderly persons are able to use a Health Manager (HM) application on their smart device for organizing their health status like requesting healthcare services or having an overview regarding their medication or nutrition plan. The EMHT is a software service hosted by the alarm call center that, in turn, is operated by a healthcare authority. Emergency notification and ambulance service, which run on mobile phones of relatives, or ambulance stations respectively, are called in order to require caregivers to provide help. An ambulance service is requested in case an ambulance should be sent to handle an emergency situation. The other case is that, based on the analyzed information sent to the EMHT, an abnormal situation is detected, and further diagnoses are necessary. Therefore, the elderly person will get an appointment and notifications for a tele-visit in her health manager application.

Step 2. Set up the goal model: Figure 7.7 captures the goals of different participants and their dependencies on each other or the realization of the goals. This is done based on the expertise of a requirements engineer and the knowledge gained during the context analysis, for example, by means of interviews. Here, we only focus on the elderly person and the alarm call center. The ambulance station is also involved because, for handling the emergency cases, the alarm call center is dependent on the ambulance as a resource.

Additionally to the SDM presented in Figure 7.7, further SRM models are created that provide more details on tasks, resources and soft goals within the actor boundaries. An example is shown in Figure 7.9. In this step (i.e. at this point of

time), we have only the white-colored elements of that SRM. The grey-colored
elements are added in Step 5 and 7.

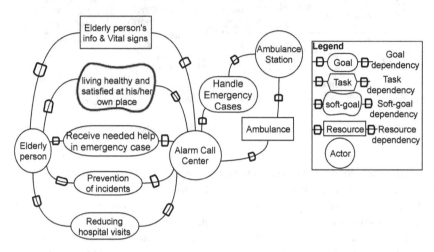

Figure 7.7: Simplified strategic dependency model with the dependencies between identified participants

Step 3. Set up the business process model: Figure 7.8 illustrates and exemplifies
the typical steps that, for example, caregivers in an alarm center have to take once
they notice that the health record of an elderly person deviates from the normal
situation and further examination is needed. This business process model targets
the satisfaction of the goals "reducing hospital visits" and "prevention of incidents"
shown in Figure 7.7.

The process starts by analyzing the elderly person's vital signs in the last seven
days. This data is examined by a physician, who decides whether the elderly person
is healthy or additional examination needs to be undertaken. In the former case, the
physician fills out the examination report. In the latter case, a tele-visit is performed
by this physician in which he/she informs the elderly person about the examination
and necessary treatment. An examination order is placed by the physician. The
physician sends out a request. This request includes information about the elderly
person, the required examination and possible labs. Furthermore, an appropriate
appointment is arranged. The process continues for taking a sample and validating
this. Eventually, the physician from the alarm call center should get the result in
order to make the diagnosis and prescribe the medication.

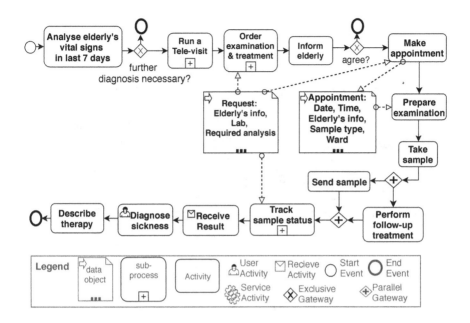

Figure 7.8: Exemplary business process model for preventing emergency cases and reducing hospital visits

Step 4. Identify trust concerns: During this step, we identify the trust concerns of our end-user Alice. She is concerned about whether she will really receive the emergency help if a similar situation happens again (heart attack experience). Alice is informed that by using the HMS, she can have regular diagnoses, which can prevent frequent hospital visits. However, Alice is concerned whether she will be able to use the service in a proper way. She is also concerned about who can get access to the data about her diseases or life habits. She indicates that she would only prefer her regular nurse and doctor to be able to see her history and health status.

Step 5. Refine goal model with including trustworthiness goals: During this step, we add trustworthiness goals to the goal model based on the identified trust concerns from Step 4. Furthermore, we refine these trustworthiness goals into trustworthiness requirements using goal-based refinement techniques. Considering the healthcare domain, reliability, availability, usability, raising awareness and privacy (providing

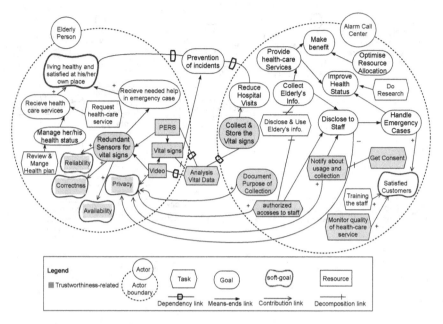

Figure 7.9: Simplified strategic rationale model including trustworthiness goals considering trust concerns

guidance and users' data protection) are crucial issues related to trustworthiness (Avancha et al., 2012; Leino-Kilpi et al., 2001; Gritzalis, 2004).

The gray-colored soft goals in Figure 7.9 are the trustworthiness goals added to the goal model in this step.

Step 6. Create business process including trustworthiness properties: Figure 7.10 illustrates the enriched business process model with the trustworthiness requirements satisfying the reliability and privacy soft goals from Figure 7.9.

In particular, we exemplify the typical steps that a human resource (e.g. a caregiver in the alarm call center) has to take or properties that a non-human resource needs to have in order to contribute to trustworthiness. We start with the activity to analyze the history of the vital signs of the elderly person in the last seven days. This activity may detect a risk in his/her health status. For addressing the trust concerns of the elderly person related to his/her confidence that she is not left alone and will get the needed healthcare when necessary, and related to his/her privacy concerns, the following trustworthiness requirements are specified: The

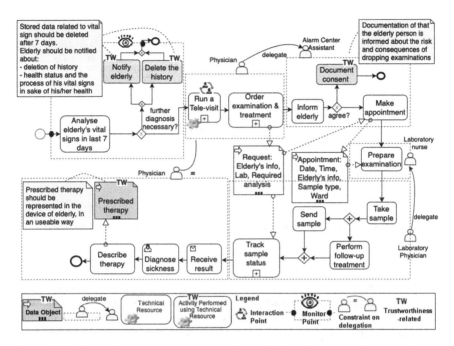

Figure 7.10: Exemplary business process model enriched with trustworthiness requirements

elderly person should receive a regular notification that informs his/her about the diagnoses that are performed on his/her vital signs. In Figure 7.10, it is added as a trustworthiness-related activity, namely "notify elderly". This activity contributes to making him/her confident that she is not left alone without care. Due to the privacy concerns, the history should be deleted, if no further diagnosis is necessary. The "delete the history" activity is also a trustworthiness-related activity added to the initial business process. This part of the business process is annotated as relevant for monitoring at run-time.

If a risk to the elderly person's health status is detected, "run a tele-visit" is offered. This activity is an interaction point supported by the HM application as a technical resource (cf. Figure 7.10). The trustworthiness properties for this interaction point are usability, response time, etc. In case of the necessity for further examination, the elderly person should be contacted by his/her physician or responsible care assistant (delegation of physician to the assistants). Furthermore, based on history, the same physician should be assigned to the activities when the

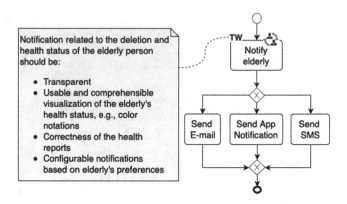

Figure 7.11: Exemplary further refinement on the business process model (within the solution peak)

elderly person is in contact with the alarm call center staff (addressing the trust concern). After processing his/her history data and if everything is alright, her last seven days of vital signs should be deleted. She/he should be informed that the processing has been performed and her health status is fine. She should be informed about the deletion of his/her history as well.

In Step 7 and Step 8, further iterative refinements of the trustworthiness goals and business processes are performed. Further grey-colored elements, i.e. additional ones to the elicited trustworthiness goals in Figure 7.9, are the result of the refinement of the goal model. For instance, in order to satisfy reliability and availability, redundant sensors for sending vital signs are considered for providing the vital signs of the elderly person to the alarm call center. The task "notify about usage and collection" is added to positively influence privacy. These refinements are further elaborated in the business process models.

Figure 7.11 shows the refinement of the trustworthiness requirements related to the "notify elderly" activity, which is related to the "notify about usage and collection" task from the goal model (cf. Figure 7.9).

Table 7.2 shows the trust concerns, corresponding requirements and activities. The column "affected resources" exemplifies possible software design decisions on resources.

Table 7.2: Examples of captured trustworthiness requirements and properties in the business process and effects on design decisions

Trust Concerns	Trustworthiness Requirements	Activities	Affected Resources
Privacy	Transparency, intervenability	Storage, deletion within 7 days, update	Private inventory system from the alarm call center, external cloud storage
Awareness	Usability, transparency, reliability, availability	Notifications, place appointments	Application on the elderly person's smart device (HM)
Safety, reliability	Reliability, availability	Raise alarm	Redundant sensors in addition to PERS
Privacy	Correctness, usability, availability	Make appointment, prescribe examination	Elderly person's details

7.6 Benefits of Our Method

The elicitation and specification of trustworthiness requirements through a user-centered requirements analysis and modelling method using a combination of goal and business process modelling is an innovative proposal. It results in the following benefits:

- Elicitation of trustworthiness requirements with a direct link to the trust concerns from which they originate as well as to the design decisions that are made based on them are key success factors for developing a trustworthy system. Tools and services developers are supported through detailed trustworthiness requirements for the software and services to be built.

- Bridging the two peaks (problem and solution) helps to elaborate the synergies between requirements and design artifacts. The benefit of interleaving the tasks of eliciting and refining requirements with the tasks of designing a software solution has long been recognized (Chung and do Prado Leite, 2009). Trustworthiness requirements together with other requirements are evolutionarily developed and will not be ignored. In a development process that incorporates just an up-front requirements engineering method, there is the risk of ignoring trust concerns. Developers might deliver solutions that fail to treat trust concerns of end-users.

It is therefore important to proactively elicit trustworthiness requirements from different participating actors during early phases and then to consider design solutions that balance and satisfy those concerns.

- Combining goal models and business process models has the benefit that we avoid gold plating. Gold plating (Pohl, 2010) is known as the implementation of irrelevant requirements, i.e. requirements that were never requested by stakeholders and are thus not backward traceable to any goals of stakeholders. Yet, our trustworthiness requirements can always be traced back to trust concerns of stakeholders. Therefore, there is always a justification for the trustworthiness requirements that are realized. This becomes even more critical, when the users pay it with the cost of their privacy or sometimes harming trust. For instance, in the home monitoring system, when the elderly person does not desire any assistance outside her/his home, the provided app (e.g. health manager) should not be provided with location information.

- The explicit consideration of conflicts on the goal level is another benefit of our approach. Sometimes some of the end-users' trust concerns are in conflict with the goals of other involved actors. For instance, the privacy goal of an elderly person in terms of transparency might be in conflict with the business goals of the hospital or insurance company. To resolve this conflict, the extent of transparency can be negotiated between the parties. In our approach, such kinds of contradictions are dealt with before the developers go into technical realizations of the goals.

- Dependencies between actors together with positive and negative links in i* describe the trustworthiness-related dependencies. However, dependencies and contribution links do not capture business relationships. These relationships are described in the business process models in our approach. One may understand the business process models also as an architectural description of the application.

- The resulting business process models with specified trustworthiness requirements can be used as a basis for designing and developing trustworthy software systems, applications and even for the evaluation of the trustworthiness properties (e.g. privacy, reliability, confidentiality or integrity) on an abstract level (cf. Chapter 10).

- Business process modelling offers an appropriate abstraction level to describe trustworthiness requirements and to later evaluate trustworthiness-related risks.

- Our approach is beneficial for the decision support during run-time adaptation as well. In an uncertain and changing environment, business processes are continuously optimized, e.g. via service substitution. To respect the overall trust-worthiness level, quality trade-offs should respect trustworthiness requirements. The business process models enhanced with trustworthiness properties are useful information during the run-time, as well.

7.7 Related Work

Systematic consideration of trustworthiness requirements is one of the key challenges that trustworthy systems must meet. However, most of the existing approaches restrict trustworthiness to security and/or privacy. Yet, in our opinion, trustworthiness is a vector of different other qualities and properties. Nevertheless, we present and discuss the most important existing approaches in this area. First, we discuss goal modelling approaches. Second, we discuss business process modelling approaches. Then, we discuss the approaches that use combinations of goal and business process modelling.

Goal Modelling Approaches

Horkoff et al. (2016) provide a systematic literature review of goal-oriented requirements engineering. They give a high-level overview of the goal-modelling field. According to their systematic literature review, i* and KAOS are the most dominant goal-modelling languages used for requirements engineering.

Both KAOS and i* have been extended by researchers to consider security and privacy requirements. An extension to KAOS for considering security requirements is presented by Lamsweerde (2004). He defines the concept of anti-goals to elicit the security goals.

An extension of the i* approach for considering security and privacy requirements is developed by Liu et al. (2003). They support the modelling of the social context of software systems and the identification of malicious intents toward the system under consideration. This work suggests a methodological framework for dealing with security and privacy requirements. Soft goals are used to model the corresponding notions of security and privacy within an agent-oriented modelling.

Secure Tropos (Giorgini et al., 2004), which extends the Tropos methodology (Bresciani et al., 2004), is an agent-oriented software development methodology tailored to describe functional, as well as security and trust requirements. However, in this approach, security is considered as the only dimension of trust. A CASE (computer-aided software engineering) tool for design and verification of functional, security and trust requirements is presented by Giorgini et al. (2006). This CASE tool supports the Secure Tropos methodology.

Business Process Modelling Approaches

De la Vara and Sánchez (2008) use BPMN to specify requirements in general. The requirements are specified by means of the description of the business processes to be realized by the system under development.

The study of related work reveals also some gaps in business process management with respect to trustworthiness.

Short and Kaluvuri (2011) provide an approach for dealing with the inclusion of internal and/or external services in a business process that contains data-handling policies. Wang et al. (2010) suggest a method to govern adaptive distributed business processes at run time with an aspect-oriented programming approach. Policies can be specified for run-time governance, such as safety constraints and how the process should react if they are violated. Several works have been done to overcome the problem of considering qualities in resource assignment. Some meta-models like (Daniel et al., 2012; der Aalst and Kumar, 2001) and an expressive resource assignment language (Cabanillas et al., 2015) have been developed. Among those, Resource Assignment Language graPH (RALPH) (Cabanillas et al., 2015) provides a graphical representation of the resource selection conditions and assignments. RALPH has formal semantics, which makes it appropriate for automated resource analysis in business process models.

There are a number of different extensions to BPMN. Stroppi et al. (2011b) present an extension for providing flexibility for resource structuring, allowing the definition of a broad range of organizational structures.

Stepien et al. (2009) present user interfaces that users can use to define conditions as policies themselves, e.g. defining privacy policies. The resource patterns provided by Russell et al. (2005) are used to support expressing criteria in resource allocation.

Business activities is a role-based access control extension of UML activity diagrams (Strembeck and Mendling, 2011) to define the separation of duties and binding of duties between the activities of a process. Wolter et al. (2009) developed a model-driven business process security requirement specification, which introduces security annotations into business process definition models for expressing security requirements for tasks. However, the current state of the art in this field neglects considering trustworthiness as a criterion for the resources and business process management.

There are BPMN extensions for the inclusion of different security requirements, e.g. non-repudiation, attack harm detection, integrity and access control (Rodríguez et al., 2007; Sang and Zhou, 2015). There are also proposed languages for the formulation of security constraints embedded in BPMN (Maines et al., 2015).

Salnitri et al. (2015) develop the Secure BPMN (SecBPMN) modelling language that extends BPMN with security annotations. SecBPMN supports establishing compliance between security-annotated business processes and security policies.

In all of these approaches, only security requirements are incorporated into a BPMN process from the perspective of a business process analyst.

Combinations of Goal and Business Process Modelling

Transforming goal models into process models provides the rationale for the design choices. Horkoff et al. (2014) conducted a systematic literature review. They created a road-map of publications that transform goal models to/from other software artifacts. According to their study, goal models are transformed into business process models in order to perform business analysis. However, our work is not transforming goal models to business process models in an automatic way. Rather, we use the combination of goal and business process models for eliciting, refining and modelling trustworthiness requirements.

Bleistein et al. (2003) use the Goal-oriented Requirement Language (GRL) to link requirements for strategic-level e-business systems to business strategies and to document patterns of best practices. They explore goal modelling for providing traceability and alignment between strategic levels, tactical and operational ones.

The linkage between goal and business process models is also applied in the context of security and privacy. For instance, the work by Salnitri et al. (2011) incorporates such an approach in the context of security. Kalloniatis et al. (2008) developed the Privacy Safeguard (PriS) method. The PriS method applies the linkage between goal and business process models for privacy requirements. PriS is a security requirements engineering method that incorporates privacy requirements into the system development process. PriS considers privacy requirements as organizational goals and uses privacy process patterns in order to describe the effect of privacy requirements on business processes. PriS captures the organizational goal in the form of goal trees, where the leaves of the tree refer to the processes that should satisfy the goal. Processes are defined in the form of activity diagrams. Argyropoulos et al. (2017) also apply the transformation of goals to service level process models. They provide a semi-automatic approach for the derivation of cloud service requirements focusing on security and privacy.

In our work, we consider a broad range of trustworthiness properties rather than just security or privacy. Furthermore, there is a rationale about from where trustworthiness requirements originate. Our approach tackles the problem of misalignments of trustworthiness requirements between the business and the system level.

7.8 Contribution and Summary of this Chapter

This chapter discussed trust issues in the context of business process management using BPMN and i*. Goal modelling provides an explicit linkage between requirements at different levels of abstraction as determined and refined by the i* diagrams. The integration with business process models offers a means of helping to ensure that requirements are in harmony with and provide support for business goals. An integration of subjective trust concerns into goal models and thereafter into the process models is provided. Our framework supports the analysis of the business processes from activity, resource and data object perspectives with respect to trustworthiness. To the best of our knowledge, we propose a novel contribution on user-centered identification of trust concerns and elicitation of trustworthiness requirements and thereafter integrating trustworthiness properties into business process design. Furthermore, our contribution includes a preparation for verification that satisfies trustworthiness constraints over resource allocation and activities execution.

Trustworthiness requirements are usually defined first on a technical level, rather than on a business process level. However, at the business process level, we are able to provide a comprehensive view on the participants, the assets/resources and their relationships regarding the satisfaction of business goals, as well as trustworthiness goals. Integrating trustworthiness-related information into business processes will support designers and developers in making their design decisions. Trustworthiness requirements on the business process level can be translated into concrete trustworthy configurations for service-based systems. Therefore, our proposed approach can be applied on different abstraction levels. Our proposed method identifies the resources and activities that are trustworthiness-related. Then, we specify the trustworthiness requirements on those resources and activities in business processes with regard to trustworthiness goals from goal models. Furthermore, our framework supports the business process lifecycle with respect to trustworthiness.

Our method presented in this chapter uses BPMN and i* as the languages. However, our approach is not limited to using i* as the goal modelling technique. For goal modelling, i* and KAOS are considered, which are used in our analysis due to their comprehensiveness.

8 Patterns for Documenting Trust and Trustworthiness

Considering trustworthiness requirements in accordance to trust concerns of the end-users during the development of software systems is a critical issue (as discussed in Chapter 7). Particularly challenging are the cross-disciplinary factors that affect trust of the end-users. Furthermore, expertise in requirements analysis is also required. It is essential for building a trustworthy software system to elicit and analyze trustworthiness requirements. Documenting these trustworthiness requirements along the other requirements that can achieve the construction of a trustworthy system is an important task.

In this chapter[1], we develop patterns to aid the documentation of trustworthiness requirements. The provided patterns are used during the requirement engineering phase to support the requirements engineer in documenting trustworthiness requirements by using linguistic templates. Using our patterns, end-users are also supported in expressing their requirements (trust concern identification pattern) and understanding which problems exist and how the problems are addressed (trustworthiness requirement pattern). These patterns provide insights into the relevant trustworthiness requirements that address the corresponding trust concerns. The application of the introduced patterns helps the requirements engineer during the trustworthiness requirement documentation in an unambiguous, understandable, traceable and verifiable way. We illustrate the patterns by applying them to the case study presented in Chapter 5.

The patterns presented in this chapter can be used optionally to enhance the RE method presented in Chapter 7.

8.1 Motivation

In this chapter, we propose a novel approach to improve the specification of trustworthiness requirements based on linguistic templates. The use of patterns for

---

[1]This chapter partially adapts Gol Mohammadi and Heisel (2016a) © 2016 ACM, with the permission of the publisher and authors.

© Springer Fachmedien Wiesbaden GmbH, part of Springer Nature 2019
N. Gol Mohammadi, *Trustworthy Cyber-Physical Systems*,
https://doi.org/10.1007/978-3-658-27488-7_8

documenting trustworthiness requirements supports structuring the knowledge related to trustworthiness requirements in a comprehensible form, reduces ambiguity, promotes reuse, and also serves as a guidance for requirements engineers to avoid a lack of relevant information. Furthermore, filling the pre-written and structured sentences, i.e. linguistic templates, is easier and less error-prone than writing them from scratch. Moreover, this approach has been successfully used in the areas of requirements engineering (Pohl, 2010), contracting Service Level Agreements (SLA) (Meland et al., 2014), and in the definition of key performance indicators in business process management (Del-Río-Ortega et al., 2012).

The benefits of using pattens to support the specification of trustworthiness requirements are the following: 1) trustworthiness requirements are unambiguous and a lack of relevant information is avoided through the use of our patterns; 2) in contrast to usual technical requirements specifications, they are more comprehensible to all stakeholders in a business process, because of the use of natural language and concepts which are closer related to the process and goal models; 3) they are traceable to the business process and to related trustworthiness goals addressing a specific trust concern of the end-user, because explicit references to business process elements and related goals are included (cf. Section 8.2); 4) they have the potential for an automated management, since a formal model can be developed to this end. In addition, the results of applying our patterns to different scenarios (cf. Section 8.5) served us in the validation and refinement of our patterns.

The RG1 and RQ1 as well as RQ3 (presented in Chapter 1) are further refined and addressed in this chapter in the following way:

- Understanding what the trust concerns of the end-user are. Understanding how the general and domain-specific trust concerns can be identified and addressed.

- Understanding what the trustworthiness goals addressing the trust concerns of the end-user are.

- Understanding what the trustworthiness properties satisfying the trustworthiness goals are, identifying whether those properties are in accordance with the identified trust concerns of the end-user, and analyzing their impact on the trustworthiness requirements.

- Identifying necessary structure for documenting gained knowledge related to trustworthiness of the system to be developed during the requirement engineering phase.

- Finding a systematic method to derive trustworthiness-related information which needs to be integrated into the business process model.

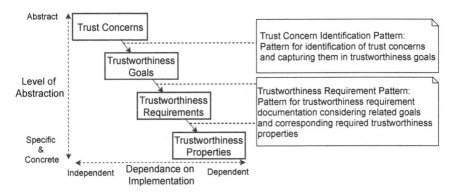

Figure 8.1: Purpose of our patterns (Gol Mohammadi and Heisel, 2016a)

The remainder of this chapter is structured as follows: In Section 8.2, we present the overview of two patterns for trust concerns identification and specifying trustworthiness requirements using linguistic templates. Section 8.3 presents the first pattern, which can be used for identification of trust concerns. Section 8.4 presents the second pattern that can be used for specification of trustworthiness requirements. Section 8.5 shows the application of our presented patterns to the AAL scenario of the application example described in Chapter 5. Section 8.6 discusses related work. Finally, Section 8.7 summarizes the contribution of our work in this chapter.

8.2 Overview of Our Patterns

In this section we will present the overview of the two patterns developed in this chapter: 1) Trust concern identification pattern and 2) Trustworthiness requirement pattern.

As shown in Figure 8.1, the trust concern identification pattern can be used by the requirement engineer to capture the trust concerns of end-users and to identify corresponding trustworthiness goals accordingly. The trustworthiness requirement pattern is used to specify trustworthiness requirements and to document their link to trustworthiness goals (modelled in the goal models), on the one hand, and trustworthiness properties in the business process models, on the other hand.

Using the patterns facilitates the specification of trustworthiness requirements for the requirement engineer. These documents will be handed to the development team to build trustworthiness right from the beginning into software components or

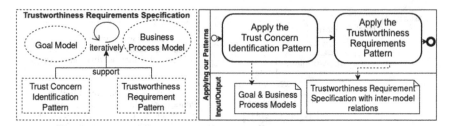

Figure 8.2: Relation between the developed patterns and the process of applying them based on (Gol Mohammadi and Heisel, 2016a)

services that are to be developed. Trustworthiness requirement descriptions can be translated to concrete trustworthy configurations for service-based systems.

We comply with the pattern format introduced in the EuroPlop community[2]. The structure of the pattern format should always capture the following components: context, problem, solution and consequences (Buschmann et al., 2007).

8.3 Trust Concerns Identification Pattern

The components of the trust concern identification pattern are described in the following. The pattern is shown in Table 8.1.

- **Context:** This pattern is applicable in the early requirement engineering phase. The requirement engineer needs to identify the trust concerns of the end-users. The identification of major trust concerns can be done either by interviewing involved stakeholders or based on the expertise of a requirements engineer. Furthermore, trustworthiness goals that address the identified trust concerns should be captured. The users of this patterns are the end-users and the requirements engineer.

  This pattern is used in the context of the *trustworthiness capability pattern 1* (cf. Chapter 6.3.4), i.e. RE method described in Chapter 7. *Trust concern identification pattern* contributes to the solution of the *trustworthiness requirements refinement method using goal and business process models* by identifying trust concerns. It also supports capturing trustworthiness goals that have to address the identified trust concerns (cf. Figure 8.2).

---

[2]http://www.europlop.net/content/introduction (accessed on 14 September 2018)

- **Problem and forces:** The challenge is the identification of trust concerns in a systematic and structured way. This pattern is used for identifying the trust concerns of the end-user and including them as trustworthiness goals in the software development process. However, these trustworthiness goals that will later be realized should be in accordance with the trust concerns of the end-users. Inadequate trustworthiness goals will cause an imbalance between the trustworthiness properties that are built into the software and the users' trust concerns. The end-users need a way to express their trust concerns and their trustworthiness requirements. Inexperienced requirements engineers need support in interviewing the end-users.

- **Solution:** Table 8.1 shows the proposed pattern for supporting requirement engineers in the identification of trust concerns of end-users. The first part of this pattern is provided in the form of a questionnaire, which is to be filled by the end-user. The questionnaire part is supporting the end-user in expressing his/her trust concerns and thereafter in communicating his/her trustworthiness requirements. The lower part of the pattern is to be filled by the requirement engineer.

Table 8.1: Trust concern identification pattern

Name	What is the name or identifier of the end-user?
Gender	**Female □ Male □**
The reason to use the product	What are the reasons to use this product?
Motivation	What objectives does the end-user follow?
Please mark the following statements with yes or no:	
Yes □ No □	I usually trust a person until there is a reason not to.
Yes □ No □	I am afraid to loose control over my personal information.
Yes □ No □	I am concerned about how my personal information is collected and used by digital applications and services.
Yes □ No □	Organisations handle the personal information they collect about me in a proper way.
Yes □ No □	Existing laws and organisational practices adequately protect me from online risks.
Yes □ No □	I am concerned that legal measures such as the ability to delete your personal informationare not put into place for increasing control.
Yes □ No □	I feel confident that encryption makes online services safe for me to use.
Yes □ No □	I am concerned about understanding my rights as described by the terms of the application provider.
Yes □ No □	I feel confident when there is a possibility to detect when my personal information has been misused.
Yes □ No □	I feel confident when there is a possibility to detect when a third party has gained access to the application without authorisation.
Yes □ No □	I feel confident when I am aware of an involved third party.

Yes ☐ No ☐	I am concerned about not knowing who is processing my information for which purpose.
Yes ☐ No ☐	Reputation of the involved organisation and third parties are important factors in my trust.
Yes ☐ No ☐	The location of the organisation and service providers are important for me.
Yes ☐ No ☐	Any guarantees regarding confidentiality of the information are important for me.
Yes ☐ No ☐	I would like to be provided with information about complaint procedures in case of problems.
Yes ☐ No ☐	I look for seals of approval when using an online service, system or application.
Yes ☐ No ☐	Is it important for me to know which type of information about me is publicly available, or to whom available?
Yes ☐ No ☐	Are your demographics sensitive information for you to reveal?
Yes ☐ No ☐	Seeing a symbol used to represent that a system, application and/or service has passed a particular set of best practice gains my trust, i.e. for quality, privacy or security, such as certification marks, authentication marks, quality assurance labels and seals of approval.
Yes ☐ No ☐	I tend to trust on above mentioned symbols when they are authoritative, i.e. they have been accredited or endorsed by a public regulator.
Yes ☐ No ☐	I am concerned about if I will be able to interact with the service properly.
Yes ☐ No ☐	I tend to doubt the correctness of instructions given by services or softwares.
Yes ☐ No ☐	I am concerned about the correct functionality of the services and softwares.
Yes ☐ No ☐	The timely receiving desired service is an important parameter in my trust on the online service.
Yes ☐ No ☐	It is important for me to see who I am interacting in the online service.
Yes ☐ No ☐	I get concerned when I lose access to my data even for a short period of time.
Credit card ☐ Debit card ☐ PayPal ☐ Invoice ☐ Via app ☐ Other?	How would you like to make online payments (e.g. credit card, debit card, PayPal, via app, invoice)?
Other points which are not mentioned above?	
The following fields are to be filled out and reviewed by a requirements engineer.	
☐ Specific	Is the stakeholder a real entity? Is the stakeholder not used to represent a group?
☐ Representative	Is the stakeholder a real existing entity? Is this stakeholder used as proxy for a group of homogeneous stakeholders?
☐ Group	Is the stakeholder not a real existing entity? Is this stakeholder used to describe a group of homogeneous stakeholders?

□ Role	Can this stakeholder be shared through groups of heterogeneous stakehold-ers? Are there well-defined rights for this stakeholder?
Trustworthiness goals for addressing trust concerns of the end-user are listed as below:	
Trustworthiness Goals	□ **Safety** □ **Security** □ **Reliability** □ **Privacy** □ **Adaptibility** □ **Testability** □ **Compliance** □ **Cost** □ **Usability** □ **Compatibility** □ **Performance** □ **Maintainability** □ **Configurabilty** □ **Complexity** □ **Data-related quality** □ **Correctness** □ **Resolution** □ **Predictability** □ **Accessibility of content and data**

- **Consequences:** The end-user answers the questions. Based on his/her answers the requirement engineer can select the relevant trustworthiness goals. Using this pattern, semi/-automated support for the trustworthiness goal selection can be provided. This can be done based on pre-analyzed dependencies between the questions and the corresponding trustworthiness goal. The requirement engineer will need to review these dependencies. The major impact of applying our pattern is that the high-level trustworthiness goals are captured in accordance with the expressed trust concerns of the end-users. The questionnaire in the natural language and the mapping to the trustworthiness goals based on the end-users' answers are a kind of linguistic templates that are used in this pattern.

As mentioned in earlier chapters (cf. Chapters 2 and 3), trustworthiness is domain- and application-dependent. The trust concerns are also different from user to user and also from project to project or application to application. The trust identification pattern can therefore be considered as a meta-pattern. This pattern can be made more concrete when considering a specific application domain. Therefore the questions in the questionnaire part of the pattern (presented in Table 8.1) are general questions. These questions be more concretized based on the project and additional questions could be added regarding the application domain.

The lower part of the pattern is based on the information collection pattern presented by Beckers et al. (2014). The questionnaire part of this pattern stems partially from the experience we gained during the European OPTET project[3] and a performed survey in the OPTET project.

8.4 Trustworthiness Requirements Pattern

The components of the *trustworthiness requirements pattern* are described in the following. The pattern is shown in Table 8.2.

---

[3]The EU-funded project with grant no. 317631 under 7th framework programme https://cordis.europa.eu/project/rcn/105733/factsheet/en (accessed on 15 August 2018)

- **Context:** The pattern is used by the requirements engineer to document trustworthiness requirements. These trustworthiness requirements will be delivered to the application and software designers and developers to get a common understanding and knowledge on the trustworthiness requirements. This pattern helps the requirement engineer to link the trustworthiness requirements to trustworthiness goals, on the one hand, and to trustworthiness properties, on the other hand. This pattern is used in the context of the *trustworthiness requirements specification* (cf. Figure 8.2). *Trustworthiness requirements pattern* covers trustworthiness requirements that should satisfy trustworthiness goals (captured using *trust concern identification pattern*). Furthermore, it links trustworthiness goals to the trustworthiness properties that should meet the trustworthiness requirements. The trustworthiness properties are capabled in business processes (cf. Figure 8.2).

- **Problem and forces:** Without capturing trustworthiness requirements in an understandable and unambiguous way, trustworthiness requirements can be misunderstood by developers and misimplemented. Furthermore, it can lead to untraceable and inconsistent requirements specification as regards trustworthiness. A lack of inter-model consistency between business process models and goal models (cf. Chapter 7) is the main problem solved by using this pattern solution.

- **Solution:** This pattern uses linguistic templates for specifying trustworthiness requirements on process elements and resources in a business process (see Table 8.2). It is inspired by the requirements templates provided in (Pohl, 2010) and performance key indicator described in (Del-Río-Ortega et al., 2012). The notation used in the template is the following: words between "<" and ">" are placeholders; words between "{" and "}" and separated by "|" are alternatives.

  The meaning of the major fields of the proposed pattern for documenting trustworthiness requirements is the following:

  Descriptive name and an identifier: Every trustworthiness requirement must be uniquely identified by a number and a descriptive name in order to allow traceability. In order to help quick identification, we suggest trustworthiness requirement identifiers should start with TW-Req.

  Process: This field refers to the process for which the trustworthiness requirement is relevant.

  Goals: This field allows the user to explicitly state the goal/s and trustworthiness goals that the trustworthiness requirement is related to. Associating a set of trustworthiness goals with a trustworthiness requirement highlights its relevance,

Table 8.2: The trustworthiness requirement pattern for capturing trustworthiness requirements with the link to trustworthiness goals and trustworthiness properties in the business process models

TW_Req_<ID>	<Descriptive name for the trustworthiness requirement>
Author Name	<Name of the author>
Process Element	<Description on the process element and its descriptive name>
Business Process	<Business process that the process element is related to, (process name and process ID)>
Goal of the Process	<Operational goals that the process supposes to address, (goal and the ID of the goal model)>
Trustworthiness Goal	<The objective goal towards enabling trustworthiness which relates to this process element (trustworthiness goal name, ID of goal model)>
Trustworthiness properties	<List of trustworthiness properties, which the process elements should be capable of>
Metrics	The metrics which can be applied in order to quantify the trustworthiness properties and calculate the metric values are: <list of metrics>
Thresholds	The metric values must: (<metric value> > <threshold value> | <metric value> < <threshold value>) | (<metric value> = <desired value> | <upper bound threshold value> > <metric value> > <lower bound threshold value>) | <upper bound threshold value> => <metric value> => <lower bound threshold value>) | Metric values fulfil the following constraint: <constraint>
Target	Lower values are desired | Higher values are desired
Source	<source on which metrics can be applied or metric values can be obtained, e.g. log files, sensors>
Responsible	role | department | organisation | person
Informed	role | department | organisation | person
Comments	<Additional information about the trustworthiness, e.g. condition assumptions, and criteria for the process elements such as activities or resource, etc.>

thus connecting to the relevant properties of the involved elements in the business process which fulfil a goal in the goal model. This field can be filled with an expression in natural language.

Process Element: This field specifies which process elements (i.e. which activities and technical resources) must hold the specified trustworthiness properties. If the process element is an actor, the actor can be a person, role, department or an organisations.

Metric Definition: This field indicates the metrics associated to this trustworthiness requirements or, more precisely, to the trustworthiness properties.

Target: This field defines the aimed-for value this trustworthiness property should keep. The target must be aligned with the goals the trustworthiness requirement is related to, so that it helps to determine the degree of goal fulfilment. Furthermore, this target value must be reasonable based on previous experiences and/or simulations when possible. During the evaluation, the process instances that must be considered for quantifying trustworthiness properties using the specified metrics should be specified as well (e.g. by considering every existing process instance, i.e. the whole set of process instances, or a specific instance (e.g. the process instances started last month)). This contributes to the time-bounded trustworthiness properties.

Source: This field references the source from which the required information to obtain the measure is gathered, e.g. event logs or sensor data.

Responsible: This field specifies the actors that are in charge of the trustworthiness requirements. This human resource can be a person, a role, a department or an organisation.

Informed This field specifies the actors that must be informed about the state of these trustworthiness properties. These actors can be persons, roles, departments or organisations.

Comments: Other information about the trustworthiness requirement that does not fit into the above mentioned fields can be mentioned here.

- **Consequences:** The major impact of applying the proposed pattern consists in structured and traceable trustworthiness requirements with adequate consistency. Furthermore, it refines the high-level trustworthiness goals (initially identified by pattern in Table 8.1) into the trustworthiness properties. These trustworthiness properties should meet the trustworthiness requirements that are defined for satisfying the trustworthiness goals.

8.5 Application of Our Patterns

For illustrating the application of our patterns, we use the home monitoring system from Chapter 7) and the same scenario that was described there.

Applying Trust Concern Identification Pattern

The trust identification pattern is used to capture the trust concerns of the end-user. Based on the questionnaire presented in Table 8.1, requirements engineers get to know that the elderly person (Alice Miller) is concerned about the fact whether she will really receive the emergency help if a similar situation happens again (heart attack experience). Table 8.3 shows the instantiated *trust concern identification pattern* for the scenario presented in Chapter 7.5. Alice is informed that by using such a service she can have regular diagnoses which can even prohibit frequent hospital visits. However, Alice is concerned if she will be able to use the service in a proper way. She is also concerned about who can get access to the data about their diseases or life habits.

Considering the trust concerns and the application domain and considering necessary legislation, the requirements engineer adds trustworthiness goals (see lower part of Table 8.3). In this case, the trustworthiness goals addressing the above-mentioned trust concerns are: security (specially availability), reliability, privacy, usability and correctness.

The existing refinement techniques (cf. Chapter 7) will be applied to refine these trustworthiness goals into trustworthiness requirements. Our proposed pattern in Table 8.2 will assist the requirement engineer in the refinement and documentation of trustworthiness requirements. This is done based on expertise of a requirements engineer and the knowledge gained during the context analysis like interviews. Please note that this pattern can be improved by the requirement engineer based on the knowledge he/she gains in the interviews and based on his/her expertise from the application domain.

Table 8.3: Trust concern identification pattern for the AAL

Name, Surname	Alice Miller
Age	71 years old
Gender	Female ☑ Male ☐
Which product are you interested in?	Assistance service in case of fall and tracking back home when I am outside home.
Motivation	
Why do you need this product?	After a heart attack at home, I do not feel confident living alone. I need help in such an emergency case. However, I would like to stay in my own home. I fear also going out, I am afraid not to find the way back home. I was once confused after shopping. It was difficult to come back home.
Please mark the following statements with yes or no and answer the questions:	

Voice ☑ Video ☐ Textual instruction on device ☑ Other?	How would you like to receive the heath care/medical instructions? I am concerned whether I would understand the textual description on a device. At first, I prefer to receive instructions with the possibility to clarify questions via a phone call. But, I would like to have also the textual description since I might forget the instructions.
Yes ☐ No ☑	I believe that the instructions made by an online health-care service are correct.
Yes ☐ No ☑	I have more confidence in an online health-care service when the service is certified and has a good reputation.
Yes ☑ No ☐	I feel more comfortable when there is an indication that an online health-care service is compliant to law and regulations (e.g. GDPR).
Yes ☑ No ☐	I am afraid to loose control over my personal information.
Yes ☐ No ☑	I am afraid to loose access to my personal information.
Yes ☑ No ☐	I am concerned about how my personal information is collected and used by online health-care services.
Yes ☑ No ☐	It is important for me to know which type of information about me is publicly available, or to whom it is available.
Yes ☐ No ☑	Are your demographics (e.g. address, age, gender, etc.) sensitive information for you to reveal?
Age ☑ Birth date ☐ Address ☑ Location ☑ Gender ☑ Marital status ☑ Education ☑ Heath records ☑ Other?	I am comfortable with sharing this information with the online health application and the involved caregivers. The examples for the involved caregivers are: staff in the alarm call center, staff in ambulance station and physicians. I am willing to share this information only if it is necessary for helping me.
Age ☑ Birth date ☑ Address ☑ Location ☐ Gender ☑ Marital status ☑ Education ☐ Heath records ☐ Prescription and Instructions ☐ Received emergency services ☐ Other?	I am comfortable with sharing this information with the contact person (one of the relatives) stored in the online health-care service. In case of emergency, I would like my daughter to be informed and to be notified about the hospital that I am delivered to.

Yes ☑ **No** ☐	I feel more confident when I am informed about who is processing my information for which purpose.

I am comfortable to allow the online health-care service to use my information in the following ways:
Demographics: Providing service ☑ Research and development ☐ Marketing and advertisement ☐
Location: Providing service ☑ Research and development ☐ Marketing and advertisement ☐
Health records: Providing service ☑ Research and development ☐ Marketing and advertisement ☐
Vital signs: Providing service ☑ Research and development ☐ Marketing and advertisement ☐
Financial information: Providing service ☑ Research and development ☐ Marketing and advertisement ☐
Log information: Providing service ☑ Research and development ☐ Marketing and advertisement ☐
Other? My health records can be used in anonymized form for the research purpose. But, I would like to be asked in advance if there is interest with this regard.

Yes ☑ **No** ☐	I feel more confident when there is transparent information about how online health-care service providers protect me from online risks.
Yes ☑ **No** ☐	I am confident when I have the control over my personal data, for example, to delete or modify my personal information when I am not willing to share this information with others any more.
Yes ☑ **No** ☐	I feel confident when there is a possibility to detect when something goes wrong, e.g. my personal information has been misused.
Yes ☑ **No** ☐	I feel confident when there is a possibility to know when a new third party will be involved in providing the online health-care service.
Yes ☑ **No** ☐	Although the health-care service is provided online, the locations of the organisation and service providers are important to me. Please note that the local law and regulations are valid within the EU countries. The online service provider is obligated to follow these regulations only if it is located within the EU borders.
Yes ☐ **No** ☑	I would agree to use an online health-care service whose provider is not located in the EU if they have cheaper prices. (Please note that your personal information can then be migrated to other countries outside the EU.)
Yes ☑ **No** ☐	I feel more confident when a guarantee is given that my personal information will be treated confidentially in the online health-care service.
Yes ☐ **No** ☑	I am confident that I will be able to interact with the online health-care service properly.
Yes ☑ **No** ☐	It would be comfortable for me when I can use the devices that I am familiar with.

Have you used smart devices before, if yes which? **Smart phone** ☑ Which? Samsung Galaxy III **Tablet** ☑ Which? Samsung Galaxy **Other?**	

Which kind of wearable devices do you prefer? **Watch-like** ☑ **Necklace-like** ☐ **Other?**	

Which kind of tutorials would help you to learn using the online health application? **User manual printed version** ☑ **User manual on smart devices** ☑ **Video tutorial** ☑ **Personal coaching session** ☑ **Learning in group** ☐ **Other?**	

Yes ☑ **No** ☐	I would like to be provided with information about complaint procedures in case of problems.
Yes ☑ **No** ☐	I am concerned about whether I will really receive help from the online health-care service when I need help.
Yes ☑ **No** ☐	I am concerned whether I will receive the necessary health-care service in time.
Yes ☑ **No** ☐	It is important for me to see who I am interacting with in the online health-care service.
Credit card ☐ **Debit card** ☐ **PayPal** ☐ **Invoice** ☑ **Via application** ☐ **Other?**	How would you like to make online payments?
Other points which are not mentioned above?	I am concerned whether someone else can abuse my information, for example, by knowing when I am out of home and knowing my location. Furthermore, I am concerned about ordering some service by mistake and being charged for it.

The following fields are to be filled out and reviewed by a requirements engineer.	

☑ **Specific**	Is the stakeholder a real entity? Is the stakeholder not used to represent a group?
☐ **Representative**	Is the stakeholder a real existing entity? Is this stakeholder used as proxy for a group of homogeneous stakeholders?
☐ **Group**	Is the stakeholder not a real existing entity? Is this stakeholder used to describe a group of homogeneous stakeholders?
☐ **Role**	Can this stakeholder be shared through groups of heterogeneous stakeholders? Are there well-defined rights for this stakeholder?

Trustworthiness goals for addressing trust concerns of the end-user are listed as below:	
Trustworthiness goals	☐ Safety ☑ Security ☑ Reliability ☑ Privacy ☐ Adaptability ☐ Testability ☐ Compliance ☐ Cost ☑ Usability ☐ Compatibility ☐ Performance ☐ Maintainability ☐ Configurability ☐ Complexity ☐ Data-related quality ☑ Correctness ☐ Resolution ☐ Predictability ☐ Accessibility of content and data

Applying the Trustworthiness Requirements Pattern

Tables 8.4, 8.5, 8.6, and 8.7 demonstrate the application of our trustworthiness requirements pattern in the presented example scenario.

Table 8.4: Instantiated *TW requirements pattern* for TW goal privacy

TW_Req-<1>	Transparency of data processing, awareness of the end-user about deletion of sensitive data after the data is not needed anymore
Author Name	Nazila Gol Mohammadi
Process Element	Analyze elderly person's vital signs from the last 7 days
Business Process	Analyzing elderly person's health status for prohibiting emergency cases modelled in Figure 8.4)
Goal of the Process	Prohibition of incidents (documented in Goal-model_1 shown in Figure 8.3)
Trustworthiness Goal	Privacy (documented in Goal-model_2 shown in Figure 8.5)
Trustworthiness properties	Notifications about data processing, deletion, documentation of purpose of collection. These properties have enriched the business process with the further elements in the business process model shown in Figure 8.6.
Metrics	For all analysed triggering events, there should be an escalation event sent to the elderly person and a deletion.
Thresholds	Fulfil the following constraint: Deletion of the vital signs should take place after analysis (expiration 7 days)
Target	
Source	Log files
Responsible	Application and software service provider
Informed	Elderly person
Comments	no comments

Note that Figures 8.3, 8.4, 8.5 and 8.6 depicts the goal and business process models for the scenario that are reprinted version from Chapter 7.5. We reprint these figures once again in this section to ease the readability of TW requirements pattern instances.

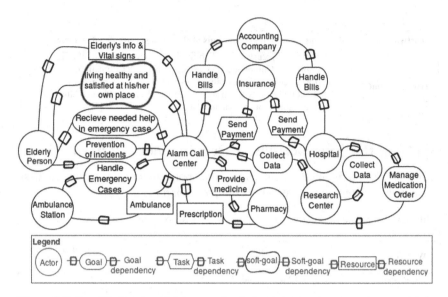

Figure 8.3: Simplified goal model (a more detailed and reprinted version of Figure 7.7)

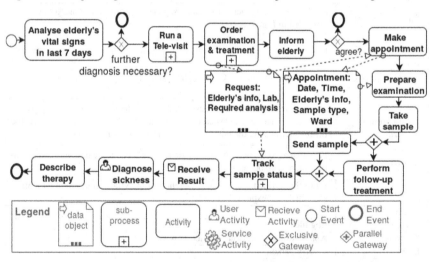

Figure 8.4: Process model (reprinted version of Figure 7.8)

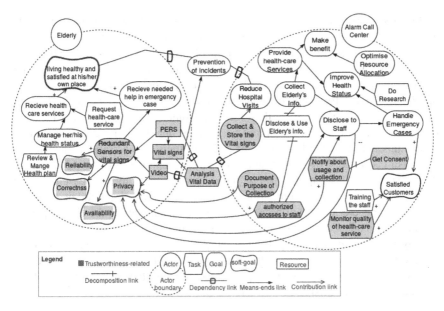

Figure 8.5: Goal model including TW goals (reprinted version of Figure 7.9)

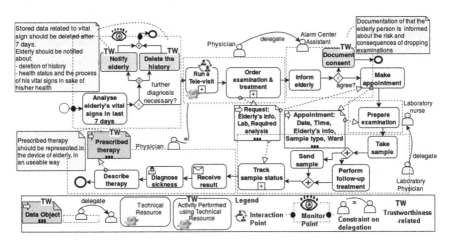

Figure 8.6: Revisited process model with TW requirements (reprinted version of Figure 7.10)

In this scenario, the activity "processing the history of the vital sign of the elderly person in the last 7 days" may detect a risk in the health status of the elderly person. For addressing trust concerns of the elderly people related to the question whether they will get the needed health-care in case it is necessary, the following trustworthiness requirements are modelled. Elderly people should receive a regular notification that informs them about the diagnose and processes that are done on their vital signs. In this way, they feel convenient and confident that they are not left alone without care. The notifications or health status reports should be understandable for elderly people. If a risk to their health status is detected, a tele-visit is offered. This can be done either by a telephone call or a video call via the "health manager" application on their device. This activity is an interaction point. The trustworthiness properties for this interaction point could be usability, response time, etc. In case of necessity for further examination, the elderly person should be contacted by his/her physician or responsible care assistant (delegation of physician to the assistants). If everything is alright after their history data has been processed, the vital signs of the last 7 days should be deleted. They should be informed that the process has been performed and their health status is fine. They should also be informed about the deletion of their history.

Table 8.5: Instantiated *TW requirements pattern* for TW goal usability

TW_Req_<2>	Learnability Effectiveness Efficiency of use Possibility of remote control for alarm call center assistant to help the elderly person with the interactions in case of problems
Author Name	Nazila Gol Mohammadi
Process Element	Tele-visit activity in Figure 8.6, an interaction point with the end-user "elderly" person as described in Chapter 7
Business Process	Analyzing elderly's health status for prohibiting emergency cases modelled in Figure 8.4)
Goal of the Process	Prohibition of incidents (documented in Goal-model_1 shown in Figure 8.3)
Trustworthiness Goal	Usability (documented in Goal-model_2 shown in Figure 8.5)
Trustworthiness properties	The technical resource supporting this activity is an interaction point with the elderly person. This technical resource is going to be installed on the smart device of the elderly person. The design-model depicts this application and its interactions with other applications in Figure 7.6.
Metrics	Rating values of the end-users in each interaction.

Thresholds	Fulfil the following constraint: Rating value for each interaction given by the elderly person should be > 4
Target	Higher values are desired
Source	Rating values
Responsible	Application, software service provider and communication provider
Informed	Health service provider
Comments	no comments

Table 8.6: Instantiated *TW requirements pattern* for TW goal reliability

TW_Req_<3>	Timeliness of receiving needed help in emergency case, Availability of service in case of emergency incident happening (elderly person as end-user)
Author Name	Nazila Gol Mohammadi
Process Element	Handle emergency request activity
Business Process	Process emergency incidents (business process model "Alarm-call-center_1")
Goal of the Process	Handle emergency cases (documented in Goal-model_1 shown in Figure 8.3)
Trustworthiness Goal	Reliability, Availability (documented in Goal-model_2 shown in Figure 8.5)
Trustworthiness properties	Redundant devices for alarm raising, Multiple services for handling emergency cases, Several ambulance resources
Metrics	Average time of duration of this activity, Duration of the activity from event "alarm rise" until ambulance arrives at the elderly person's home
Thresholds	Duration < 10 minutes
Target	Lower value is desired
Source	Log files
Responsible	Technology provider, health service provider
Informed	Alarm call center, elderly person
Comments	no comments

Table 8.7: Instantiated *TW requirements pattern* for TW goal correctness

TW_Req_<4>	Correctness of alarms for the alarm call center (caregiver in the alarm call center)
Author Name	Nazila Gol Mohammadi
Process Element	Handle emergency request activity
Business Process	Process emergency incidents (business process model "Alarm-call-center_1")
Goal of the Process	Handle emergency cases (documented in Figure 8.3)
Trustworthiness Goal	Correctness of raised alarm (documented in Goal-model_3)
Trustworthiness properties	Redundant devices for alarm registration, Testability function for elderly to reduce their false alarms
Metrics	Percentage of false alarms: Nr. of false alarms / all emergency requests $* 100$
Thresholds	Percentage of false alarms $< 5\%$
Target	Lower value is desired
Source	Log files
Responsible	Technology provider, application provider
Informed	Alarm call center
Comments	During holidays, number of false alarms triggered by elderly people increase.Function status and network status indicators may be helpful to reduce the number of false alarms triggered by elderly people.

8.6 Related Work

According to Withall (2007), there are three types of requirements patterns: functional, pervasive, and affects database. He identifies 37 requirement patterns. All of the 37 requirement patterns are divided into eight domains: fundamental requirement patterns, information requirement patterns, data entity requirement patterns, user function requirement patterns, performance requirement patterns, flexibility requirement patterns, access control requirement patterns, and commercial requirement patterns. Withall proposes the following core components for structuring software requirements patterns: domain, author, classification, context (in which the pattern can be applied), discussion, content (that describes what is necessary and the type of requirement), examples, information regarding how to use the pattern for implementation purposes and information regarding how to use the pattern for testing purposes.

Da Silva et al. (2015) use use cases as a requirements modelling technique. The proposed use case patterns include the following elements: pattern name, context, problem, solution, examples, consequence, related patterns, and known uses. These works have been used as a basis for our patterns. We included the suggested core elements in our patterns. However, our patterns have a different purpose. Furthermore, our patterns consider a tighter integration of trust concerns and trustworthiness requirements.

Pohl (2010) introduces patterns which describe scenarios in a structured textual format. Pohl's requirements templates include possible exception scenarios as well. The idea of using a structured textual format in our trustworthiness requirements pattern is similar to Pohl's requirements templates. He does not provide specific notations to document trustworthiness or any other non-functional requirements, and only consider functional requirements.

Del-Río-Ortega et al. (2012) develop some patterns for defining process performance indicators. The authors also proposed and an ontology-based linguistic pattern. This pattern relies on a formal descriptive logic. Therefore, it is possible to perform automated analysis and infer knowledge regarding the relationships between different key performance indicators in business process management (Del-Río-Ortega et al., 2012). The idea of using a linguistic pattern in our trustworthiness requirements pattern is similar to this work. Del-Río-Ortega et al. do not provide specific notations to document and model trustworthiness requirements, and only consider key performance indicators in business process management.

For analysing software quality, Alebrahim et al. (2014) propose a structured approach for modelling domain knowledge. The domain knowledge is captured by using patterns in addition to exploring the requirements for avoiding an incorrect specification. Our pattern can be used complementarily to the approach of Alebrahim et al.. Their pattern can be used prior to ours for capturing and modelling trustworthiness-related domain knowledge.

Beckers et al. (2015) propose a meta-model for describing context patterns. The meta-model contains components that can be used to structure and describe domain knowledge in a generic form. These context patterns can afterwards be instantiated with the domain knowledge required for software engineering. The pattern presented here for the identification of trust concerns used the meta-model from Beckers et al. (2015). However, we extend this meta-model based on the needs for documenting trust-related knowledge.

8.7 Contribution and Summary of this Chapter

This chapter provides two patterns for capturing trust concerns and bridging the gap from the trustworthiness goals to trustworthiness properties. The patterns are easy to learn, promote reuse, reduce ambiguities and avoid the lack of information related to trustworthiness. They are understandable to all stakeholders and maintain traceability between the goal models and the business process model. Furthermore, they provide the basis for an automatic analysis.

9 Problem-based Derivation of Trustworthiness Requirements from Users' Trust Concerns

In this chapter[1], we present a problem-based requirements engineering method that supports the systematic derivation of trustworthiness requirements from end-users' trust concerns. Based on identified trust concerns of users, trust assumptions are made explicit in problem diagrams. They express the conditions under which users are willing to trust. The problem diagrams and trust assumptions are then refined until they are concrete enough to derive trustworthiness requirements from them. During the refinement process, trust assumptions may influence and modify the system design (and vice versa, i.e. due to a certain system design, new trust concerns may arise that need to be addressed). In this way, users' trust concerns are considered right from the beginning and trustworthiness is designed into the CPS. The case study from Chapter 5 and the corresponding scenario described in Chapter 7 are again used to demonstrate our approach.

The problem-based requirements engineering method presented in this chapter can be used alternatively to the RE method presented in Chapter 7. The trust concern identification pattern from Chapter 8 can also be used with the problem-based RE method presented in this chapter.

9.1 Motivation

There are two challenges when aiming to achieve that a CPS is considered trustworthy: (i) trust and trust concerns are subjective and thus differ from user group to user group and (ii) trustworthiness is achieved by satisfying a set of other qualities or properties (cf. Chapter 4).

Traditional development methodologies did not respect users' trust concerns in dynamic, heterogeneous, and distributed settings. Therefore, trustworthiness-by-design methodologies (cf. Chapter 6) have been introduced. Requirements

---

[1]This chapter partially adapts Gol Mohammadi et al. (2018a) © 2015 IEEE, with the permission of the publisher.

© Springer Fachmedien Wiesbaden GmbH, part of Springer Nature 2019
N. Gol Mohammadi, *Trustworthy Cyber-Physical Systems*,
https://doi.org/10.1007/978-3-658-27488-7_9

engineering is a critical activity in these "by-design" methodologies. However, there is only a small set of well-accepted requirement refinement methods and complementary decision support (supporting design decisions), which can be applied in a systematic way for considering trustworthiness (cf. Haley et al. (2004); Giorgini et al. (2006)). We believe that trustworthiness of CPS is strongly dependent on their development processes, especially the elaboration of trustworthiness requirements during the requirements engineering phase.

In this chapter, we suggest a problem-based requirements engineering method that supports specifically the systematic derivation of trustworthiness requirements from end-users' trust concerns. Based on the users' trust concerns, trust assumptions are made explicit in problem diagrams. Trust assumptions express the conditions under which users are willing to trust. The problem diagrams and trust assumptions are then refined until they are concrete enough to derive trustworthiness requirements from them. During the refinement process, trust assumptions may influence and modify the system design (and vice versa, i.e. due to a certain system design, new trust concerns may arise that need to be addressed). In this way, users' trust concerns are considered right from the beginning and trustworthiness is designed into the CPS.

The chapter is structured as follows. In Section 9.2, we explain the fundamentals of our work. In Section 9.3, we present our method for systematically deriving trustworthiness requirements from trust concerns. In Section 9.4, we demonstrate the application of our method using the AAL case study (cf. Chapter 5). In Section 9.5, we describe tool support. In Section 9.6, related work is discussed. In Section 9.7, we draw conclusions.

9.2 Background

In this section, we first introduce problem-based requirements engineering and explain its advantages. Then, we describe the so-called Six-Variable Model that we will use as a support in making trust assumptions explicit.

9.2.1 Problem-based Requirements Engineering

Problem-based requirements engineering was introduced by (Jackson, 2001). He considers the software to be developed in a software development project as a solution. The software is developed to solve a problem in the environment. The environment is a portion of the real world whose current behaviour is unsatisfactory. The software will be developed and integrated into this environment to achieve that the behaviour is satisfactory then. The software and its environment together make up the system (in Jackson's terms).

A major benefit of problem-based requirements engineering is its focus on problem analysis. Jackson (2001) criticizes that developers frequently focus too much on developing the solution, without having analysed the problem thoroughly beforehand. However, it is quite hard to develop a proper solution without having understood the problem correctly. To prevent that, he suggests analysing and decomposing software development problems as a first step in requirements engineering, i.e. before focussing on the solution.

Jackson differentiates between three types of statements (based on Zave and Jackson (1997)): requirements R, domain knowledge K, specifications S. *Requirements* are optative statements, i.e. statements describing the environment as we would like it to be because of the machine. They shall express the desires of the customer concerning the software development project. *Domain knowledge* consists of indicative statements, i.e. statements describing the environment as it would be without or in spite of the machine. The *specification* consists again of optative statements, however, in contrast to the above-mentioned requirements, these need to be directly implementable and to support satisfaction of the requirements. The relation between requirements, domain knowledge, and specifications is defined by means of the satisfaction argument: $S, K \vdash R$. The argument mainly says that, if a machine is developed that satisfies S and is inserted into the environment described by K, and S and K are consistent each internally and with each other, then the set of requirements R is satisfied.

A problem diagram shows the machine (i.e. the software-to-be), its environment, and the requirement to be satisfied (see Figure 9.1 for an example). A problem diagram contains the following modelling elements: a machine domain, problem domains, a requirement, interfaces, requirement references, and constraining references. A problem domain represents a material or immaterial object in the machine's environment that is relevant for satisfying the requirement. The requirement is to be satisfied by the machine together with the problem domains. Interfaces exist between machine domain and problem domains or among problem domains. At the interfaces, phenomena (e.g. events, states, values) are shared. Sharing means that one domain controls a phenomenon, while the other observes it. At an interface, not only the phenomena are annotated but also an abbreviation of the domain controlling them followed by an exclamation mark (e.g. CM!). A requirement is connected to problem domains by means of a requirement reference or a constraining reference. A requirement reference expresses that the requirement refers to phenomena of the domain, while a constraining reference expresses that the requirement constrains (i.e. influences) them.

9.2.2 The Six-Variable Model

The Six-Variable Model (Ulfat-Bunyadi et al., 2016) (shown in Figure 9.1) extends the well-known Four-Variable Model (Parnas and Madey, 1995) and focuses on control systems.

A control system consists of some control software which uses sensors and actuators to monitor/control certain quantities in the environment. However, frequently, it is not possible to monitor/control exactly those variables one is interested in. This is especially the case, when sensors and actuators for monitoring and controlling are selected. The selection of sensors/actuators/other systems for monitoring/controlling often results in the situation that a different set of variables is monitored/controlled, whose variables are related to the ones of real interest. Therefore, the Six-Variable Model demands that the variables of real interest should be documented as well beside the classical four variables: m (monitored), c (controlled), i (input), and o (output). The two new variables are the so-called *referenced* and *desired* variables. r (referenced) variables are environmental quantities that should originally be observed in the environment, i.e. before deciding which sensors/actuators/other systems to use for monitoring/controlling. d (desired) variables are environmental quantities that should originally be influenced in the environment. In addition to the six variables, it should also be documented how the variables are related to each other. The Six-Variable Model is depicted in Figure 9.1 as a problem diagram.

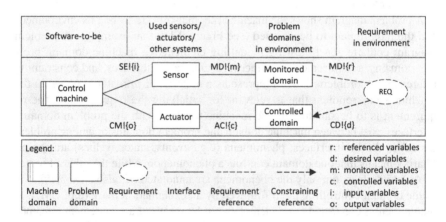

Figure 9.1: The Six-Variable Model (Ulfat-Bunyadi et al., 2016)

9.3 Trustworthiness Requirement Analysis Method using the Six-Variable Model

Before describing our method for the systematic derivation of trustworthiness requirements, we introduce the conceptual model that is underlying our method.

9.3.1 Conceptual Model

Figure 9.2 shows the main concepts that are used in our method and the relationships between them. Since our method is based on problem diagrams, problem diagram concepts are shown in white, while our extensions are shown in grey.

As mentioned above, there are two types of *statements* about a system according to the terminology of Zave and Jackson (1997): *indicative* and *optative* statements. The *requirements* and the *specification* represent optative statements, while *domain knowledge* is indicative. The requirements need to be satisfied by the system. This means that the specification must be satisfied by the *machine domain*, the domain knowledge needs to be valid, and specification and domain knowledge have to be consistent with each other. Domain knowledge is often divided into facts and assumptions (cf. Lamsweerde (2009); Hatebur and Heisel (2010)). *Facts* hold always regardless of the system (e.g. physical laws). *Assumptions* describe things that cannot always be guaranteed, but which are needed to satisfy the requirements (e.g. rules for user behaviour). The *system* consists of different types of *system elements*. In the figure, we show only those elements that are relevant for us, i.e. there are further system elements that are not shown here. Important system elements are the *machine domain, problem domains*, and the *phenomena* that are shared.

Our extensions consist of the following concepts. *System users* use the system (CPS) and have *trust concerns* which need to be elicited. To address these trust concerns, a *trustworthiness (TW) vector* must be defined which consists of all the *TW properties* the system must possess in order to be trustworthy from the user's point of view. During the requirements engineering process, requirements need to be specified which ensure that the system will be trustworthy. We call these requirements *TW requirements*. Trustworthiness requirements address trust concerns of system users. They represent a specialisation of Zave and Jackson's *requirements*. Trustworthiness properties satisfy the trustworthiness requirements.

During this refinement process, we consider mainly one specific type of assumptions: trust assumptions. We define *trust assumptions* as assumptions made by developers expressing the conditions under which the users will trust the system. These trust assumptions may refer to problem domains, to the machine domain, and

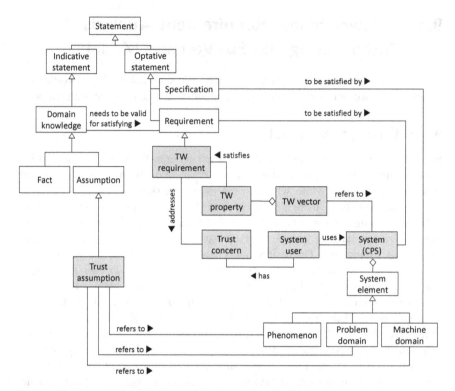

Figure 9.2: Conceptual model (Gol Mohammadi et al., 2018a)

even to phenomena annotated in the problem diagram. We use the trust assumptions to bridge the gap between trust concerns, on the one hand, and TW requirements, on the other hand.

9.3.2 Method Steps

In order to address users' trust concerns, the concerns have to be elicited and trustworthiness requirements have to be derived from them, i.e. requirements which ensure that the CPS is trustworthy once it is developed. This has to be done in addition to traditional requirements engineering. Our method supports developers in deriving trustworthiness requirements from trust concerns in a systematic and structured way. Figure 9.3 provides an overview of our method showing the steps to be performed as well as input and output of these steps. In the following, we describe each step in detail.

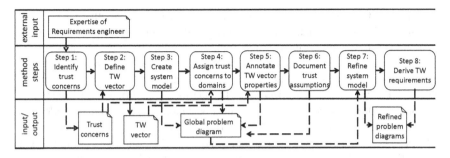

Figure 9.3: Overview of our method (Gol Mohammadi et al., 2018a)

Step 1. Identify trust concerns: As a first step, trust concerns (TC) of end-users must be identified. To this end, elicitation techniques such as interviews and questionnaires like the one provided in pervious chapter (cf. Chapter 8) can be used. Furthermore, trust concerns may also be identified based on the expertise of the requirements engineer.

Step 2. Define TW vector: During this step, a trustworthiness (TW) vector is defined which can address the trust concerns. The TW vector comprises all trustworthiness properties (i.e. system qualities) the CPS must possess in order to be trustworthy. Desired degrees for these properties do not need to be specified. However, they can be specified.

Step 3. Create system model: During this step, a global system model is created. We suggest creating a high level problem diagram based on the Six-Variable Model. A CPS can be understood as a complex control system. The Six-Variable Model supports focussing on the real world and the effects that shall be achieved there. Developers frequently focus on the solution they are developing and therefore tend to neglect modelling the real world. The Six-Variable Model reminds developers of documenting referenced and desired variables as well, in addition to the classical four variables (monitored, controlled, input, and output variables). The resulting global system model serves as a foundation for the next three steps.

Step 4. Assign trust concerns to model elements: During this step, the trust concerns that have been elicited in Step 1 are assigned to the relevant elements in the global system model. A trust concern may refer to one or several domains, one or several phenomena, and even to the requirement. A user may, for example, have a trust concern regarding the reliability or usability of a certain device. He/she may also have a trust concern regarding the privacy of his/her data that is exchanged and stored in the CPS. Similarly, he/she may be concerned about whether CPS will be able to satisfy its functional requirement(s). For documenting trust concerns in the system model, we suggest using annotations and relating them by means of arrows to their source (e.g. the user), on the one hand, and to the element to which they refer, on the other hand (see Figure 9.5 for an example).

Step 5. Annotate TW vector properties: During this step, properties from the TW vector for addressing the trust concerns must be annotated in the system model. For each trust concern, at least one TW property must be annotated. However, several TW properties may also be annotated at one trust concern. Annotating the TW properties from the vector at the trust concerns has the advantage that it becomes traceable why certain TW properties are relevant, i.e. due to which trust concerns, and which elements they affect in the system model (namely the ones affected by the trust concerns).

Step 6. Document trust assumptions: During this step, trust assumptions that are relevant for addressing the trust concerns are documented in the system model. They are made by the developers based on the trust concerns and the TW vector properties. We recommend documenting them in the problem diagrams because they also serve as justifications for design decisions that are made (e.g. having redundant sensors). For annotating trust assumptions, we suggest using the notation suggested by Haley et al. (2004). Note that although we use the notation suggested by Haley et al., our trust assumptions differ from their trust assumptions, which focus mainly on security-related trust issues. Our trust assumptions are more general, referring to all TW properties defined in the TW vector (i.e. not only security). Beside the assumptions, the complete TW vector is also modelled in the system model. It is annotated as a dashed oval (i.e. in the same way as the requirement) and is related to the requirement by means of a dashed arrow expressing that the TW vector extends the requirement.

Step 7. Refine system model: During this step, the problem shown in the global system model is decomposed into subproblems, and each subproblem is modelled in a separate problem diagram. The trust concerns, TW vector properties, and trust assumptions are refined as well. This is done until detailed trust assumptions are defined.

Step 8. Derive TW requirements: During this step, TW requirements are derived from the detailed trust assumptions in the refined problem diagrams. Note that the TW requirements might be quite similar to the trust assumptions. However, in contrast to trust assumptions (which have rather the character of justifications), TW requirements represent requirements and are thus to be satisfied by the system. Yet, it will not always be visible in the problem diagrams how they are satisfied. Some of them might be satisfied in later development phases (e.g. during architectural design, detailed design, etc.). TW requirements are modelled as dashed ovals (just as the requirement) and are related to the TW vector by means of dashed arrows, annotated with "satisfies" to express that they contribute to satisfying the TW vector.

The final result of our method are the refined problem diagrams which contain trust assumptions and TW requirements. These diagrams are input to subsequent development phases like architectural design, detailed design, etc. In this way, it is ensured that trustworthiness is designed into the CPS right from the beginning and that it even may influence the system model (problem diagram) resulting in extensions and modifications.

9.4 Application Example

To illustrate our method, we use again the AAL case study from Chapter 5 and the scenario used in Chapter 7 (cf. Section 7.5).

Step 1. Identify trust concerns: Alice is concerned about the fact whether she will really receive the emergency help if she has a heart attack (or similar) again (TC1). Furthermore, she is concerned whether she will be able to use the system in a proper way (TC2) and about who can access the data about her diseases or life habits (TC3). She would prefer only her regular nurse and doctor to be able to see her history and health status.

Step 2. Define TW vector: The trust concerns TC1 to TC3 can be addressed by a TW vector consisting of reliability, usability, and privacy. Note that this is a simplified version of a TW vector that we use for illustration purposes. Usually, a TW vector is more complex.

Step 3. Create system model: Figure 9.4 depicts the global system model for the EMHT (emergency monitoring and handling tool). It shows the machine domain, sensors and actuators used by the machine domain as well as relevant real world domains. At the connections (interfaces and references), the six variables are annotated. Referenced variables (i.e. the variables of real interest) are, for example, the health status of a patient and his/her need for help. The corresponding monitored variable is "call for help". The machine is informed about the patient's call for help by the PERS device (personal emergency response system), i.e. the patient has to press the alarm button of the device if he/she needs help.

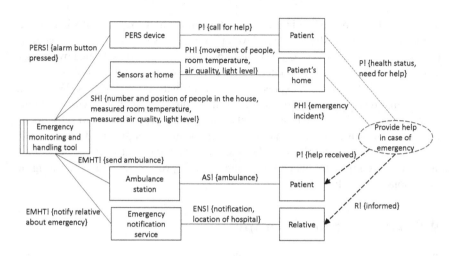

Figure 9.4: Global system model (Gol Mohammadi et al., 2018a)

Another referenced variable is an emergency incident which might occur at the patient's home. To observe the referenced variable "emergency incident", the following variables are monitored at the patient's home: movement of people, room temperature, and air quality. The sensors at the patient's home provide the following information to the EMHT (i.e. these are the input variables for the EMHT): the number and position of people in the house, the measured room temperature, and the measured air quality. Based on the information from these sensors and the information from the PERS device, the EMHT decides whether an emergency incident has occurred or not and sends an ambulance to the patient, if necessary. At the same time, it informs the patient's relatives that an emergency incident has occurred and that the patient is brought to a certain hospital. Thus, the effects that shall be achieved in the real world are that the patient is helped and his/her relatives are informed, if an incident occurs.

Step 4. Assign trust concerns to model elements: Figure 9.5 shows how we assigned the trust concerns of our patient Alice to elements of the system model. TC1 is quite general because Alice questions whether the system will be able to satisfy its requirement. Therefore, we assigned it to the requirement. Since this requirement is to be satisfied by the machine and all shown problem domains, it refers actually to all these elements. TC2 refers to the PERS device, since the PERS device is the only shown device that is directly used by the patient. TC3 refers to phenomena at three interfaces, because at all these interfaces user data is exchanged.

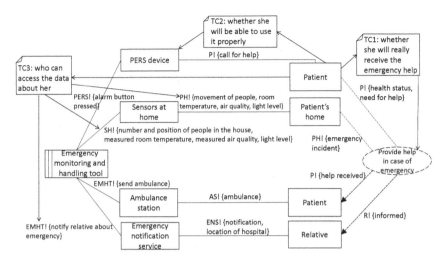

Figure 9.5: Trust concerns (Gol Mohammadi et al., 2018a)

Step 5: Annotate TW vector properties: Figure 9.6 shows the properties of the TW vector for each trust concern. TC1 can be addressed by the TW property reliability. TC2 can be addressed by usability and TC3 can be addressed by privacy.

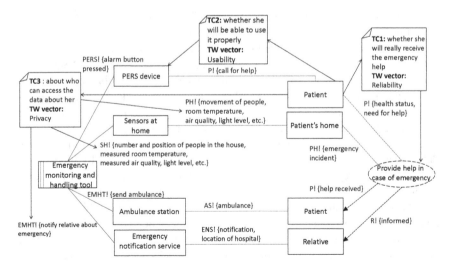

Figure 9.6: Trust concerns and trustworthiness properties (Gol Mohammadi et al., 2018a)

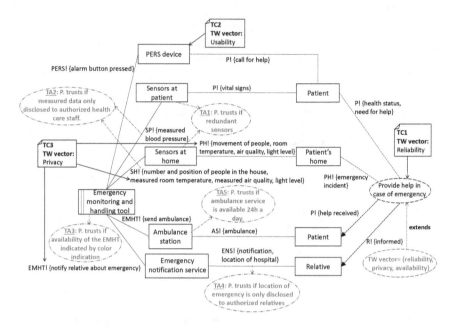

Figure 9.7: Trust assumptions (Gol Mohammadi et al., 2018a)

Step 6. Document trust assumptions: Figure 9.7 shows five trust assumptions that
we defined for addressing the three trust concerns. The first trust assumption is TA1
that says "Patient trusts if redundant sensors are used". As shown in Figure 9.7, TA1
had an impact on the system design: due to TA1, the problem domain "Sensors at
patient" is introduced. These sensors are responsible for monitoring the vital signs
of the patient. Based on this data, the EMHT machine is able to detect the patient's
need for help. In this way, redundancy is achieved as regards the way the EMHT is
informed about the patient's need for help: either by the patient him-/herself who
presses the alarm button at the PERS device, or by the sensors at the patient which
detect that the vital signs deviate from their usual/normal values. Redundancy is
also achieved as regards the way the EMHT is able to detect emergency incidents:
by the sensors installed at the patient's home and by the sensors at the patient
him-/herself. The introduction of these sensors addresses TC2 (usability concern)
and TC1 (reliability concern). Because our patient Alice was, on the one hand,
concerned about whether she will receive emergency help when needed and, on the
other hand, whether she will be able to use the PERS device when she needs help –

there might be situations, in which she is no more able to press the alarm button. By means of the additional sensors at the patient, both concerns are addressed now. TA2 ("Patient trusts if measured data is only disclosed to authorised health care staff.") and TA4 ("Patient trusts if location of hospital is only disclosed to authorised relatives."), both, address TC3 (privacy concern). TA3 ("Patient trusts if availability of the EMHT is indicated by colour indication.") and TA5 ("Patient trusts if ambulance service is available 24 hours a day.") contribute to addressing TC1 (reliability concern).

Step 7. Refine system model: The overall software development problem shown in the global system model is "Provide help in case of emergency". We decomposed this problem into the following subproblems which represent mainly functional requirements (FR):

FR1: Provide patients with means for calling help.

FR2: Monitor patient (to detect emergency situation).

FR3: Send ambulance to patient in case of emergency.

FR4: Inform relatives about emergency.

The problem diagram for FR2 is shown in Figure 9.8. To improve readability, we omitted the trust concerns in this diagram. The diagram shows the sensors that are used for monitoring the patient him-/herself as well as his/her house. A blood pressure meter, that the patient must wear, measures his/her blood pressure regularly. In his/her home, a video sensor, smoke detectors as well as temperature sensors are used to monitor the number and movement of people in the house, to detect fire, and to measure the room temperature. The machine is called "Monitor machine" and is part of the overall machine (the EMHT). It stores the patient's measured blood pressure and health status in a data store called patient data (shown as so-called designed domain in the problem diagram). If it detects an emergency incident, it stores the type of the detected incident in the data store "Emergency incidents". These two designed domains are then used by other domains in other problem diagrams (not shown here).

Step 8. Derive TW requirements: Figure 9.8 shows two TW requirements which have been defined based on the trust assumptions TA1 and TA2. Although the TW-Req1 and TW-Req2 are quite similar to TA1 and TA2, they differ in their nature, since the latter are only statements that are assumed and serve as justifications for certain design decisions, and the former are requirements which need to be satisfied somehow by the system. For satisfying TW-Req1, it is, for example, visible in the problem diagram that a video sensor and a blood pressure meter are both used

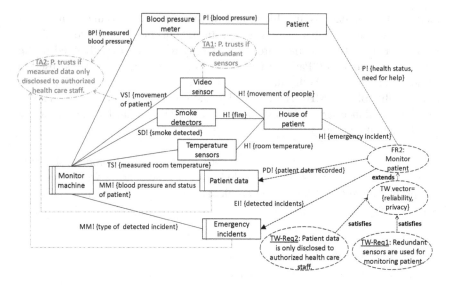

Figure 9.8: Trustworthiness requirements (Gol Mohammadi et al., 2018a)

to ensure redundancy. For TW-Req2, on the other hand, it is not visible how this requirement is satisfied. The satisfaction of this requirement is deferred to later development phases, when data access rights are defined as assigned to certain user groups.

9.5 Tool Support

The creation of problem diagrams is supported by the UML4PF profile that was proposed by Hatebur and Heisel (2010). This profile allows for modelling problem diagrams as UML class diagrams. The profile can also be used to create the problem diagrams resulting from our method. The extensions that we made to the problem diagram notation to enable modelling of trustworthiness-related issues can be represented in the following way, when using the UML4PF profile:

- trust concerns can be modelled as UML comments

- trust assumptions can be modelled as classes with the stereotype ≪*domain knowledge*≫

- TW requirements can be modelled as classes with the stereotype ≪*requirement*≫

- the TW vector can also be modelled as classes wit the stereotype ≪*requirement*≫

- the *satisfies* relationship between TW requirements and the TW vector can be modelled as a dependency

- the *extends* relationship between TW vector and the requirement in the problem diagram can be modelled as a dependency

- the relationship between trust assumptions and the domains and phenomena they affect can be modelled as a dependency with the stereotype ≪*refersTo*≫

In this way, our extended problem diagrams can be modelled as UML class diagrams with corresponding stereotypes at the model elements.

9.6 Related Work

There are several existing approaches that restrict trustworthiness to security and/or privacy. Although we do not share this opinion, we provide a brief overview of the most important existing approaches in this area.

Mellado et al. (2010) carry out a systematic literature review on security requirements engineering. They summarize the approaches considering security in all stages of information system development, especially during the requirements engineering phase. Indeed, there is plenty of work regarding requirements refinement processes considering trust. Therein, first, systems are specified consisting of functionalities with no security features. Then, the next refinement includes encryption, access control and authentication. However, there is no clear reasoning why encryption, access control and authentication are necessary and sufficient with respect to trust.

An extension of problem frames (Jackson, 2001) has been developed for the elaboration and analysis of security requirements. Haley et al. (2004) consider trust assumptions during analysis of security requirements. They define trust assumptions in a different way than we do: in a problem diagram for a security requirement, the requirements engineer trusts a problem domain to participate competently and honestly in the satisfaction of the security requirement. The requirements engineer trusts this assumption to be true. These assumed properties act as domain restrictions, i.e. they restrict the dependent problem domain in some way. Therefore, Haley et al. suggest modelling them as ovals with an arc from the dependent problem domain to the oval describing the properties being depended upon. As described in Section 9.3, we also use the notation suggested by Haley et al. in our method. Yet, we define trust assumptions in a different way, since it is not the requirements engineer who needs to trust but the users, and we do not consider trust assumptions only in the context of security requirements but in the context of any type of requirements.

Horkoff et al. (2016) provide a systematic literature review of goal-oriented requirements engineering methods. According to this review, i* and KAOS are the most dominant goal modelling languages and both have been extended to consider security and privacy requirements. Lamsweerde (2004), for example, extends KAOS by defining the concept of anti-goals to support elicitation of security goals. Liu et al. (2003) extend i* for considering security and privacy requirements. They support modelling of the social context of software systems and identification of malicious intents toward the system. They use softgoals for modelling the corresponding notions of security and privacy within this agent-oriented modelling approach. Elahi and Yu (2009) extend i* as well. They state that trust assumptions (i.e. assumptions about trust relationships among actors) should be made explicit so that trust trade-off decisions (between gaining some benefits from a second party and being exposed to security and privacy risks) can be analysed and made by analysts in a systematic way. Therefore, Elahi and Yu extend i* models with different types of trust and distrust relationships. Another agent-oriented software development methodology is Tropos (Bresciani et al., 2004). It was extended by Secure Tropos (Giorgini et al., 2004), which is tailored to describe functional, security, and trust requirements. However, in this approach, security is again considered as the only dimension of trust.

9.7 Contribution and Summary of this Chapter

In this chapter, we presented a method that supports the systematic derivation of trustworthiness requirements from users' trust concerns. Our method has the following advantages and benefits:

First, we understand trustworthiness as a vector of properties/qualities that the system must possess in order to be trustworthy. This vector can be defined for different user groups. In this chapter, we mainly focussed on the end-users. However, a CPS is usually used by different user groups. In case of the AAL, doctors, hospitals, operators in the ambulance call center, and even relatives of the patients represent other user groups beside patients. Our method can be used in the same way to address the trust concerns of these groups as well.

Second, our method is problem-based, and this means that we can exploit all the benefits of the problem frames approach (Jackson, 2001) and the extensions made to it. A major benefit of the method itself is that it supports focussing and analysing the software development problem first, before developing the solution. A proper solution can only be defined if the problem has been understood thoroughly. Our method enables that trust concerns are analysed as part of the problem and that they influence the solution and its design right from the beginning.

Third, the artefacts that result from our method ensure traceability from trust concerns, to TW properties (in the TW vector), to trust assumptions, and finally to TW requirements. Thus, the rationale and justification for TW requirements is documented and can be traced back at any time. A major benefit of this traceability is, of course, that it allows for impact analysis in case of changes to TW requirements and facilitates systematic change integration. If a TW requirement must, for example, be modified because it is not feasible, it is backward-traceable from which trust concerns it was derived. Based on this information, it can also be decided whether the trust concern is still sufficiently addressed by the modified TW requirement.

In Chapter 7, we proposed another RE method which is similarly intended for systematically eliciting and refining trustworthiness requirements. However, there, we used a combination of goal and business process models. The main difference between our two methods consists in the models used. The benefit of using problem diagrams (as in this chapter) is that they show the system design and thus facilitate making modifications to it, if required due to users' trust concerns. The two RE methods presented in this book are alternative, they even can be used complementarily.

10 Computational Approach towards End-to-End Trustworthiness Evaluation

In this chapter[1], we present an approach for evaluating the trustworthiness of a CPS. If desired, this approach can be enhanced with risk assessment approach presented in Chapter 11. The combined approach and the advantages of combining the two approaches are presented in Chapter 11.

10.1 Motivation

A cyber-physical system is shaped by technologies and services that contain software as core elements. The software elements in these systems should be designed and manufactured in such a way that they reliably satisfy trustworthiness requirements. It is not only essential to use constructive quality assurance techniques, such as best practices for development processes, but also to analytically evaluate the trustworthiness of a desired system early in the design phase.

As introduced in Chapter 2, trustworthiness can be seen as an objective system property reflecting the system's ability to perform as expected (Avizienis et al., 2004). In order to achieve objectivity, we need to measure certain system qualities that are relevant to achieve trustworthiness. To this end, metrics can be used in order to quantify trustworthiness attributes. A metric is a function that allows for measuring and quantifying certain trustworthiness attributes and more concrete trustworthiness properties of a system. According to IEEE 1061 (IEEE Standards Board, 1993), a software quality metric is a "function whose inputs are software data and whose output is a single numerical value that can be interpreted as the degree to which software possesses a given attribute that affects its quality". Thus, metrics allow for measuring and quantifying certain trustworthiness attributes by means of more concrete properties of a system. Furthermore, measurements and

[1]This chapter partially adapts Di Cerbo et al. (2013) © Springer-Verlag Berlin Heidelberg 2013, Gol Mohammadi et al. (2015b) © 2015 IEEE, and Di Cerbo et al. (2015) © Springer International Publishing Switzerland 2015, with the permission of the publishers.

corresponding metric values can be used as evidence for certifying a certain quality level (Di Cerbo et al., 2012).

Systems are often composed of existing software services or components that are certified and provided on a software marketplace (cf., e.g. Di Cerbo et al. (2012)). Component-based development (Lenzini et al., 2007) poses the challenge of considering different component structures for determining the "End-to-End" (E2E) trustworthiness of the overall system. Different certified metric values of all the involved components have to be aggregated considering the specific system topology, in which they are embedded. Particularly, redundancy is often introduced in system design, for instance, as means to increase trustworthiness in terms of higher reliability or availability.

Another challenge consists in aggregating the resulting end-to-end trustworthiness values on different levels of granularity or abstraction, e.g. on the level of each trustworthiness attribute or on the overall trustworthiness as a whole. Despite a large number of suggestions in the literature on evaluation and documentation of the design decisions, the end-to-end evaluation of multifaceted trustworthiness remains an open research question. There are approaches that merely focus on, for example, reliability (Raheja and Gullo, 2012).

Thus, there are two dimensions that need to be taken into account when evaluating the overall system trustworthiness. The first dimension is the overall system structure while the second is the level of granularity of the end-to-end calculation, e.g. regarding a hierarchy of trustworthiness attributes and sets of different metrics. Our approach builds upon available formulae that consider different system structures for calculating the overall trustworthiness.

This chapter addresses the problem of evaluating the overall trustworthiness of online CPS with a particular focus on software assets that are accessible via an online marketplace. Some software marketplaces allow integrators and service providers to deploy a new composite system by selecting system assets and compose them in order to create a new system based on their trustworthiness certificates (Di Cerbo et al., 2012; Ali et al., 2013).

We use different metrics to quantify system trustworthiness attributes, and use the trustworthiness metric values in the certificate of each software component as parameters for calculating the overall end-to-end trustworthiness. To this end, workflow models serve as adequate abstractions to specify sequences of assets that are involved in achieving a certain goal with a system composition. Based on these low-level end-to-end trustworthiness values, more aggregate values can be calculated, eventually resulting in an overall trustworthiness value. The end-to-end values can be used as evidence of the system's trustworthiness, and to compare different candidate system compositions.

We propose an approach that supports designers in composing end-to-end formulae and performing the trustworthiness evaluation process. We provide metric skeletons and templates as well as guidance for determining aggregated values on different abstraction levels. As a sample evaluation, we present the application of our approach to evaluate the end-to-end trustworthiness of an exemplary system from the ambient assisted living domain (cf. Chapter 5). We also show how the proposed framework (TW-Man) supports end-to-end trustworthiness evaluation.

The remainder of this chapter is structured as follows: In Section 10.2, we present the background and definitions of the main concepts. A brief overview of existing techniques for evaluating trustworthiness of software is provided in Section 10.3. Section 10.4 describes our approach in evaluating end-to-end trustworthiness. Section 10.5 presents a proof of concept implementation. Section 10.6 presents an application example using two scenarios. Section 10.8 concludes with the contribution of this chapter.

10.2 Background

This section presents the background concepts that form the basis for our approach presented in this chapter.

10.2.1 Component-based System Design

Component-based software engineering aims at extensively reusing existing components in software development, and, for example, focuses on components and interface models (Sommerville, 2016). In the area of Service-Oriented Architectures (SOA), software components, which are independent of their environment and loosely coupled, are used to build systems that support business processes.

Concerning the modelling of component-based systems, the so-called Reliability Block Diagram, as used in reliability engineering for complex systems, allows the designer to model different composition types, i.e. series, parallel, and combined series-parallel structures (Raheja and Gullo, 2012). Related to web service composition, there are some more specialised modelling and description languages such as the Business Process Execution Language (BPEL) (Khalaf et al., 2003). Decker et al. (2008) use BPMN as a modelling language for representing business processes and control flows for web service orchestration.

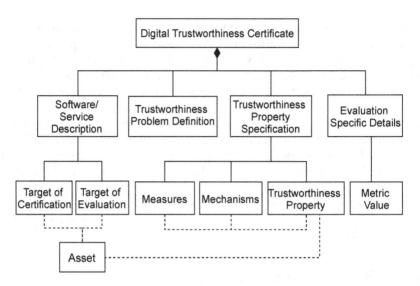

Figure 10.1: A simplified schematic representation of a digital trustworthiness certificate and its structure based on (Di Cerbo et al., 2013)

10.2.2 Digital Trustworthiness Certificates and Trustworthy Service Marketplace

Today, machine-readable security certificates (Ali et al., 2013) are used to document the security properties of a service. However, these do not include trustworthiness information. We argue that these certificates can be extended to include multi-faceted trustworthiness attributes (cf. Chapter 4) that are quantifiable by means of metrics (Avizienis et al., 2004). In the OPTET project, the concept of digital trust-worthiness certificates was developed. Di Cerbo et al. extended machine-readable security certificates to include trustworthiness information (Di Cerbo et al. (2013, 2015)). These certificates are called digital trustworthiness certificates (DTWC). The DTWC concept (Di Cerbo et al., 2014) allows to include trustworthiness metric values and their interpretation as a kind of evidence on achieved trustworthiness qualities of a software or service. Such trustworthiness metric values may be generated by applying product metrics. Di Cerbo et al. use our definition of trustworthiness and therefore consider trustworthiness also as a vector of quality attributes as we do.

In contrast to traditional certificates that are documented often in legal terms, the DTWC is a machine-readable digital artefact. The DTWC is realized based on a Linked Data vocabulary, and it is composed of four main components (see Figure 10.1): software or service description, trustworthiness problem definition, trustworthiness property specification and evaluation specific details. The system description is scalable in granularity (from methods, libraries, and modules, up to the whole architecture) and allows for including references to other DTWCs in order to represent a software system exhaustively. The problem definition captures the threats for software qualities that have been considered for a software during its design, development process, and run-time execution, similar to what ISO/IEC 27000 (2018) suggests for threat modelling. The trustworthiness property specification expresses claims about the qualities of the software (or its specific parts), while the evaluation part supports such claims by providing objectively measured atomic metric values. Metric values are captured as DTWC evidences, that have an explicit link to claims on software/process qualities (the trustworthiness properties) associated to a software or its parts (assets).

Software marketplaces, such as the Amazon Web Services Marketplace (Amazon, 2014), provide platforms for distributing and offering software services to organizations. In order to address the problem of trustworthiness of the offered services, certification is a mechanism to guarantee certain levels of service (Lotz et al., 2015). For instance, Ali et al. (2013) present a marketplace system that enables the provision of security certificates. The concept of a Trustworthy Software Marketplace (Di Cerbo et al., 2012) uses DTWC, and allows for matching this form of trustworthiness evidence to user requirements.

In this chapter, we use the concept of DTWC. From here on, we call them simply certificates. These certificates may be provided in a trustworthy service marketplace. The designer may compare and select candidate asset instances by querying a trustworthy service marketplace that includes these certificates.

10.3 Related Work

Service composition and evaluation with respect to quality of service has been examined in the past.

Klatt et al. (2012) propose to use a service quality prediction of composed services in order to support service composition under consideration of service quality. Quality evaluation is also an integral part of the service composition framework proposed by Liu et al. (2009). Elshaafi et al. (2012) present an approach towards measuring the trustworthiness of a service composition with focus on run-time monitoring. Elshaafi et al. provide formulae that allow for calculating the trustworthiness (in terms of reputation, reliability, and security) of composite services, taking into account several service composition constructs such as sequence, parallel, loop, choice, discriminator, and multichoice-multimerge patterns. Zhao et al. (2009) propose a framework for trustworthy web service management, which also involves formulae for aggregating the availability, reliability, and response time of services composed in sequence, parallel, conditional, and loop structures. Other approaches, such as Malik and Bouguettaya (2009), focus on reputation by aggregating service ratings in order to determine a provider's rating.

Quality of Service (QoS) aggregation can be applied in order to determine the QoS of a web service workflow based on the QoS of each involved or executed web service (Hwang et al., 2007; Jaeger et al., 2004). Cardoso et al. (2004) utilize graph reduction mechanisms and respective formulae for aggregating time, cost, and reliability of service workflows. Jaeger et al. (2004) provide also workflow composition patterns and aggregation schemes. Hwang et al. (2007) propose a probabilistic approach for estimating the QoS of service compositions, which is based on more elaborate metrics, and addresses uncertainty given for QoS values. They consider sequence, parallel, choice, discriminator, and loop structures in addition to interleaved parallel, multiple choices, and m-out-of-n constructs.

Related to the use of metrics, Wang and Crowcroft (2006) distinguish additive, multiplicative, and concave metrics for QoS routing, which can be considered as a problem that also applies to service composition. Raheja and Gullo (2012) consider that the reliability of the whole system depends on the reliability of its components, thus, formulae that represent the different component structures are used in order to calculate the overall reliability.

Regarding software-intensive systems, Kan (2002) distinguishes three types of software metrics: product metrics, process metrics, and project metrics. In our approach, we concentrate on product metrics which are focusing on characteristics of software products.

Although the related approaches summarized above support a wide range of system structures, they focus on a limited set of trustworthiness metrics neglecting the system trustworthiness dimension previously described (cf. Chapter 4). Furthermore, we identified the need for establishing a comprehensive framework that supports a large set of trustworthiness metrics (cf. Chapters 4 and 3). More specifically, each trustworthiness metric is mapped to a metric type (multiplicative, concave, and additive) and has either a positive or a negative interpretation (whether higher values are desirable or not).

Wang and Crowcroft (2006) and Almerhag et al. (2010) define three types of metrics as follows:

Definition of metric types: let $m(x_i)$ be a metric for measuring a quality of x_i, where x_i is represented in a graph G either by a node or an edge. The employment of the metric $m(x_i)$ will output the metric value v_i. Aggregation of the metric values over a set of nodes or edges (say S) depends on the type of the metric.

A metric whose value over S is the sum of the values is an *additive metric*. A metric whose value over S is the minimum value observed in S is a *concave metric*.
A metric whose value over S is the product of the values is a *multiplicative metric*.

For example, availability is of multiplicative type and has a positive interpretation. In case we have the measure of the unavailability, it also is of multiplicative type but it has a negative interpretation. The positive interpretation means that higher values with regard to metric values are desired, where as the negative interpretation means lower values are desired. Furthermore, each trustworthiness metric belongs to one trustworthiness attribute. The information above (type of metric and its interpretation), together with the system structure, is used to calculate the overall trustworthiness metric. Even though we start with sequential topologies, we can also support more complex structures by allowing redundancy in specific asset instances (namely parallel and "m out of n" constructs).

10.4 Evaluating End-to-End Trustworthiness

This section describes our end-to-end trustworthiness evaluation approach. We build upon existing approaches towards evaluation and formulae for composite system structures, and unify them into a comprehensive framework that provides system designers with guidance for evaluating trustworthiness on different layers of abstraction (shown in Figure 10.2). The aim of the framework is to facilitate the evaluation process, and to structure evaluation reports as the basis for selecting a certain design alternative.

Our framework covers two dimensions of end-to-end trustworthiness evaluation, as depicted in Figure 10.2. On the one hand, the structure or topology of the entire software system involves many different assets that participate in a certain control or data flow relation to support a business process or to achieve some business goal. This structure is described in terms of workflows. For instance, parallel or redundant structures are often used to increase trustworthiness properties such as performance, reliability, or availability. The different possible compositions of the

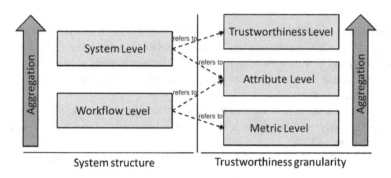

Figure 10.2: Overview of the End-to-End Trustworthiness Evaluation framework based on (Gol Mohammadi et al., 2015b)

system structure need to be taken into account when determining trustworthiness values of entire systems, and can be abstracted by focusing on a complete system which may be characterized by multiple workflows. On the other hand, the trustworthiness of both, single software services and overall system structures, can be evaluated on different levels of abstraction or granularity. For instance, at the lowest level, metrics are used to provide detailed evidence of specific trustworthiness properties, while these values have to be aggregated on the more abstract level of trustworthiness attributes such as "availability". The highest level of trustworthiness granularity provides an overall trustworthiness value for the whole system. As regards the system structure granularity, workflow level refers either to the metric level or to the attribute level, whereas system level either refers to the attribute level or to the trustworthiness level.

The framework consists of two parts. First, an ontology is presented that provides general concepts for end-to-end trustworthiness evaluation. These concepts form the basis for establishing calculation-based trustworthiness evaluation of composite system structures on different levels of granularity. Second, a method is given for objectively evaluating end-to-end trustworthiness of each system quality attribute based on the aggregation of partial trustworthiness measurements of each asset instance making up a CPS. Specifically, we describe abstraction mechanisms and a related process of successively aggregating trustworthiness values on different levels of granularity, which takes into account the system structure or topology. In the following, we describe the parts of the framework in more detail.

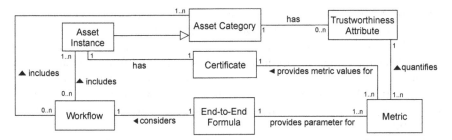

Figure 10.3: Concepts of the End-to-End Trustworthiness Evaluation (Gol Mohammadi et al., 2015b)

10.4.1 Conceptual Model of Design-Time End-to-End Trustworthiness Evaluation

In order to establish a sound theoretical foundation for our end-to-end trustworthiness evaluation approach, we define some basic concepts that need to be considered when assessing the multi-faceted trustworthiness of composite systems. Figure 10.3 shows the relevant concepts as well as their relations. This figure details the parts of the overall conceptual model of the TW-Man framework (cf. Figure 3.4, Chapter 3) that are related to the end-to-end trustworthiness evaluation.

A CPS consists of several assets, i.e. anything of value in a CPS (Surridge et al., 2013), including physical, technical, or logical parts, as well as humans. An asset is an abstract, basic building block of a system that may manifest in different implementations (i.e. asset instances from different vendors).

We use the term "Asset Category" to distinguish between generic types of system building blocks on an abstract level, and concrete instances pertaining to a certain category. An "Asset Instance" is a concrete manifestation of an "Asset Category", e.g. a concrete software application and implementation that is provided on an online marketplace. For example, "DBMS_1" could be a software service offered on the marketplace as an instance of the asset "Database Management System".

A "Metric" is a standard way for measuring and quantifying certain trustworthiness attributes and more concrete quality properties of a system. Metric values of a specific asset instance are provided in terms of trustworthiness certificate that is often provided together with the software itself on a marketplace.

The asset instance has a "Certificate". Such a "Certificate" is created by a certification authority that evaluates a software system or asset instance in order to confirm that it meets some trustworthiness goals. A certificate describes all observed trustworthiness properties of the software as well as related evidence in terms of certified metric values (cf. Di Cerbo et al. (2014)).

A "Workflow" represents the automation of a business process, in whole or part, during which documents, information or tasks are passed from one participant to another for action, according to a set of procedural rules (Object Management Group, 2011). Participants are the asset instances. A workflow model specifies the interplay among asset instances and their interrelations in the control flow of performing some business process.

The workflow concept is an appropriate abstraction mechanism to focus on the aspects that are necessary for determining end-to-end trustworthiness formulae.

An "End-to-End Formula" is a template or function that allows for calculating the trustworthiness of composite system structures represented in terms of workflows. It requires metric values for each involved asset instance as arguments, and returns one value that characterizes the trustworthiness of the whole workflow.

10.4.2 End-to-End Trustworthiness Computation

This section presents our approach towards calculating end-to-end trustworthiness using our framework. Specifically, we describe the steps of an evaluation process that takes into account different system structures as well as different levels of granularity. First, we show how adequate models are created in order to depict system and redundancy structures. Then, we describe how aggregation mechanisms are used in order to abstract from certain trustworthiness details to eventually derive an overall system trustworthiness value.

1) Workflow Modelling and End-to-End Formula Creation

The computational approach towards end-to-end trustworthiness evaluation relies upon the availability of metric values for each asset of the system as a means to quantitatively express trustworthiness. The metric values can be found, for instance, in certificates of the asset instances that are available on a marketplace. Thus, the end-to-end computation is performed for concrete instances of the general assets that build up a system.

Depending on the characteristics of its intended usage scenarios, a system can have arbitrary structures (sequential, tree, network, etc.), where the system building blocks can be seen as nodes in the structure. A workflow is a specific composition (or sequence) of asset instances that are invoked and orchestrated in order to achieve a certain goal or to support some business process. A graphical workflow model (i.e. the workflow graph) aims at guiding the evaluation process by modelling and determining which objects (i.e. asset instances) are functionally connected and

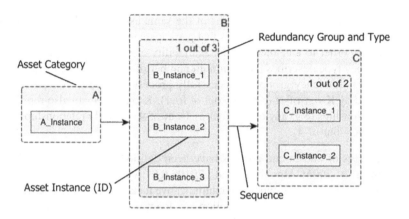

Figure 10.4: Example workflow graph and modelling concepts (OPTET Consortium, 2014b)

should thus be evaluated together in an end-to-end configuration. Hence, a system can be described by multiple workflows. Each workflow determines a particular part of the system that is under consideration of evaluation, and contains vital redundancy information.

We depict this information in a workflow graph, as illustrated in Figure 10.4 (created using the yEd[2] Graph Editor). A concrete example of such a workflow graph is illustrated in Section 10.6. We propose to represent the following elements and concepts in an appropriate workflow model:

- (Sub-)System topology: the topology includes the asset categories and their relations.

- Assets categories and asset instances: Asset categories are abstract building blocks of a system, while asset instances denote concrete implementations or realizations of them.

- Boundary of trustworthiness evaluation: End-to-end trustworthiness evaluation requires the definition of two nodes (i.e. system assets) of a workflow sequence for specifying the boundary of evaluation. Please note that the order of the individual assets does not matter in the end-to-end formula creation.

- Redundancy group and type: In addition to the interaction relations of asset instances (e.g. control flow, data flow), it is also necessary to model the redun-

---

[2]yWorks GmbH: yEd Graph Editor. http://www.yworks.com/products/yed (accessed on 12 September 2018)

dancy among several asset instances of the same asset. A redundancy group contains a number of asset instances that participate in some kind of redundancy relation in order to e.g. increase the availability of the provided service. The redundancy type describes the minimum number of required asset instances in a certain redundancy group to successfully process a request. A type can be described by K-out-of-N (e.g. two out of four). K-out-of-N can also represent OR-relationships (e.g. any one of four as 1-out-of-4) or AND-relationships (e.g. all four as 4-out-of-4).

Three types of end-to-end metrics have been defined in the literature (Wang and Crowcroft, 2006; Almerhag et al., 2010) (cf. Section 10.3): the additive metrics (e.g. cost, response time), the multiplicative metrics (e.g. mean availability) and the concave metrics (e.g. encryption key length). The metrics' type has to be considered when determining the respective end-to-end formula. Table 10.1 provides skeletons of the mathematical formula (F) (Gol Mohammadi et al., 2015b) that can be constructed for computing the trustworthiness value of a single asset category j. The skeletons of the mathematical formulae are based on (Wang and Crowcroft, 2006; Almerhag et al., 2010; Elshaafi et al., 2012).

Such an asset category is assumed to be consisting of $i = 1, \ldots, n$ asset instances, where m_i is the trustworthiness metric value that characterizes the trustworthiness of the i-th asset instance, and consequently appears in its trustworthiness certificate. Depending on the metric type (concave, multiplicative, or additive) as well as the metric target type (interpretation type of the metric: higher or lower values), we get a different formula, e.g. concave metrics depend on the bottleneck asset instance and thus the minimum or maximum of the asset instance metric values is needed (e.g. the asset employing the smallest encryption key length).

We should note that the formulae appearing for multiplicative metrics refer to the K-out-of-N case, which can be used to create the "extreme" constructs as well. More specifically, if $K = 1$ then it refers to the "OR" construct, while if $K = N$ we get "AND".

For simplification and better readability of the multiplicative formula skeleton, we assume that all asset instances within a redundancy group belong to the same asset category, i.e. m_i for $i = 1, \ldots, n$, in contrast to the general case where $m_i \neq m_j$. Furthermore, we consider all the combinations where at least one asset instance will complete a certain task with the expected trustworthiness value. Thus, in the example of a redundancy group composed of three asset instances following the 2-out-of-3 construct, we would consider only the combination and not a special arrangement of asset instances. Following a binary representation: 0 refers to the event where a certain asset instance is not able to satisfy the required trustworthiness value; and 1 refers to the event where a certain asset instance is able to complete the task with satisfaction. The following cases would be considered: $011, 101, 110$ and 111.

Table 10.1: Composition of formulae for the asset category and End-to-End Trustworthiness (Gol Mohammadi et al., 2015b)

Metric Type	Metric Target Type	Asset Category Redundancy Type	Formula of Asset Category j	Formula for E2E Metric
Concave	Higher values	-	$F1)\ a_j = min\ m_i$	$F2)\ e = min\ a_j$
	Lower values		$F3)\ a_j = max\ m_i$	$F4)\ e = max\ a_j$
Multipl-icative	Higher values	N-out-of-N (AND)	$F5)\ a_j = \prod_{i=1}^{n} m_i$	$F8)\ e = \prod_j a_j$
		1-out-of-N (OR)	$F6)\ a_j = 1 - \prod_{i=1}^{n}(1 - m_i)$	
		K-out-of-N	$F7)\ a_j = \sum_{i=k}^{n}\binom{n}{i}m^i \times (1-m)^{n-i}$	
	Lower values	N-out-of-N (AND)	$F9)\ a_j = \prod_{i=1}^{n} m_i$	$F12)\ e = 1 - \prod_j a_j$
		1-out-of-N (OR)	$F10)\ a_j = 1 - \prod_{i=1}^{n}(1 - m_i)$	
		K-out-of-N	$F11)\ a_j = \sum_{i=k}^{n}\binom{n}{i}m^i \times (1-m)^{n-i}$	
Additive	Both Lower/ Higher values	-	$F13)\ a_j = \sum_{i=k}^{n} m_i$	$F14)\ e = \sum_j a_j$

Given that a workflow usually contains more than one asset category, the next step is to compose the end-to-end formula, denoted e. Table 10.1 provides a skeleton of the formula for all asset categories, say $j = 1, \ldots, k$ depending on the metric type.

The formula skeletons provide valuable guidance for representing different system structures and asset redundancy types in the form of a mathematical model for calculating end-to-end trustworthiness metric values with respect to related metrics. Metric values of single asset instances are then used as parameters for the end-to-end metrics that have been defined based on the workflows. In particular,

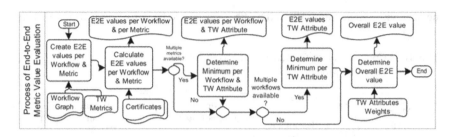

Figure 10.5: Process of calculating end-to-end metric values (Gol Mohammadi et al., 2015b)

an end-to-end metric value is derived for each workflow of the system, and each provided metric.

2) Aggregation of Trustworthiness Values

So far, the focus of evaluation was limited to a certain number of separate workflows, and individual metrics. As mentioned above, our end-to-end trustworthiness evaluation framework also considers different levels of granularity with respect to the trustworthiness of a system. To this end, the concept of trustworthiness attributes is an appropriate means to abstract from different metrics that may be available for a certain attribute in the first place. Since the resulting metric values still pertain to certain workflows, they can be aggregated by focusing on a trustworthiness attribute related to the whole system, which may be characterized by multiple workflows. Calculating the minimum of all the different values pertaining to the workflows is an adequate mechanism, and in order to guarantee consistency, the metrics where lower values are desirable are transformed into higher ones (by complementing the metric value). Another approach could be to determine the weighted average among the different values. Note that these are applicable only if the values are of the same metric type. Finally, the last step is to abstract from multiple workflows and calculate one overall end-to-end value. To this end, the designer can specify weights for each attribute, and calculate the weighted average. Figure 10.5 illustrates the steps of aggregating trustworthiness values on different levels of granularity.

To summarize, our approach allows for calculating end-to-end trustworthiness metric values on the following layers of abstraction:

- End-to-end values per workflow and metric: Given a workflow and a particular metric that can be used to estimate a certain trustworthiness attribute, we calculate an end-to-end metric using the end-to-end formula skeleton.

- End-to-end values per workflow and attribute: For determining the end-to-end value related to a certain workflow and trustworthiness attribute, the minimum value of all end-to-end values that are available for each of the metrics pertaining to that attribute, is calculated.

- End-to-end values per attribute: The end-to-end value per trustworthiness attribute is determined by calculating the minimum value for all the given workflows, related to this attribute.

- An end-to-end value per system (overall end-to-end trustworthiness): In order to calculate one end-to-end trustworthiness metric value for the whole system described by several trustworthiness attributes and workflows, weights are specified by the designer for each trustworthiness attribute.

10.5 Proof-of-Concept Implementation of End-to-End Trustworthiness Evaluation

In this section, we provide an overview of the design of the end-to-end trustworthiness evaluation tool and describe its context, components, and interfaces.

More details on the information that is (graphically) modelled in a workflow are presented in the next subsection. We decided to use workflow graphs with the modelling editor "yEd" that provides an intuitive user interface for creating workflows and encoding the necessary information for our approach, such as asset instances with their identifiers and quantities, redundancy type between assets of the same category, etc. The produced workflow graph can be exported in an XML-based format that can be further processed by the components of our provided tool. Please note that the tool supports multiple workflows when computing an overall value so as to capture all features of the system in question.

The tool consists of two main components, namely an "End-to-End Trustworthiness Calculator" and a "Metric tool". The metric tool provides the definition of the metrics for each trustworthiness attributes presented in Chapter 4. We use the metric tool to get the metrics for each trustworthiness attribute.

10.5.1 Context View of the End-to-End Trustworthiness Evaluation Tool

The aim of the End-to-End Trustworthiness Evaluation (E2E TWE) tool is to help the system designer make informed design choices with regard to the constructed system's trustworthiness. The tool supports two use cases: (1) evaluating a system

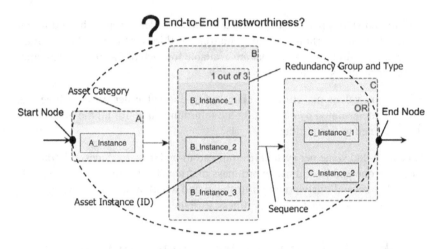

Figure 10.6: Determining end-to-end trustworthiness of the system or a composition

configuration based on the design-time system model. The designer may compare different configurations and select a system configuration; and (2) determining the trustworthiness profile of new assets.

Use case 1 supports selecting a set of asset instances to materialize the asset categories in the system model, as well as specify their structure (especially regarding redundancy).

Use case 2 supports situations in which a new asset is to be developed. The goal is to aid in specifying its trustworthiness requirements (in terms of specifying which values should be promised for which trustworthiness attributes), so that when combined with the other assets, the desired E2E trustworthiness levels are met.

Figure 10.6 and Figure 10.7 show the two use cases, respectively. Figure 10.7 shows the application of our approach in use case 2 to determine requirements for system asset instances that shall be developed and embedded into a system configuration consisting of existing asset instances. The designer can include a placeholder node in the workflow graph, so that the end-to-end formula can be transformed. This allows the designer to identify the minimum trustworthiness requirements with respect to a certain metric, which is required to meet the overall trustworthiness requirements or expectations.

Figure 10.8 shows the actor and functionalities for the end-to-end trustworthiness evaluation tool. The tool is able to compute and compare the end-to-end trustworthiness of different CPS compositions considering structure and assets. In addition, the tool is able to guide developers and propose trustworthiness metric values for a

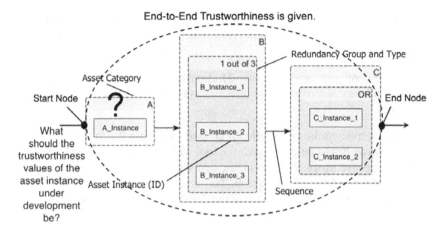

Figure 10.7: Determining trustworthiness values in the form of a Trustworthiness Profile of an asset to be selected or developed for a specific composition

missing asset such that a complete system will achieve the overall requirements. More specifically, the tool supports the following functionalities:

- Evaluate system (Use case 1): Using our tool, the CPS designer selects the asset instances from the marketplace, models the structure and connectivity of these

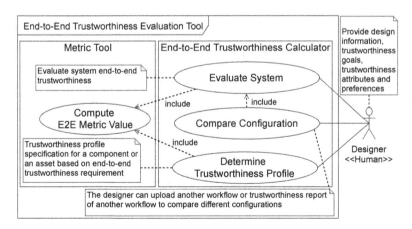

Figure 10.8: UML use case diagram for the End-to-End Trustworthiness Evaluation Tool based on (OPTET Consortium, 2014b)

parts and produces a report that allows the designer to evaluate its trustworthiness (for a set of selected trustworthiness attributes). The result of the evaluation is captured in trustworthiness reports generated by the tool.

- Compare configurations (Use case 1): Enables the designer to compare the trustworthiness of two or more different system configurations and make a decision.

- Determine trustworthiness profile for an asset (Use case 2): In the case where a single asset has to be developed, the tool will report the minimum level for every respective trustworthiness metric that should be reached in order to meet the global (or end-to-end) constraint. This is useful for the designer in order to verify in a user-friendly manner that the developers have produced a software which meets the trustworthiness specification.

10.5.2 Architecture of the End-to-End Trustworthiness Evaluation Tool

In this section, we provide an overview of the tool's architecture (shown in Figure 10.9) and describe its components and functionality.

The system designer interacts with the tool through a web-based user interface. First, the designer specifies a set of trustworthiness attributes that are of interest for the particular system, as well as a weight for each attribute that represents her/his

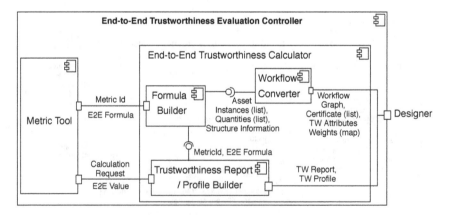

Figure 10.9: Component diagram of the End-to-End Trustworthiness Evaluation Tool based on (OPTET Consortium, 2014b)

preferences for the specific system evaluated. These are used for calculating the overall trustworthiness score of the system from the individual attribute values. The designer then uploads a design-time system model and continues by providing workflows, which specify sequences of system asset instances that collaborate in order to realize a certain goal or support some business process. For each asset instance involved in the workflows, the designer must also supply a trustworthiness certificate containing metric values that are provided as evidence for trustworthiness. These can either be retrieved directly from some software marketplace or uploaded manually. The workflows and metric values contained in the asset certificates will be used by the "End-to-End Trustworthiness Calculator" to compute end-to-end trustworthiness values for the whole system.

In use case 1, the result of the evaluation is a trustworthiness report containing the overall end-to-end trustworthiness values for the system. These reports can be saved for future reference, documentation, or for comparing different system configurations to make an informed decision.

In use case 2, the designer needs to specify the trustworthiness requirements for the whole system, and to designate which one of the components is yet to be developed. The result is a trustworthiness profile detailing the required metric values for the to-be-developed components in order to achieve the overall trustworthiness requirements for the system. This provides an easy way to communicate to the software developers how to produce a new component that meets the trustworthiness specification.

Figure 10.9 shows the component diagram of the trustworthiness evaluation tool. The tool is composed of three main components:

- The End-to-End Trustworthiness Calculator (E2E TW Calculator) accepts a list of workflows derived from a design-time system model describing data flow paths in the system, a trustworthiness specification assigning a desired weight to each trustworthiness attribute, and the trustworthiness certificates of each asset instance in the system. By interacting with other sub-components, it produces a set of calculated trustworthiness metrics and attributes for the overall system, as well as an overall trustworthiness score. In the second use case it receives a list of trustworthiness requirements for the overall system and returns a trustworthiness profile, which includes the target values of the different trustworthiness metrics for the asset that is to be developed. The end-to-end trustworthiness calculator is composed of several sub-components called "Workflow Converter", "Formula Builder" and "Trustworthiness Report/ Trustworthiness Profile Builder". The description of these components is as follows:

  – The workflow converter accepts a set of the workflow files in an XML-based format. The workflow files are provided by the designer. Each workflow that is part of the system in question, includes information about asset categories used including their structure and their sequence as well as the asset instances (including their IDs and their quantities).

- The Formula builder receives the output of the workflow converter and pre-pares an end-to-end metric formula for a set of trustworthiness metrics. The set of trustworthiness metrics is retrieved from the metric tool based on the trustworthiness attributes that appear in the trustworthiness specification. The latter is provided by the designer and contains the desired weight for each trustworthiness attribute (metrics whose attributes have zero weight are ig-nored).

- The TW report/ TW profile builder produces a file containing the main output for the use-cases of the tool following the process outlined in Figure 10.5. More specifically, a TW report is produced whenever the user wants to evaluate a system's trustworthiness (Use Case 1), while a TW profile is created for a software asset to be developed (Use Case 2). In order to do so it accepts a set of end-to-end metric formulae from the "Formula Builder", retrieves the certificates for each asset instance found in the workflows and finally instructs the "Metric Tool" to perform the necessary computations (for TW metrics, TW attributes, and overall TW value). In case of a TW profile, the designer has to supply the targeted system requirements as an input.

• The metric tool supports the trustworthiness evaluation. It contains the trustwor-thiness attributes and metrics to calculate the end-to-end metric values based on the supplied formulae and individual asset metric values. Please note that the de-tailed information related to this component can be found in OPTET Consortium (2014b).

• In addition, there is an End-to-End Trustworthiness Evaluation Controller (E2E TWE Controller) component that is responsible for orchestrating the flow of data between the internal components and interacting with the web user interface.

Figure 10.10 defines the interactions between the components considering the first use case, i.e. the computation of a final E2E TW value for the overall system.

As shown in the UML sequence diagram (Figure 10.10), the designer provides workflow graphs which specify sequences of system asset instances that collaborate in order to realize a certain goal or support some business process. The definition of workflow graphs can be based on design-time system models.

For each asset instance involved in the workflows, the designer manually uploads certificates to the E2E TW Evaluation Controller. Note that ideally these can be queried from a marketplace and should include metric values.

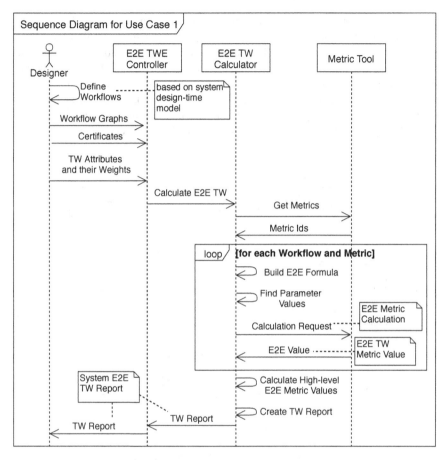

Figure 10.10: UML sequence diagram of E2E TW Evaluation for Use Case 1 based on (OPTET Consortium, 2014b)

The designer continues with providing weights of a set of trustworthiness attributes that are of interest for the particular system.

Based on these inputs, the E2E TW Calculator is invoked, which, in turn, builds an E2E formula according to the concepts presented in Section 10.4.2, and forwards it to the metric tool (Get Metrics). The metric tool returns the Metric Ids. After extracting the parameters, i.e. the certified metric values from the certificate of each involved asset instance, the E2E TW Calculator sends an E2E metric calculation request to the metric tool in order to receive respective E2E values. This first E2E calculation step on the level of metrics is performed for each workflow. Then, these values are the starting point for determining more abstract and high-level E2E trustworthiness values such as E2E values for each workflow and TW attribute (in the case that multiple metrics are available), as well as one E2E TW value for the whole system. All these calculated E2E values on the different layers of abstraction will be composed and a corresponding TW report for the designer is created.

The interactions among the E2E TWE tool components related to the second use case (cf. Figure 10.8) are illustrated in the UML sequence diagram in Figure 10.11.

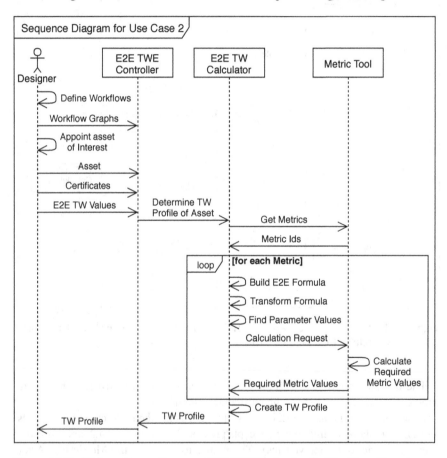

Figure 10.11: UML sequence diagram of E2E TW Evaluation for Use Case 2 based on (OPTET Consortium, 2014b)

Here, the designer uses the tool to determine required TW values for an asset that is yet to be developed but is expected to be part in an E2E system configuration. The TW profile of a concrete instance is described in terms of threshold metric values. In addition to a workflow and certificates of the existing asset instances, the designer has to provide the Asset ID of the workflow asset for which the TW profile shall be created. Also, a set of threshold TW metric values for the E2E system configuration must be specified, i.e. the overall system requirements are specified (cf. Figure 10.7). The E2E TW Calculator builds, as requested by the controller via the user interface, an E2E metrics formula similar to the first use case. However, this formula needs to be transformed in a way that allows for determining the target metric values for the asset under development (i.e. the minimum required values that meet the overall TW requirements). This calculation is conducted by the Metric Tool for each metric given as part of the system requirements. All the required minimum TW metric values are then used to return the TW profile of the missing asset to the designer. These values will be useful as a guideline for the developers in the subsequent design and implementation phases.

More detailed information related to the interfaces and a user guide are provided in OPTET Consortium (2014b).

10.6 Application Example

We consider again the AAL example from Chapter 5. However, here we focus on a so-called fall management system. The Fall Management System (FMS) monitors an elderly person at his or her home with respect to emergency situations, such as an incident. Detected emergency situations are reported to a central alarm handling service that will decide upon the actions to be taken. Depending on the severity of the emergency, relatives can be notified, or ambulances requested. Figure 10.12 shows an exemplary design-time system model of the fall management system, and includes the main (software) components.

Using our end-to-end trustworthiness approach, the designer is able to perform "what-if" scenarios and can adjust the system structure and its redundancy levels in order to meet the goals.

In an initial step, the designer selects the evaluation criteria to be used, i.e. the weights of relevant trustworthiness attributes with respect to the overall end-to-end trustworthiness of the complete system. The weights represent the preferences regarding the relevance of each attribute, and can be specified e.g. as percentage values. For the fall management system, the following list of trustworthiness attributes and associated weights are specified by the designer: privacy (40%), availability (100%), reliability (80%), response time (100%), learnability (40 %), effectiveness (60%) and functional correctness (60%).

Then, the designer creates a set of workflow graphs, each representing a certain feature or describing a usage scenario of the system. The workflows are based on the design-time system model shown in Figure 10.12.

The designer has the flexibility to exclude some asset categories that are less important, or make assumptions about the trustworthiness of the relevant asset instances. Even though humans play a key role in CPS, the workflow concept allows us to focus only on certified software assets that are available on a marketplace. The resulting two workflow graphs for the fall management system are shown in Figure 10.13.

Workflow 1 consists of three asset categories: PERS, EMHT and Ambulance Service. For each one, the designer has selected concrete asset instances that are available as implementations or realizations of the assets, as well as their redundancy relations (i.e. cardinality and redundancy type). In our scenario, the selected system composition consists of a single instance of the PERS device, i.e. "PERS_App_1" which is a PERS implementation for mobile phones, two EMHT instances, including the main "EMHT_1" and a backup "EMHT_2" (indicated by the "1 out of 2" (OR) type in the graph), and a pool of three "Ambulance Service" instances, one of which should be available at a certain point in time (denoted by the "1 out of 3" redundancy type). These asset instances or instance groups are modelled in a sequential order, indicated by the directed edges between them. This workflow specifies that the "PERS_App_1" has some functional dependency with either "EMHT_1" or "EMHT_2", which in turn calls one out of three Ambulance

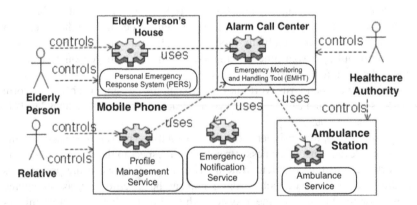

Figure 10.12: Design-time system model of the Fall Management System (Gol Mohammadi et al., 2015b)

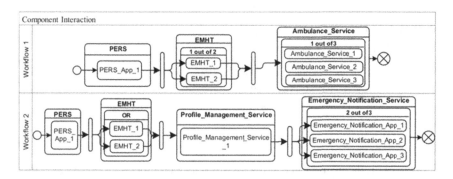

Figure 10.13: Workflow graphs of the Fall Management System (Gol Mohammadi et al., 2015b)

Services. Thereby, the overall system functionality is provided, i.e. the request of an ambulance as reaction to an emergency alarm handled by the EMHT.

The second workflow graph shown in Figure 10.13 describes another scenario or functionality, which should also be provided by the FMS. It involves a slightly different set of asset categories that are used to notify relatives in an emergency situation. Again, we focus on software assets, so the notification is performed by instances of the "Emergency Notification Service" asset in this workflow. We assume that at least two out of three relatives should be informed in this concrete case, so that a minimum of two respective applications are involved in successfully carrying out the scenario described in this workflow.

The next step includes providing a trustworthiness certificate for each asset instance involved in the workflows. Certificates carry the trustworthiness metric values that have been approved by a certification authority, and are used as the basis for the end-to-end trustworthiness calculation. Then, as depicted in the loop construct in Figure 10.10, the first step of trustworthiness computation consists of creating an end-to-end formula for each trustworthiness metric and workflow. Based on the metric type and interpretation as well as information about the involved component's interactions present in the workflow graphs, an end-to-end formula for each trustworthiness metric and workflow is created.

In case of Workflow 1, the following end-to-end formula is created for multiplicative metrics (Formula F8 from Table 10.1) that have a positive interpretation (Metric Target Type: higher values):

$$e_{Workflow_1,m} = \prod_{i=1}^{n} a_{i,m}$$

$$= tw_{PERSApp1,m} \times [1 - (1 - tw_{EMHT1,m})(1 - tw_{EMHT2,m})]$$

$$\times \left[1 - (1 - tw_{AmbulanceService1,m})(1 - tw_{AmbulanceService2,m})(1 - tw_{AmbulanceService3,m})\right]$$

$$= 0.8 \times [1 - (1 - 0.98)(1 - 0.92)]$$

$$\times [1 - (1 - 0.95)(1 - 0.85)(1 - 0.35)]$$

$$\approx 0.79$$

$$(10.1)$$

where tw, is the metric value of the asset instance i for metric m. Please note that some asset instance names from Figure 10.13 have been abbreviated. The metric values extracted from certificates are used to calculate separate end-to-end values for each metric and workflow. For the asset category of EMHT and Ambulance Service the formula F6 from Table 10.1 is used for each (Asset Category Redundancy Type: 1-out-of-N). This formula represents a generic template that needs to be filled with metric values for each involved asset instance. In our example, the "mean run-time availability" metric, which belongs to the "availability" attribute, is a multiplicative one, has positive interpretation, and is composed and calculated using the formula above (Formula 10.1). The resulting value is approximately 79%. All involved software assets in the system composition, and redundancies are taken into account.

Another example for this multiplicative metric is calculated for Workflow 2 in Formula 10.2. Similar to Workflow 1, the metric has a positive interpretation that higher values are desired (Metric Target Type). Therefore, the end-to-end formula is created for multiplicative metrics based on formula F8 from Table 10.1. For the asset category of EMHT, the formula F6 is used, whereas for the Emergency_Notification_Service (Asset Category Redundancy Type: K-out-of-N), the formula F7 is used.

$$e_{Workflow2,m} = tw_{PERSApp1,m} \times \left\{1 - [(1 - tw_{EMHT1,m}) \times (1 - tw_{EMHT2,m})]\right\} \times tw_{ProfManSer1,m}$$

$$\times \left\{\left[(1 - tw_{EmNotApp1,m}) \times tw_{EmNotApp2,m} \times tw_{EmNotApp3,m}\right]\right.$$

$$\times \left[tw_{EmNotApp1,m} \times (1 - tw_{EmNotApp2,m}) \times tw_{EmNotApp3,m}\right]$$

$$+ \left[tw_{EmNotApp1,m} \times tw_{EmNotApp2,m} \times (1 - tw_{EmNotApp3,m})\right]$$

$$\left. + \left[tw_{EmNotApp1,m} \times tw_{EmNotApp2,m} \times tw_{EmNotApp3,m}\right]\right\}$$

$$= 0.8 \times \left\{1 - [(1 - 0.98) \times (1 - 0.92)]\right\} \times 0.75 \times \left\{[(1 - 0.99) \times 0.5 \times 0.87]\right.$$

$$\times [0.99 \times (1 - 0.5) \times 0.87] + [0.99 \times 0.5 \times (1 - 0.87)] + [0.99 \times 0.5 \times 0.87]\}$$

$$\approx 0.3$$

$$(10.2)$$

Similarly, for each metric, a separate end-to-end metric is created, and corresponding trustworthiness values is calculated respectively. For instance, in the case of concave metrics where lower values are desirable, the following end-to-end formula is created as shown in Formula 10.3.

$$
\begin{aligned}
e_{Workflow1,m} &= \max(a_{PERS,m}, a_{EMHT,m}, a_{Ambulance,m}) \\
&= \max(a_{PERS1,m}, a_{EMHT1,m}, a_{EMHT2,m}, a_{AmbServ1,m}, a_{AmbServ2,m}, a_{AmbServ3,m})
\end{aligned}
\tag{10.3}
$$

The formulae for all other metrics are created in a similar way, according to Table 10.1. Trustworthiness attributes can be quantified by multiple metrics. Hence, the E2E TWE approach presented in Section 10.4 allows for aggregating and calculating end-to-end metrics on different levels of granularity.

The next step is to abstract from metrics and calculate an end-to-end value on the level of trustworthiness attributes per workflow. More specifically, if multiple metrics characterize an attribute, we use the minimum value per workflow and metric as the end-to-end value for that attribute and workflow combination.

In order to do so, metrics with negative interpretation are transformed into ones with a positive interpretation by taking the residual complementary probability value.

Considering a trustworthiness attribute, e.g. availability identified by "Attr", which contains the trustworthiness metrics $m1, ..., m6$, its value for the workflow 1 is computed as follows:

$$
\begin{aligned}
tw_{Workflow1,Attr} &= \min(tw_{Workflow1,m1}, tw_{Workflow1,m2}, tw_{Workflow1,m3}, \\
&\quad tw_{Workflow1,m4}, tw_{Workflow1,m5}, tw_{Workflow1,m6}) \\
&= \min(0.9, 0.63, 0.385, 0.5, 0.89, 0.48) = 0.385
\end{aligned}
\tag{10.4}
$$

Please note that for the "Availability" attribute there are several metrics. We have created an E2E formula for each metric for Workflow 1 similar to the E2E Formula 10.1. The resulting E2E values are shown in Formula 10.4.

According to the E2E TWE approach, the next step is to abstract from several workflows and to compute the overall end-to-end values of the whole system per trustworthiness attribute. Following a similar "pessimistic" approach, this value is determined accordingly by calculating the minimum value of all workflows. For the attribute "Availability", this will result in the following end-to-end value:

$$
\begin{aligned}
tw_{Attr} &= \min(tw_{Workflow1,Attr}, tw_{Workflow2,Attr}) \\
&= \min(0.79, 0.3) \\
&= 0.3
\end{aligned}
\tag{10.5}
$$

Finally, the overall end-to-end trustworthiness of the whole system has to be calculated, as an abstraction from separate attribute values. To this end, the weights that have been initially assigned to each attribute are taken into account in order to compute the weighted average (privacy (40%), availability (100%), reliability (80%), response time (100%), learnability (40%), effectiveness (60%) and functional correctness (60%)). This calculation is reflected in the following formula for our example:

$$
\begin{aligned}
& \frac{\sum tw_{Attr} \times tw_{Attr}}{\sum tw_{Attr}} \\
&= \frac{0.4 \times 0.385 + 1 \times 0.3 + 0.8 \times 0.41 + 1 \times 0.34 + 0.4 \times 0.5 + 0.6 \times 0.4 + 0.6 \times 0.36}{0.4 + 1 + 0.8 + 1 + 0.4 + 0.6 + 0.6} \\
&= \frac{1.784}{4.8} \\
&\approx 0.37
\end{aligned}
\tag{10.6}
$$

The resulting end-to-end trustworthiness values on different levels of granularity (i.e. per workflow and metric, per workflow and attribute, per attribute, as well as one overall value) allow the designer to evaluate and document the trustworthiness of different alternative system compositions on the instance level, and consequently help in making informed design decisions.

10.7 Limitations and Threats to Validity

Our computational approach is performed on an asset instance level and relies on metric values of trustworthiness attributes which are available in a certificate. We assume that the atomic metric values provided in the certificates are correct. If not, then the calculated E2E values will not be accurate and correct as well. Furthermore, we use the metrics provided by the used metric tool[3] and we assume that these metrics are correctly defined and deliver a meaningful expression on measuring trustworthiness attributes. Some trustworthiness attributes may be difficult to measure or to express in terms of numeric values. However, using these quantitative values may help the designer to further analyze and improve these properties of the system under consideration. Defining metrics is not in the scope of this book, and the ones employed in this chapter were not deeply evaluated.

Several decisions were also made in the formula composition, with respect to the presented end-to-end trustworthiness calculation. These decisions have restricted the emerging structure of the system. For instance, the metric types, their interpretation types and redundancy groups are simplified and generalized

---

[3]The used metric tool was developed in the OPTET project (cf. OPTET Consortium (2014b)).

for reducing complexity. These simplifications may well remove complexity from the aggregation mechanism (cf. Figure 10.2), but the drawback is that it will not be appropriate for complex trustworthiness metrics with other distribution models. Investigation of different metric types and aggregations of these metrics into a meaningful interpretation is an important aspect of future work. Therefore, the end-to-end metrics which were selected for the computation of end-to-end trustworthiness values per trustworthiness attribute are in fact limited. The metric types should be further extended to cover other metrics which do not belong to the three categories presented in this chapter. For example, metrics with the metric type "average", "additive probabilities", or other probability distribution types (e.g. Poisson processes) may be addressed in the future work (for more details see Section 14.3).

10.8 Contribution and Summary of this Chapter

In this chapter, we addressed the problems of commonly used evaluation approaches for evaluating end-to-end trustworthiness. Component-based software development introduces the challenge of considering different component structures for determining an "end-to-end" trustworthiness value based on metrics. The system structure needs to be considered and reflected in the end-to-end trustworthiness metric that is used to calculate these values. Especially, redundancy structures, which are introduced at design-time to assure correct system performance and thereby increase trustworthiness levels, require consideration in the end-to-end trustworthiness calculation. The explicit description of respective metrics, which can provide meaningful statements about the trustworthiness, is a precondition for the calculation of an end-to-end trustworthiness value, which requires certified metric values of each involved asset instance as parameters. This evaluation result will be documented and used to support making informed design decisions.

Furthermore, our computational approach, which is performed on the application level and relies on measurements of trustworthiness attributes of software asset instances available on the marketplace, can be complemented by a risk-management approach. The latter is helpful on the higher level of abstract assets, i.e. asset categories that can be realized by multiple instance implementations. Specifically, at design-time it is essential to identify potential threats to trustworthiness, and related controls to prevent threat activity at run-time. Using a risk assessment method in a complementary way to the E2E trustworthiness computation approach allows for a more comprehensive trustworthiness evaluation of CPS. The initial steps and concepts towards complementing this direction are sketched in Chapter 11.

11 Enhancing Trustworthiness Evaluation with Risk Assessment

In this chapter[1], we aim at combining our computational approach presented in Chapter 10 with a risk management approach. The risk-based approach identifies threats to trustworthiness on the abstract level of generic building blocks. Our hybrid approach for trustworthiness evaluation and the complementary tool prototype support the assessment of risks related to trustworthiness as well as the evaluation of trustworthiness requirements. The result of the evaluation can be used as trustworthiness evidence enabling the designer to compare different system configurations during design-time.

11.1 Motivation

Lack of expertise and market pressures are only some of the challenges developers of cyber-physical systems face, which may adversely affect the quality of the systems and hinder risk assessment. This, in turn, may damage the trustworthiness of the cyber-physical systems and consequently reduce the trust of end-users.

Hence, it is crucial to be able to analytically evaluate and estimate the trustworthiness of a system early in the design phase through a thorough analysis of risks and mitigation actions. This includes identifying controls to prevent threat activities at run-time. The results of this analysis should be addressed appropriately in subsequent development phases when implementing the system. For instance, the selection and reuse of existing components or services may be introduce potential threats that yield certain trustworthiness requirements in terms of controls. Explicit documentation of design decisions that may affect the trustworthiness of a system is also essential.

Furthermore, CPS designers may need guidance when deciding whether including a certain mitigation mechanism in the system will result in an actual increase

---

[1]This chapter partially adapts Gol Mohammadi et al. (2015a), with the permission of the publisher.

© Springer Fachmedien Wiesbaden GmbH, part of Springer Nature 2019
N. Gol Mohammadi, *Trustworthy Cyber-Physical Systems*,
https://doi.org/10.1007/978-3-658-27488-7_11

of trustworthiness, and eventually pay off. Therefore, there is a need to enable evaluation of the end-to-end trustworthiness of different system configurations in order to gain some confidence in the realization of controls, and consequently the prevention of potential threats that may occur in system operation.

To the best of our knowledge, there are no existing approaches that combine risk-assessment and computational evaluation techniques in such a way that the consideration of threats and potential mitigations are evaluated once concrete assets are available and composed in order to build the system. In this chapter, we address the problem of evaluating the overall trustworthiness of cyber-physical systems. We employ two complementary techniques for evaluating trustworthiness at design-time. Specifically, we combine risk-based and computational analysis techniques and propose a comprehensive evaluation approach that is applicable on many levels of granularity.

The risk-based approach is applied at a very early stage to an abstract model of the system (system model) which is independent of concrete component realizations. It focuses on the identification and analysis of general threats that may affect the correct system functionality and cause behaviour that is not acceptable for the trustors. These threats constitute risks that need to be mitigated to assure that the system will perform as expected at run-time. Complementary, the computational approach is performed at a later stage, on a more concrete level. It uses trustworthiness metrics, and involves calculating and aggregating them according to the system structure, to produce end-to-end metric values. In this stage, we focus particularly on software assets that are accessible via an online marketplace. Previous works aimed at establishing a software marketplace to allow designers to select trustworthy system assets based on their certificates and compose them to create a new system (Ali et al., 2013). The computational approach relies on the trustworthiness metric values present within each asset certificate to calculate end-to-end metric values (cf. Chapter 10).

The main contribution of this chapter is a hybrid approach that allows designers to evaluate a system's trustworthiness at design-time and make good design choices based on risk assessment and trustworthiness metrics.

The remainder of this chapter is structured as follows: In Section 11.2, we present the background concepts used throughout this chapter. A brief overview of existing techniques for a risk-based trustworthiness evaluation is presented in Section 11.3. Section 11.4 presents our approach toward end-to-end trustworthiness evaluation enhanced with risk assessment. Section 11.5 presents the extensions made in the architecture and proof of concept implementation of our evaluation tool (presented in Chapter 10) to support our proposed hybrid approach. Section 11.6 evaluates the method using the AAL example. Section 11.7 summarizes the contribution of this chapter.

11.2 Background

First, we provide an overview of the modelling approaches that are used to design and compose CPS. Then, we present the risk assessment technique that we use in our approach for the overall evaluation of trustworthiness.

11.2.1 System Model as an Input for Evaluation of Trustworthiness

Architectural modelling of CPS systems is still in its infancy (Broy et al., 2012; Lock and Sommerville, 2010). Traditional modelling approaches are insufficient as they focus mainly on the technical aspects of a CPS, and on modelling system functionalities. Furthermore, they do not include any information on the deployment, and relation between different types of technical parts of systems, e.g. hosts of applications. These models are designed to help system designers to graphically identify and analyze the threats that can arise in a system (Lock and Sommerville, 2010). In CPS, there is a particular need on explicitly specifying the role of component dependencies, especially regarding the relation between different kinds of assets. A CPS consists of several assets, including physical, technical or logical parts, as well as human stakeholders. From this perspective, the connections between several system assets, including especially non-software assets such as hardware or humans, have to be considered. A design-time system model needs to represent the individual system components within a CPS which are responsible for supporting a given task or business process. The design-time model of CPS allows the domain expertise (in terms of asset types, threats, and controls) to be encoded and reused in the systems' design. For this reason, a set of generic asset classes exists for CPS, as well as a comprehensive knowledge base of associated threats and controls.

To cope with the complexity of CPS, different models of the CPS can be established on different levels of abstraction. This allows the designer to model and consider different compositions, e.g. series, inclusion of redundant assets, and more complex structures. As shown in Chapter 10, a workflow model can be used in order to specify a set of asset instances as well as their interrelations, e.g. in the control flow of performing some business process, or to provide a particular system functionality. Workflow models are often used in the context of service composition to model how composite structures (e.g. sequences) of different services cooperate in order to achieve some business goal (cf. e.g. Hwang et al. (2007)).

11.2.2 Risk Assessment for Identification of Threats and Controls using the System Analyser

The *"System Analyser"*[2] is a risk assessment tool that details the relationships between the assets of a system (OPTET Consortium, 2014b). We combine this risk assessment approach with our computational evaluation approach presented in the previous chapter (cf. Chapter 10). While the computational approach indicates what trustworthiness level is expected in terms of the different trustworthiness attributes and metric values, the risk assessment method allows the identification of threats that may compromise the system and affect its trustworthiness, and can hence be considered complementary to the end-to-end trustworthiness calculation approach. The threats are linked to one or more assets, and their impact is specified in terms of assets misbehavior.

The *System Analyser* is a model-based risk assessment approach. As a first step in performing a risk assessment, the assets of the system and their relations must be identified. The *System Analyser* (Surridge et al., 2013) uses graphs for representing system assets and their relations. The assets in a system represent the nodes in a graph, and the relations among them are the edges. The *System Analyser* tool uses three distinct layers that build on each other:

A core model: The core model captures the fundamental concepts, e.g. assets, roles and threats, and the relationships between them, that the system model builds upon. A simplified version is shown in Figure 11.1. Asset, Threat, Control and Misbehavior are the major concepts. A "Threat" threatens an "Asset", a "Threat" causes a "Misbehavior", and a "Control" blocks a "Threat". In addition to the

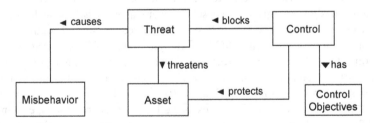

Figure 11.1: The core model (simplified version based on Surridge et al. (2013))

---

[2]This tool was initially developed in the OPTET project. Now, it is called Secure System Designer. http://www.it-innovation.soton.ac.uk/projects/optet (accessed on 10 August 2018)
It is further developed in the context of RestAssured project. RestAssured project is funded by the EU's Horizon 2020 research and innovation programme under grant agreement 731678. https://restassuredh2020.eu (accessed on 10 August 2018)

threat, the model provide the associated "Control Objective" to manage threats. This can happen by blocking the threat so that it cannot occur in the first place, or by reducing the threat impact so that any disruption of the functionality is minimal. The System Analyser approach is based on semantic modelling. The model's stack allows the domain expertise (in terms of asset types, threats and controls) to be encoded and reused in the systems' design.

Domain models: Domain models encode domain-specific knowledge, e.g. detailed threats and their possible controls. The major point is a definition of the different possible asset classes that might exist in a given domain. These will typically always include things like hosts, processes, data, stakeholders, etc.

The main asset classes that can be used by a designer to model the system are the following (see Figure 11.2):

- Logical Asset: A logical asset might be used directly by the designer to describe system processes. At this stage, there is no distinction between software and other processes;

- Human: A human is an individual user of the system. A human asset is a type of stakeholder asset with independent acts towards her/his own interests;

- Organization: An organization can be a commercial or non-commercial business. Organization is also a type of stakeholder asset, but it is made up of many people acting according to some organizational objectives and control;

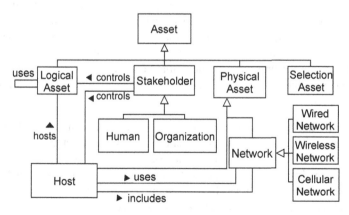

Figure 11.2: The main asset classes and their relations based on (OPTET Consortium, 2014b)

- Host: A host is a collection of physical apparatuses (technical equipments) including one or more connected ICT systems that support logical processes;

- Wired Network: A wired network is a network that uses physical (wired) connections to transmit data between hosts;

- Wireless Network: A wireless network is a network that uses radio signals to transmit data between hosts;

- Cellular Network: A cellular network is a network in which radio signals are used to transmit data between hosts and the network, but wired connections are used within the network.

- Selection Asset: The selection asset class represents a special case. Some types of selection asset are used to model the options for communicating between hosts over networks. This is a "fine-grained" detail that does not need to be asserted by the system designer as it can be inferred from the other "main" asset classes and relationships. Other types of selection asset are used to model the options for composing logical assets. These cannot be deduced from the rest of the structure, so their subclasses and relationships have to be asserted to fully define a composition (e.g. redundancy and backup server compositions).

Other concepts from the core model like Control or Misbehavior need to be specified for each domain model. For example, for each asset class, the domain model also needs to define the different roles it can perform in a system model (e.g. client or service, master or slave), its possible misbehavior (e.g. loss of availability), and the controls that can be applied to it. A part of a domain model consists of a catalogue of threat patterns. These represent the different possible ways that assets of the classes defined in the domain model can be threatened. The threat pattern catalogue therefore encodes knowledge about the threats that exist within the domain represented by the domain model. The System Analyser uses this knowledge base to generate a comprehensive catalogue of threats for each system model.

System models: The system model represents a system upon which the risk assessment is being executed. A system model is constructed from the asset classes in a domain model. Each system model can only use one domain model, but each domain model can be used by any number of system models. The relationships between the assets in a system model are expressed using properties defined in the domain model, e.g. that a web service uses a database.

Figure 11.3 shows the graphical interface of the system designer tool and its trustworthiness system model editor that allows designers to create design-time models of their systems. The System Analyser allows a designer to browse the

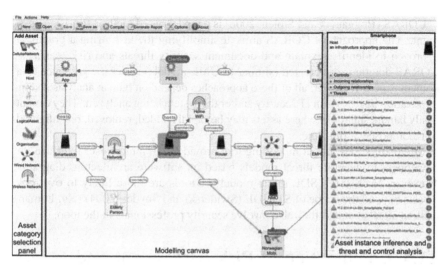

Figure 11.3: Screenshot of the Trustworthiness System Model Editor of the System Analyser tool for our AAL scenario based on (IT-innovation, 2013)

list of identified threats to trustworthiness and to specify controls that should be implemented in the system to block these identified threats. Figure 11.3 shows the design-time model with assets and their relationships for the fall management system (based on Figure 10.12 from Chapter 10.6). A more detailed description of this model is given in Section 11.6.

11.3 Related Work

This section gives an overview of related work in the areas of risk identification and mitigation.

There are many standards and methods such as the ones provided by Alberts and Dorofee (2002); El Fray (2012) that describe risk management methodologies and provide support in the process of identifying the system assets and the relevant threats. Many of these tools and methodologies provide generic threats (e.g. theft of media, fire, tampering with software, exceeding limits of operation) while others provide catalogues of specific threats per asset type (e.g. file, operating system, application software). Risk management is defined as the coordinated activities to direct and control an organization with regard to risk (ISO/IEC 27005, 2011).

CORAS (Hogganvik and Stølen, 2006) is a model-based method for risk assessment. The approach of CORAS aims at simplifying the task using a graphical approach to identify, explain and document security threats and risk scenarios. CORAS diagrams are created (similar to UML models) under the guidance of a domain expert. However, all of these approaches depend on human analysis and interpretation by experts in IT security and/or the system being analyzed. They cannot easily handle situations where assets may be rapidly added, removed, reconfigured or recomposed at run-time.

Microsoft's SDL threat modelling tool provides a graphical user interface for developers to generate threat models based on software architecture diagrams. However, Microsoft's SDL threat modelling tools are more likely to overlook threats beyond the scope of STRIDE (Swiderski and Snyder, 2004) (e.g. human-centred attacks) unless they also involve security professionals in the loop.

11.4 Combination of Risk Assessment and End-to-End Trustworthiness Evaluation

In this section, we describe how how we combined the E2E TW evaluation with a risk assessment approach. First, we present the conceptual model that describes general concepts for the two-fold evaluation. Second, we describe our approach which consists of two techniques performed at two different abstraction levels of evaluation and assessment. Our approach complements threat analysis and control identification (at the asset category level) with metric calculation based on the trustworthiness measures of each of the system's software assets (at the asset instance level).

11.4.1 Conceptual Model for Design-Time Trustworthiness Evaluation

We define the fundamental concepts and their relations in form of a conceptual model that is depicted in Figure 11.4. The conceptual model includes also the risk assessment concepts of the initial conceptual model presented in Chapter 10. Gray colored elements stem from the conceptual model described in Chapter 10 (cf. Figure 10.3). Hence, we describe here only the new elements (white colored) related to risk assessment.

A "Threat" is a situation or event that, if active at run-time, could undermine the value of an asset by altering its behavior. A "Control" can be specified to protect an

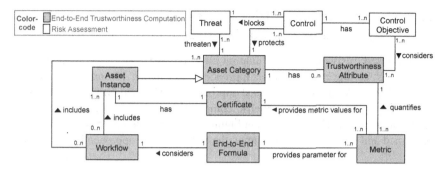

Figure 11.4: Conceptual model for trustworthiness evaluation based on (Gol Mohammadi et al., 2015a)

asset category by blocking threats. Each control has some "Control Objective" that considers the "Trustworthiness Attribute" that an asset category has.

The CPS designer can use the system model editor (cf. Figure 11.3) to map the system assets (and their relationships) to the different available asset classes and relationships. At this level, the system assets can be abstract (i.e. use "elderly person" as an asset and not necessarily individuals e.g. Alice, Bob). This is useful since in the design phase one may not have such information. The individual people who may use the system will be known at a later stage, i.e. when the system is deployed and running. We assume the same concerning the services (e.g. the ambulance service can be provided by the Red Cross or another organization). The System Analyser is configured with the domain knowledge and allows analysing the produced system model. It receives the produced system asset model as input and produces the list of threats that may compromise the different assets. This is done by associating the threats of the generic class (e.g. human) to the associated abstract asset (e.g. elderly person). The inference does not stop at this stage. It also takes into consideration the asset relations (the structure of the system) in order to identify threats that are associated with the interaction patterns.

The designer can use the System Analyser in order to identify the threats to the system assets and come up with a list of controls that mitigate or block the threats. In order to detect these threats during run-time, they are also mapped to asset misbehaviors. This provides guidance to the designer as to what kind of instrumentation should be put in place in order to maintain the system (further detailed information is provided in Chapter 12).

We use the System Analyser as a risk assessment tool for identification of threats and controls. However, any other model-based risk assessment method that is able to provide the threats and controls could be used as well.

11.4.2 Combination of Risk Assessment and Computational Approaches toward Trustworthiness Evaluation

Our proposed trustworthiness evaluation method consists of two complementary approaches, i.e. the computational approach from Chapter 10 and a risk management approach. While the risk-based approach is performed on the level of asset categories, the trustworthiness metric computation is based on metric values of asset instances, which is illustrated in Figure 11.5. First, the risk-based approach is performed and then, based on its output, the computational approach is performed.

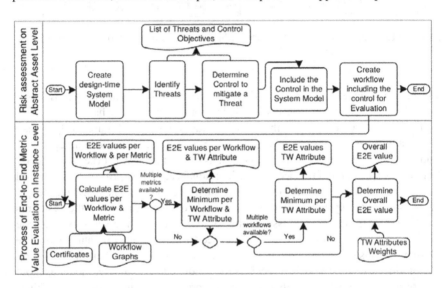

Figure 11.5: Trustworthiness evaluation in two different abstraction layers (Gol Moham-madi et al., 2015a)

The starting point for the risk-based approach is a design-time system model on an abstract level, which describes the general building blocks of an envisioned CPS on a high level of abstraction. It includes both physical and logical assets (e.g. software), as well as humans that interact with the system. This model is independent of concrete realizations, i.e. it includes asset categories without considering which asset instances shall be deployed as implementations of software assets. However, at this early stage our approach already allows us to identify threats that may cause misbehavior. With the determination of controls to block these threats, one has an opportunity to correct system behavior at run-time. To this end, a knowledge base of threats is used to identify relevant threats to the asset based on its type (e.g. logical asset, physical asset, etc.) and its relation patterns (e.g. client-service relation). Given the threats and potential controls, the designer is provided with a statement on the risks and corresponding actions that can be taken or at least planned for at design-time. Based on this information, asset structures may be revised, or informed decisions on the concrete asset instances can be made.

Once concrete asset instances (available on a marketplace) are selected for the asset categories and modelled in terms of one or multiple workflows, the designer can use the computational trustworthiness evaluation approach described in Chapter 10 to calculate the end-to-end trustworthiness based on the certified metric values of each of the asset instances and the end-to-end formulas for each relevant workflow. The resulting end-to-end trustworthiness values provide detailed information about the aggregated trustworthiness of the asset instances that are involved in a certain workflow. This allows the designer to relate the threats to the affected trustworthiness values, and also to evaluate and substantiate the effectiveness of applied design-time controls. If the metric values reflect the existence of controls (e.g. cryptography, authentication), the quantification enhances the evaluation. In order to facilitate the interpretation of the calculated end-to-end trustworthiness, the initial values that are particular to a certain workflow can again be aggregated so that finally one value for the whole system trustworthiness can be obtained. The relation of the process shown in Figure 11.5 to the one from Chapter 10 (cf. Figure 10.5) is that the step of providing the workflow graphs and creating E2E value per workflow is performed using the model-based risk assessment. The system model is enhanced with suggested controls. The designer can create the workflows based of the system models created using the System Analyser.

A precondition for combining the risk-based approach with the computational approach as shown in Figure 11.5 is that the value ranges of different metrics are comparable. In the following, we describe this combination in more detail.

Trustworthiness Evaluation using Threats and Controls Analysis at Abstract Asset Level

To perform the risk assessment as shown in Figure 11.5, the approaches of Surridge et al. (2013); Lock and Sommerville (2010) can be applied. The approaches allow the identification of threats that may compromise the system and affect its trustworthiness. These approaches can be enhanced with our E2E trustworthiness computational approach from Chapter 10. The threats are linked to one or more assets and their impact is specified in terms of asset misbehaviors. In addition to the threats, the models provide the associated control objectives to manage those threats. This can be by blocking the threat so that it cannot occur in the first place, or by reducing the threat impact so that any disruption of the functionality is minimal.

The CPS designer can use the design-time system model to map the system assets (and their relationships) to the different available asset categories and relationships. At this level, the involved assets can be abstract (i.e. use "elderly person" as an asset instead individuals).

Trustworthiness Evaluation using Computational Approaches at Asset Instance Level

Our computational approach for evaluating system trustworthiness runs across two dimensions. The first dimension consists of the trustworthiness values, which can refer to metrics, attributes (as a set of relevant metrics) or the overall trustworthiness. The second dimension is the system level that includes asset instances, asset categories, workflows and, finally, the overall system. Asset instances are the individual offerings present in the marketplace and can belong to a certain asset category. Combining several asset categories into a sequence results in a workflow that represents the steps to be completed to perform a system task successfully, e.g. as part of a business process. By modelling both, asset instances and asset categories, the connection to the risk-based evaluation of trustworthiness, as described in the previous section, is established. In contrast to Chapter 10, the system model is created in a systematic way. Including controls in the system model is supported by the automatic identification of threat to trustworthiness and list of possible controls. In contrast to that, in Chapter 10, this step was performed in ad hoc manner and was dependent on the designer's expertise.

For complex systems, we would expect that the designer defines multiple workflows. Note that when more than one asset instance exists as realization of an asset category, then it is necessary to specify the minimum number that is required to successfully process a request. Redundant structures can be specified at the asset instance level. There are three broad cases of redundancy type, namely "any of the asset instances" (OR), "all asset instances" (AND) and "any subset of a certain number of asset instances" (K-Out-Of-N).

We follow a bottom-up approach as shown in Figure 11.5. The first step consists of computing end-to-end metric values for a specific workflow. In order to perform this step, we depend on the availability of trustworthiness metric values for each asset instance involved. The metric values for each asset instance that is available on a marketplace are encoded in their certificates. Multiple metrics may be used to characterize a certain trustworthiness attribute. Hence, the next step is to aggregate all the metric values pertaining to an attribute into a single trustworthiness attribute value for that particular workflow. Given that multiple workflows may be necessary to describe all system features, the next step is to aggregate all trustworthiness attributes per workflow into a single attribute value for the overall system. Finally,

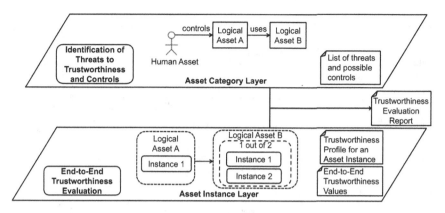

Figure 11.6: The relation between the complementary approaches for trustworthiness evaluation

a single trustworthiness value is found as the weighted average of the attribute values and their weights, which are provided by the designer. Figure 11.6 presents a summary of the major activities and artifacts for providing an overall trustworthiness evaluation of a CPS.

11.5 Proof-of-Concept Implementation for our Trustworthiness Evaluation Approach

In this section, we show how our "End-to-End Trustworthiness Evaluation" presented in Chapter 10 can actually be extended with a concrete risk assessment technique.

11.5.1 Context View of End-to-End Trustworthiness Evaluation Tool Enabled with Risk Assessment

Figure 11.7 shows the actor and functionalities for the end-to-end trustworthiness evaluation tool that now includes a risk assessment technique as well. Here, we extend the Use Case 1 (*evaluate system*) presented in the previous chapter (cf. Section 10.5.1). The gray colored elements are already described in Chapter 10. The use case intends to evaluate and/or compare system configurations based on the design-time system model. It supports selecting a set of asset instances to materialize the abstract assets in the system model, as well as specify their structure.

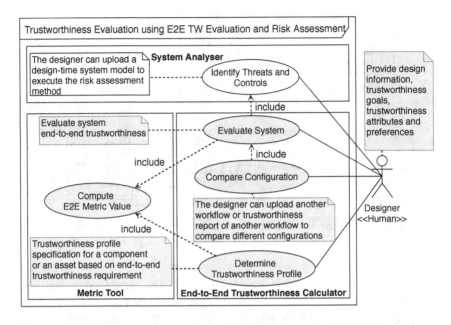

Figure 11.7: UML use case diagram for our TW Evaluation using E2E TW Evaluation and Risk Assessment methods based on (OPTET Consortium, 2014b)

Now, with involving the risk assessment, the design-time system model may serve as input. Based on the model-based risk assessment, the threats will be identified and the controls will be suggested. The designer can select from these controls. She/he can evaluate the system model in which a control for blocking a threat has been included (e.g. new asset is introduced to the structure of the system). As a support in this selection and decision-making process different alternatives can be evaluated and compared, so that when the controls are integrated with the rest of the assets, the desired E2E trustworthiness levels are met.

11.5.2 Architecture of End-to-End Trustworthiness Evaluation Tool including Risk Assessment Components

In this section, we provide an overview of the corresponding extension to the tool's architecture (shown in Figure 11.8) and describe the new components and functionality. First, the designer specifies a set of trustworthiness attributes that

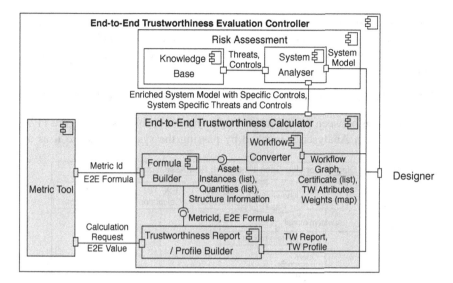

Figure 11.8: Component diagram of E2E TW Evaluation tool including Risk Assessment components based on (OPTET Consortium, 2014b)

are of interest for the particular system, as well as a weight for each attribute that represents her/his preferences for the specific system evaluated. These are used for calculating the overall trustworthiness score of the system from the individual attribute values. The designer then uploads a design-time system model, which is used by the *System Analyser* to identify threats and controls. The designer continues with the process that the E2E TW calculator needs and provides workflows. For each asset instance involved in the workflows, the designer must also supply a trustworthiness certificate containing metric values that are provided as evidence for trustworthiness. These can either be retrieved directly from some software marketplace or can be uploaded manually. The workflows and metric values contained in the asset certificates will be used by the E2E Trustworthiness Calculator to compute end-to-end trustworthiness values for the whole system.

As defined in Use Case 1 in Section 10.5.1, the result of the evaluation is a trustworthiness report. The trustworthiness report now contains the threats and controls in addition to the overall end-to-end trustworthiness values for the system. This report can be saved for future reference, documentation, or for comparing different system alternatives based on controls to make a cost-effective decision.

Figure 11.8 shows the component diagram of the trustworthiness evaluation tool with the extension consisting of the following two risk assessment components:

- The System Analyser takes as input the system model of interest and produces an enriched system model containing threats and candidate control objectives, based on an existing knowledge base. These candidate threats and control objectives are also put into the trustworthiness report.

- The knowledge base includes the core model, domain models and threat patterns.

The interactions between the different components are as follows (see Figure 11.9): First the System Analyser is invoked by passing the system model to it as an

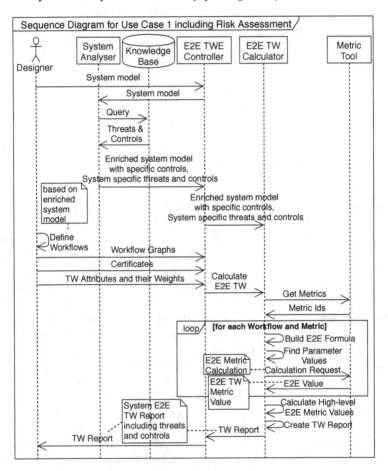

Figure 11.9: UML sequence diagram of E2E TW Evaluation tool for Use Case 1 including Risk Assessment components based on (OPTET Consortium, 2014b)

argument. After querying its knowledge base, it enriches the model with potential threats and suitable controls, and returns it to the E2E TWE Controller. Then the E2E TW Calculator is invoked, with providing the workflow graphs, asset certificates and trustworthiness specification. It starts by building an E2E formula for each metric and workflow. It then extracts the metric values from the certificates of each involved asset instance, and requests the metric tool to provide respective E2E metric values. After this, a first E2E calculation step is performed for each workflow. These values serve as a starting point for determining more high-level E2E trustworthiness values (cf. Figure 11.5). These include E2E trustworthiness attribute values for each workflow, E2E trustworthiness attribute values for the whole system, and in the end one E2E trustworthiness value for the whole system based on the weights assigned to each attribute by the designer. All these values are then composed, together with the system-specific threats and controls, to provide a comprehensive E2E Trustworthiness Report.

Figure 11.9 defines the interactions between the components for the Use Case 1 (*evaluate system*). This use case has been extended to include the *System Analyser* and its *Knowledge Base*, i.e. the system trustworthiness evaluation computes a final E2E TW value including the threats and the selected controls for blocking those threats for the overall system.

11.6 Application Example

We use the same that was presented in Chapter 10. The starting point for evaluating the trustworthiness of such a CPS is a design-time system model that includes physical, logical, and human assets of that system. This is depicted in Figure 11.10. This diagram includes the concepts that are important for risk assessment, for example, network information. This information is important in the identification of threats. For simplicity, the relatives and used services by them are not considered here. In addition to the elderly person, alarm call center, PERS, EMHT, and ambulance service assets that were shown in Figure 10.12, the designer specifies several assets that are necessary, for example, for communicating such as the following: Internet gateway, Phone network, Mobile phone, Ambulance, etc. *Elderly person* controls the *smartphone* and *smartwatch*. Both, *smartphone* and *smartwatch*, are connected to an *adhoc network*. *Smartwatch* hosts *smartwatch application*. The elderly person's *smartphone* hosts the *PERS* (personal emergency response system). The *PERS* uses the *EMHT* (emergency monitoring and handling tool) *service* that is hosted by *EMHT host*. The *EMHT* host is controlled by the *Caregiver*. The *caregiver* works as health authority in an alarm call center or in an ambulance station (cf. Figure 10.12). *Smartphone* and *router* in the elderly person's home are

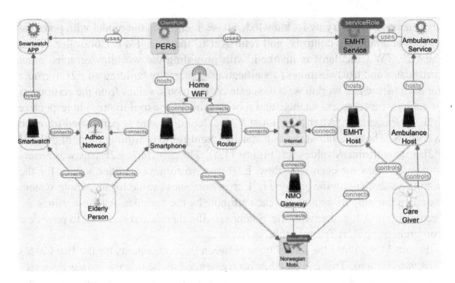

Figure 11.10: A simplified and human-readable version of the system model of the FMS based on (IT-innovation, 2013)

connected to the *home Wi-Fi*. Through the router, they are connected to the Internet. The *EMHT* host is also connected to the *Internet*. The Internet service provider is the *Norwegian mobile* provider using the *NMO gateway*. The *Ambulance service* is hosted by the *Ambulance host*. This model is stored in a machine-readable form as an RDF (resource description framework) ontology file.

11.6.1 Identification of Threats and Controls

Based on the system model, which specifies the relevant asset types of the system, and their relations, the trustworthiness evaluation is first performed on the abstraction layer of asset categories. Use Case 1 (evaluate system) of our prototype tool supports the designer in this task. The model file is uploaded via the E2E TWE user interface and passed to the System Analyser which in turn analyses the threats that may affect each system asset that is included in the system model. The System Analyser reports for each asset type the related threats as well as the potential controls that can be applied to prevent or mitigate the threats.

A threat that may arise at run-time is the unavailability of the EMHT asset (see Figure 11.12). This threat is identified based on the threat patterns in the *knowledge base* (shown in Figure 11.11). This will probably lead to a failure of the whole FMS, since the EMHT is a central service that enables and facilitates handling of

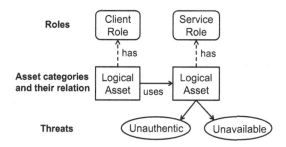

Figure 11.11: The Client-Service pattern and example threats based on (OPTET Consortium, 2014a)

incoming calls for help. Hence, a possible control to react to this threat at run-time is service substitution, i.e. to switch to another backup service that may also be a different implementation of the asset category. In order to address and implement this control at design-time, two or more concrete EMHT realizations have to be considered as redundant instances of the EMHT asset. The identified control will be considered and the designer will configure the system to include redundant asset instances of an asset category. This composition will be modelled as a workflow, which is used in the end-to-end trustworthiness calculation.

11.6.2 Trustworthiness Calculation for Asset Instance Configurations

In order to address the control requirements for blocking the unavailability threat related to a failure of the *EMHT* asset category, a redundant asset instance structure needs to be chosen. This may also apply to the *Ambulance Service* asset category. Hence, the designer specifies the redundant asset instances *EMHT_1* and *EMHT_2* and *Ambulance_Service_1* to *3* for the asset category *"EMHT"* and *"Ambulance Service"* respectively. These relations between the two complementary approaches for our example are illustrated in Figure 11.12, which also shows how the generated output supports the evaluation. Several workflows can be specified in order to describe different sequences of component interactions on asset instance level based on the system model. Figure 10.13 (presented in Chapter 10.6) shows exemplary workflows for this example.

Please note that we also included these redundancies in the previous chapter (cf. Chapter 10) in an ad hoc manner to illustrate the formula creation for end-to-end formulas and also for asset categories. In this chapter, using the System Analyser, the redundancies are included in a systematic way.

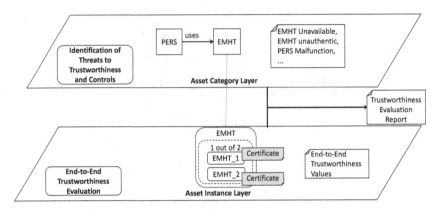

Figure 11.12: The relation between the complementary approaches for trustworthiness evaluation in our exemplary FMS

More details related to the computation of E2E trustworthiness for the possible workflows is presented in Chapter 10.

11.7 Contribution and Summary of this Chapter

In this chapter, we addressed the problems of commonly used evaluation techniques for evaluating the overall trustworthiness of a CPS. We suggest a combination of two complementary techniques: a computational approach and a risk management approach.

To summarize, our two-fold approach allows for evaluating the trustworthiness of a desired CPS first on the level of generic assets as CPS building blocks, which results in a set of threats and controls that embody the output of a risk-based assessment. These results are used to introduce redundancy on the more concrete level of asset instances. Redundant structures of asset instances (that are certified to show some relevant trustworthiness attributes in terms of metrics) result in end-to-end trustworthiness values that are calculated using the computational approach towards trustworthiness evaluation.

12 Maintenance of Trustworthiness in a Cyber-Physical System and Preparation for Run-Time

In cyber-physical systems, sub-optimal or incorrect functioning of the system may have detrimental effects. In addition to designing systems with trustworthiness in mind, maintaining trustworthiness at run-time is a critical task to identify issues that could negatively affect the trustworthiness of a system. Therefore, it is necessary to provide means to maintain trustworthiness of cyber-physical systems during run-time. However, today trustworthiness characteristics are poorly monitored, diagnosed and assessed by existing methods and technologies. In this chapter[1], we address this problem and provide support for semi-automatic trustworthiness maintenance. We propose a trustworthiness maintenance approach for monitoring and managing the system's trustworthiness properties in order to preserve the overall established trustworthiness during run-time. The TW-Man framework (presented in Chapter 3) provides a conceptual model for run-time trustworthiness maintenance, and respective business processes for identifying threats and enacting control decisions to mitigate these threats. Hence, this chapter focuses on the part of the TW-Man framework for trustworthiness maintenance at run-time and examines the challenges in planning for run-time activities, e.g. defining the needed monitoring interfaces and action steps, as well as determining the execution interfaces for performing the actions. We also present use cases and an architecture for developing trustworthiness maintenance systems that support system providers. Then, we present an operational tool for system trustworthiness maintenance.

---

[1]This chapter partially adapts Gol Mohammadi et al. (2014a) © Springer International Publishing Switzerland 2014, Alebrahim et al. (2015), Bandyszak et al. (2015), and Goldsteen et al. (2015), with the permission of the publishers.

12.1 Motivation

Stakeholders expect a system to stay trustworthy during its execution. The trustworthiness might be compromised by security attacks or system failures at run-time. Furthermore, changes in the system context may affect the trustworthiness of a CPS by violating its trustworthiness requirements. Therefore, it is crucial to monitor and assure trustworthiness at run-time, following defined processes that build upon a sound theoretical basis.

Trustworthiness requirements evolve either by new trust concerns of the end-users over a long period of time or by modifications in the environmental settings such as the change of using a third-party provider, infrastructure migration, and new regulations. Consider, for example, if you consider service provisioning or service substitution. Service-Level Agreements (SLAs) are documented in a contract between the customer and the service provider (Alhamad et al., 2010). A new service substitution has to guarantee the agreed (trustworthiness) SLA. However, new service or service provider policies may not respect the established trust relation.

The CPS providers should have the capacity to evaluate the run-time trustworthiness in order to enforce the agreed service terms and trust relation conditions.

In the following, we give examples of changes which may affect the trustworthiness of the system with respect to the established trust relation. Trustworthiness properties of the software can be compromised by different parties within the system boundary. For example, the substitution of a service by another service (which is more advanced with regard to performance), might cause a violation of the trustworthiness in terms of privacy. Therefore, an analysis of the effects of such an adaptation action on the trustworthiness of the system has to be performed beforehand. Such an examination has to consider the different types of changes that can be made to a system and affect its trustworthiness (Alebrahim et al., 2015). Some changes can be observable by the software, e.g. reconfiguration, substitution of third party services, while others go by undetected, e.g. changes in regulations and trust expectations of the end-user. For example, an end-user has already engaged in using a software. This end-user then obtains awareness of the consequences of sharing sensitive data. Subsequently, she/he raises concerns about privacy. This may lead to changes in the trustworthiness requirements. Another example is a software that provides new features to the end-user requiring access to location data. If the end-user is not willing to share her/his location data, updating the software with the new features will result in a violation of the trustworthiness, as the old features did not require access to the location data.

By studying existing trustworthiness maintenance approaches, we identified a lack of generally applicable and domain-independent concepts. In addition, existing frameworks and technologies do not appropriately address all facets of trustworthiness. There is also insufficient guidance for service providers to understand and conduct maintenance processes, and to build corresponding tools. We seek to go beyond the state-of-the-art of run-time trustworthiness maintenance by establishing a better understanding of key concepts for measuring and controlling trustworthiness at run-time, and by providing process guidance to maintain the trustworthiness of a CPS.

The remainder of this chapter is structured as follows. In Section 12.2, we describe the background concepts with respect to the underlying run-time maintenance approach. In Section 12.3, we briefly discuss related work. Section 12.4 presents the contribution of this chapter which consists of four parts: 1) a domain-independent conceptual model that describes the key concepts of our run-time approach, 2) business processes for monitoring, measuring, and managing trustworthiness, as well as mitigating trustworthiness issues at run-time, and 3) + 4) use cases and an architecture for trustworthiness maintenance systems. In Section 12.5, we present an application example for demonstrating our trustworthiness maintenance approach. Finally, in Section 12.6, we give a summary and a brief discussion of our research activities.

12.2 Background: Run-time Maintenance in Autonomic Computing

This section presents the fundamental concepts that form the basis for our run-time approach. We briefly introduce the concept of run-time maintenance in autonomic systems. Our approach to maintain trustworthiness at run-time is mainly based on the vision of Autonomic Computing (Kephart and Chess, 2003). The goal of Autonomic Computing is to design and develop distributed and service-oriented systems that can easily adapt to changes. Considering assets of CPS as managed elements of an autonomic system allows us to apply the concepts of Autonomic Computing to trustworthiness maintenance. MAPE-K (Monitor, Analyze, Plan, Execute, and Knowledge) is a reference model for control loops in Autonomic Computing with the objective of supporting the concepts of self-management, specifically: self-configuration, self-optimization, self-healing, and self-protection (Kephart and Chess, 2003; IBM, 2005). Figure 12.1 shows the elements of an autonomic system: the control loop activities, sensor and effector interfaces, and the system being managed.

The monitor component of the control loop provides mechanisms to collect events from the managed element (in our case, the CPS). It is also able to filter

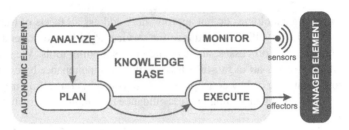

Figure 12.1: Autonomic computing and MAPE-K loop

and aggregate the data and to report details or metrics (IBM, 2005). To this end, system-specific sensors provide interfaces for gathering the required monitoring data and they can also raise events when the system configuration changes (IBM, 2005). The analyze component of the control loop provides means to correlate and model the reported details or measures. It is able to handle complex situations and predicts future situations. The next component, plan, provides mechanisms to construct the set of actions required to achieve a certain goal or objective, or to respond to a certain event. Finally, the execute component offers mechanisms to realize the actions determined in the planning phase, i.e. to control the system by means of effectors that modify the managed element (Kephart and Chess, 2003). A system is a managed element (e.g. software) that contains resources and provides services. In our case, managed elements are assets of the CPS. Additionally, a common knowledge base acts as the central part of the control loop, and is shared by the activities to store and access collected and analyzed data.

12.3 Related Work

So far in this book (in previous chapters), related work has been discussed from several areas. For example, methodologies for designing and developing trustworthy systems, such as (Amoroso et al., 1994) or from our work from Chapters 6 to 11, focus on best practices, techniques, and tools that can be applied at design-time, including the trustworthiness evaluation of development artifacts and processes. However, these trustworthiness-by-design approaches do not consider the issues related to run-time trustworthiness assessment. In Chapter 10, we used design-time metrics to evaluate the trustworthiness of developed CPS. However, run-time metrics as a means for quantifying software quality attributes can be found in several publications, e.g. related to security and dependability (Arlitt et al., 2001), personalization (Bassin et al., 2002), or resource consumption (Zivkovic et al., 2011). The problem of run-time trustworthiness maintenance that we address in this chapter has many similarities with the monitoring and adaption of web services in Service-Oriented Architectures, responding to the violation of quality criteria. Users generally favor web services that can be expected to perform as described in Service Level Agreements. To this end, reputation mechanisms can be used (e.g. Rana et al. (2008)). However, these are not appropriate for objectively measuring trustworthiness based on system characteristics. In contrast, using online monitoring approaches, analyzes and conflict resolution can be carried out based on logging the service interactions. Online monitoring can be performed by the service provider, service consumer, or trusted third parties (Clark et al., 2010; Quillinan et al., 2010). The ANIKETOS trustworthiness module (Elshaafi et al., 2012) allows for monitoring the dependability of service-oriented systems, considering system composition as well as specific component characteristics. However, in this book, dependability is only one of the trustworthiness attributes (cf. Chapter 4).

Zhao et al. (2009) also consider service composition related to availability, reliability, response time, reputation, and security. Service composition plays an important role in evaluation, as well as in management. For example, Elshaafi et al. (2012) consider the substitution of services as the major means of restoring trustworthiness. Decisions to change the system composition should not only consider system qualities (Yu et al., 2007), but also related costs and profits (Zivkovic et al., 2011; Elshaafi et al., 2012). Lenzini et al. (2007) propose a trustworthiness management framework in the domain of component-based embedded systems, which aims at evaluating and controlling trustworthiness, e.g. with respect to dependability and security characteristics such as CPU consumption, memory usage, or presence of encryption mechanisms. Conceptually, their framework is closely related to ours, since it provides a software system that allows for monitoring multiple quality attributes based on metrics and compliance to user-specific trustworthiness profiles.

However, there are no comprehensive approaches towards trustworthiness maintenance, which consider a multitude of system qualities and different types of CPS. Furthermore, there is also a lack of a common terminology of relevant run-time trustworthiness concepts. Additionally, appropriate tool support for enabling monitoring and management processes is rare. There is insufficient guidance for service providers to understand and establish maintenance processes, and to develop supporting systems.

12.4 Maintaining Trustworthiness at Run-Time

This section presents our approach for maintaining trustworthiness at run-time. We describe a framework that consists of the following parts: 1) a conceptual model that provides general concepts for our run-time trustworthiness maintenance, 2) processes for monitoring and managing trustworthiness, 3) functional use cases of a system for supporting the execution of these processes, and 4) a reference architecture that guides the development of such maintenance systems. The reference architecture is based on MAPE-K, which in principle allows for realization of automated maintenance. However, our approach focuses on semi-automatic trustworthiness maintenance, which involves decisions made by a human maintenance operator. In the following subsections, we elaborate on the elements of the framework in detail.

12.4.1 Conceptual Model for Run-Time Trustworthiness Maintenance

This section outlines the underlying conceptual model on which the development of the run-time trustworthiness maintenance is based. Rather than focusing on a specific domain, our approach provides a meta-model that abstracts from concrete system characteristics in such a way that it can be interpreted by different stakeholders and applied across disciplines. Figure 12.2 illustrates the key concepts and their interrelations. This figure details the parts of the overall conceptual model of the TW-Man framework (cf. Figure 3.4) presented in Chapter 3 that are related to the run-time trustworthiness maintenance.

The definition of trustworthiness attributes forms the basis for identifying the concepts, since they allow for assessing the trustworthiness of a CPS. However, trustworthiness attributes are not modelled directly; instead they are encoded implicitly using a set of quantitative concepts. The core elements abstract from common concepts that are used to model trustworthiness of CPS, while the run-time concepts are particularly required for our maintenance approach.

Trustworthiness attributes of an "Asset", are concretized by "Trustworthiness Properties" that describe the system's quality at a lower abstraction level with measurable values of a certain data type, e.g. the response time related to a specific input, or current availability of an asset[2]. These properties are atomic in the sense that they refer to a particular system snapshot in time. The relation between

---

[2]Availability is the ability of the system to deliver expected functionality when it is required. The major metrics used in the state of the art for measuring availability are Mean Time Between Failure (MTBF), also called Mean Time to Failure (MTTF), and Mean Time to Repair (MTTR). Probing the system can be used to check whether it is available. By probing the system a number of times during a

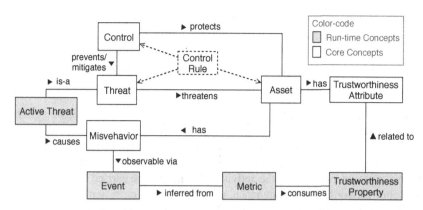

Figure 12.2: Conceptual model for Run-Time Trustworthiness Maintenance based on based on (Gol Mohammadi et al., 2014a)

trustworthiness attributes and properties is many to many; an attribute can potentially be concretized by means of multiple properties, whereas a property might be an indicator for various trustworthiness attributes. Values of trustworthiness properties can be read and processed by metrics in order to estimate the current levels of trustworthiness attributes. A metric is a function that consumes a set of properties and produces a measure related to trustworthiness attributes. Based on metrics, statements about the behavior of a CPS can be derived. They also allow for specifying reference threshold values captured in Trustworthiness Service-Level Agreements (TSLAs).

A system's behavior is observed by means of "Events", i.e. induced asset behaviors perceivable from interaction with the system. Events can indicate either normal or abnormal behavior, e.g. underperformance or unaccountable accesses. Misbehavior observed from an event or a sequence of events may manifest in a "Threat" which undermines an asset's value and reduces the trustworthiness of the CPS. This in turn leads to an output that is unacceptable for the system's stakeholders, reducing their level of trust in the system. Given these consequences, we denote a threat "active". Threats (e.g. loss of data) can be mitigated by either preventing them from becoming active, or counteracting their effects (e.g. corrupted outputs). Therefore, "Controls" (e.g. service substitution) are to be executed. "Control Rules" specify which controls can block or mitigate a given type of threat. Identifying and analyzing potential threats, their consequences, and adequate controls is a

---

certain period of time, this data can be used to calculate the mean availability and compare it with the expected value.

challenging task that should be tackled in the early phases of requirements analysis (cf. Section 6.3.4 and Chapter 11).

12.4.2 Processes for Run-Time Trustworthiness Maintenance

In order to provide guidance for realizing trustworthiness maintenance, we define two complementary reference processes, namely trustworthiness monitoring and management. These processes illustrate the utilization of the concepts described in Section 12.4.1. We denote them as "reference processes" since they provide a high-level and generic view on the activities that need to be carried out in order to implement trustworthiness maintenance, without considering system-specific characteristics. Instantiating the processes will require analyzing these characteristics and defining, e.g. appropriate metric thresholds to identify CPS misbehavior(s). Our approach is semi-automatic, i.e. we assume a human maintenance operator to be consulted for taking critical decisions.

Trustworthiness Monitoring

The process of monitoring is responsible for observing the behavior of the CPS in order to identify and report misbehaviors to the management, which will then analyze the CPS state for potential threats and enact corrective actions, if necessary. Our monitoring approach is based on metrics. The reference process for trustworthiness monitoring is shown in the BPMN diagram depicted in Figure 12.3.

The first step involves collecting all relevant trustworthiness properties (e.g. properties indicating system usage). These can be either 1) system properties that are necessary to compute the metrics for the set of relevant trustworthiness attributes or 2) system topology changes, such as the inclusion of a new asset. Atomic system events indicate changes of properties. For each system asset, trustworthiness metrics are computed. Having enough monitoring data, statistical analysis can be used for aggregating atomic measurements into composite ones, e.g. the mean response time of an asset. These measures are further processed in order to identify violations of trustworthiness requirements that are captured in user-specific TSLAs. For each trustworthiness metric, it is observed whether the required threshold(s) are exceeded. If so, the critical assets are consequently reported to the management, so that potentially active threats can be identified and mitigation actions can be triggered.

Each CPS has its individual characteristics and requirements for trustworthiness. At run-time, system characteristics may change, e.g. due to adaptations to the

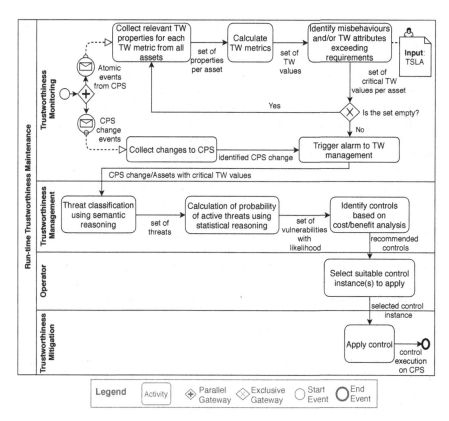

Figure 12.3: Trustworthiness Monitoring, Management and Mitigation process

environment. Consequently, another important monitoring task is to accept change notifications from the CPS and to forward them to the trustworthiness management.

Trustworthiness Management and Mitigation

The key objective of trustworthiness management (see Figure 12.3) is to guarantee correct system and service behavior at run-time by continuously analyzing system behavior, identifying potential threats, as well as recommending and executing possible mitigation actions. Note that we do not provide a separate mitigation process, since the actual mitigation execution is rather a technical issue that does not involve complex logic.

The reference management and mitigation process is triggered by incoming events (i.e. misbehaviors or system changes) reported by the trustworthiness monitoring. Misbehaviors identified in the form of deviations from required trustworthiness levels indicate an abnormal status, e.g. underperformance due to insufficient resources, or malicious attacks. The management process keeps track of the system status over time and analyzes the causes of misbehaviors. Once threats are classified, it is necessary (i) to analyze their effect on the asset's behavior and to understand the links between them in order to analyze complex observations and sequences of threats that may be active, and (iii) to identify suitable controls. Statistical reasoning is necessary for estimating threat probabilities (for each trustworthiness attribute).

Regarding control selection and deployment, we focus on semi-automated threat mitigation, as illustrated in Figure 12.3, which requires human intervention. The maintenance operator is notified whenever new threats are identified. These threats may be active, indicating vulnerabilities due to a lack of necessary controls. Each threat is given a likelihood based on the observed system behaviors. It is then the maintenance operator's responsibility to select appropriate controls that can be applied to the CPS in order to realize mitigation. These controls involve, e.g. authentication or encryption. Several control instances may be available for each control (e.g. different encryption technologies), having different benefits and costs. Based on cost-effective recommendations, the operator selects control instances to be deployed. More information about the trustworthiness cost optimization problem can be found in the work by Kalogiros et al. (2015). As a consequence, previously identified active threats should be classified as blocked or mitigated. The system may be dynamic, i.e. assets can be added or removed. Thus, notifications about changes of the CPS topology will also trigger the management process (see Figure 12.3).

12.4.3 Functional Requirements of a Run-Time Trustworthiness Maintenance System

Based on the reference processes introduced in Section 12.4.2, we elicit functional requirements for a tool that supports CPS providers in maintaining trustworthiness. Such a tool is supposed to facilitate and realize the business processes in a semi-automatic manner, i.e. with a human operator in the loop. We distinguish three main areas of functionality: monitoring, management, and mitigation. The latter is included for a better separation of concerns, although we did not define a separate reference process for mitigation (only "apply control" activity in Figure 12.3). We analyzed possible maintenance functionalities, and actors that interact with the system. The results of this analysis are shown in the UML use case diagram in Figure 12.4.

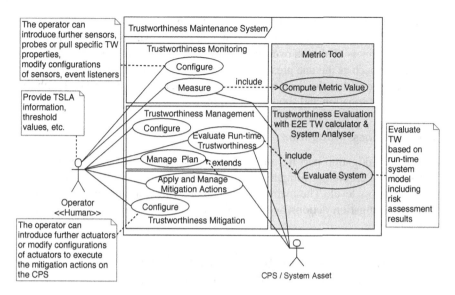

Figure 12.4: Trustworthiness maintenance use cases

Trustworthiness Monitoring

The monitoring functionality is responsible for collecting events and properties from the CPS and computing trustworthiness values (using run-time metrics). The measuring use case includes the compute metric value use case from the metric tool that was described in Chapter 10. The inputs to the monitoring component are system properties and atomic events that are collected from the CPS. The output, i.e. metric values or measures, is provided to the management. The operator is able to start and stop the measuring and to configure the monitoring. Specifically, the operator can use the concept of trustworthiness requirements specified in TSLAs or in a trustworthiness profile (cf. Chapter 10) from the design-time evaluation (cf. Figure 12.3) to derive an appropriate configuration.

Trustworthiness Management

The management part provides the means to assess current trustworthiness attributes using the metrics provided from monitoring, choose an appropriate plan (if needed) and forward it to mitigation. The operator is able to configure the management component and provides a list of monitor(s) from which measures should be read, a list of trustworthiness attributes that are of interest, as well as management processes.

Additionally, the operator is able to start and stop the management process, retrieve trustworthiness metric values, and to generate reports which contain summaries of trustworthiness evolution over time. For evaluating run-time trustworthiness, a similar approach as the one presented in Chapter 11 could be included. However, the difference is that the design-time system model should be updated with the monitored information and should be used for evaluation.

Trustworthiness Mitigation

Lastly, the mitigation part has one main purpose: to control the CPS assets by realizing and enforcing mitigation actions, i.e. executing controls to adjust the trustworthiness level. The maintenance operator will configure the service with available mitigation actions and controls that are to be executed by means of effectors.

12.4.4 Reference Architecture for Run-Time Trustworthiness Maintenance Systems

As mentioned above, we consider the trustworthiness maintenance system as an autonomic computing system (see Section 12.2). The autonomic system elements can be mapped to three maintenance components, similar to the distribution of functionality in the use case diagram in Figure 12.4. The monitor and mitigation components are each responsible for a single functionality; monitoring and executing controls respectively. Analyze and plan functionalities are mapped to a single management package, since they are closely related. Furthermore, it simplifies the interfaces. Figure 12.5 shows the reference architecture of a maintenance system as a UML component diagram.

Trustworthiness maintenance systems are designed around one centralized management component and support distributed monitoring and mitigation. This modular architecture enables instantiating multiple monitors on different systems, each reporting to a single centralized management component. Likewise, mitigation can be distributed among multiple systems, too. This allows for greater scalability and flexibility.

Monitor

The monitor package contains three components. The monitor component provides an API to administer and configure the package, while the measurement producer is responsible for interfacing with the CPS via sensors. The latter supports both passive sensors listening to events, as well as active sensors that actively measure

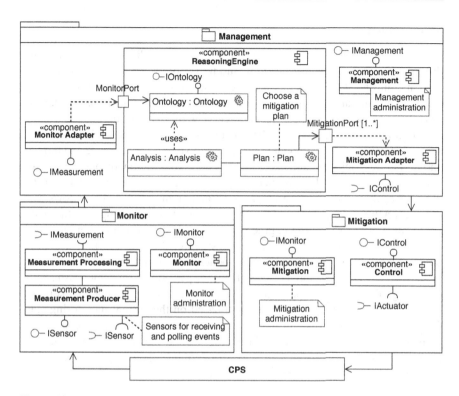

Figure 12.5: Reference system architecture for run-time TW Maintenance based on (Gol Mohammadi et al., 2014a)

the CPS (e.g. to check if the system is available). Hence, the CPS-specific event capturing implementation is decoupled from the more generic measurement processing component which gathers and processes all events. It is able to compute metrics and forward summarized information to the management. In addition, it may adjust the processes controlling the sensors (e.g. with respect to the frequency of measurements).

One way to implement the monitor component is using an event-based approach like Complex Event Processing (CEP) (Luckham, 2001). CEP handles events in a processing unit in order to perform monitoring activities, and to identify unexpected and abnormal situations at run-time. This offers the ability of taking actions based on enclosed information in events about the current situation of a CPS.

Management

The management package is responsible for gathering all information from the different monitors, store it, analyze it, and find appropriate plans to execute mitigation controls. It contains monitor and mitigation adapters that allow multiple monitors or mitigation packages to interact with the management package. They provide the reasoning engine with a unified view of all input sources and a single view of all mitigation packages. The management package also includes the management administration component that is used to configure all connected monitor and mitigation packages, and exposes APIs for configuration, display, and report generation. The central component, the reasoning engine, encapsulates all the logic for analyzing the measurements and planning the actions. This allows us to define an API for the engine and then replace it with different engines. Internally, an instance of the reasoning engine contains analysis and plan components, as expected from an autonomic computing system (cf. Section 12.2), as well as an ontology component. The ontology component encapsulates all required system models which define e.g. threats. This allows for performing semantic reasoning by executing rules against the provisional system status and estimating the likelihood of threat activeness (e.g. vulnerabilities) based on the current monitoring state. Given active threats, probabilities and a knowledge base of candidate controls for each threat, the plan component can instruct mitigation on what action(s) to perform in order to restore or maintain the CPS's trustworthiness in a cost-effective manner, following the maintenance operator's confirmation.

Mitigation

The mitigation package contains a control component that encapsulates all interaction with the CPS and a mitigation administration component. This allows us to separate CPS control details from mitigation configuration and expose a generic API. The mitigation package is responsible for executing mitigation actions by means of appropriate CPS-specific effectors. These actions may be complex such as deploying another instance of a service or as simple as presenting a warning to the maintenance operator including information for him to act on.

12.5 Tool Architecture of the Run-Time Trustworthiness Maintenance

This section describes an application example for demonstrating our trustworthiness maintenance approach of providing run-time support. We also illustrate the instantiation of the proposed reference architecture and of the general processes by providing examples that apply to our proposed approach.

12.5.1 Low-Level Architecture

The tool's architecture (see Figure 12.6) is based on the concept of our reference architecture. It includes a monitor component responsible for collecting events from the system assets, storing them in a database and performing initial processing to compute trustworthiness metrics and misbehaviors, a management component that receives alerts from the monitor, identifies relevant threats and controls and selects the best controls to deploy, and a mitigation component that actually executes the selected controls.

Events may be sent to the monitor component in several ways. One option is to pre-configure the monitored system to send such events to the maintenance tool. This requires placing the support for run-time maintenance into the system design so that observation and control interfaces are built into the system. In Chapter 6, we describe how this could be achieved. Another option is to use specialized sensors that collect events in a specific environment or a generic monitoring framework such as Zabbix (2009). The latter option also enables monitoring existing systems and applications. The main processing sub-component within the monitor is a CEP which receives all low-level events and fires a misbehavior event whenever a single measurement reaches its pre-defined threshold or some more complex rule is triggered. The CEP depends on system-specific configuration that is based on observable system properties. For the AAL example (see Section 12.5.2), as a CEP engine the IBM[3] **Pro**active Technology **On**line[4] (Proton) has been used (cf. OPTET Consortium (2014c)).

The main analysis within the management component is performed by a Trustworthiness Evaluator (TWE) which maintains and incrementally updates a semantic run-time model of the system. The model includes the different system assets and the connections between them, system threats and vulnerabilities, and controls that have been deployed. This model comprises not only software assets, but also physical assets such as hardware and humans interacting with the system. The TWE utilizes machine reasoning based on a generic threat ontology that incorporates relevant security knowledge. This semantic model should encode as many common attack patterns as possible to be able to correctly identify threats to the system.

The TWE uses a Bayesian network approach to analyze threat activity likelihood given the reported system behavior. Bayesian networks are a powerful tool for

---

[3]`https://www.ibm.com` (accessed on 22 October 2018)

[4]`https://proactive-technology-online.readthedocs.io/en/latest/ProtonUserGuide_FI_WARE5_4_1/index.html` (accessed on 22 October 2018)

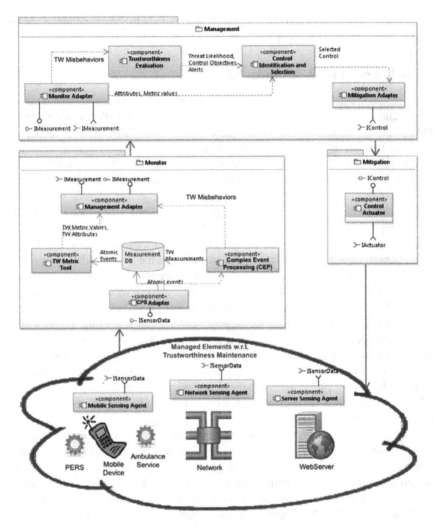

Figure 12.6: Low-level architecture of the TW Maintenance tool based on (Goldsteen et al., 2015)

constructing models of phenomena involving uncertainty. Bayesian models can combine expert knowledge with observational data, and can be refined over time through learning from observation. In our case, we encode the expert knowledge (e.g. prior threat likelihoods, causational probabilities, etc.) in the model, and use events observed at run-time as evidence to reason the threat activity likelihood and perform predictive analysis. As a result of system events, the TWE performs a comprehensive threat analysis, including finding possible threats given the observed system status, determining their likelihoods, and deciding whether they constitute a secondary effect due to the activity of other threats.

The trustworthiness evaluation process is triggered each time a meaningful system event is detected by the monitor including misbehaviors and system topology updates. The output consists of threats with a likelihood to pass a pre-defined threshold along with control options for mitigating the threat. Then, the "Control Identification and Selection" component selects one or more controls to deploy, taking into consideration both cost and different trustworthiness metrics. The mitigation component, which encompasses system-specific information on how to execute each control, actually deploys the selected controls.

Each one of the above-mentioned components needs to be configured to support the specific system that will be monitored: the monitor needs to be configured to recognize the events arriving from the system (or monitoring framework) and to derive metric values and misbehaviors; the TWE receives a model of the deployed system assets and how they are connected; and the mitigation needs to be configured with system-specific information on how to execute each control. The amount of monitoring information required from the system depends on the attack patterns one wants to detect. The more complex the patterns, the more information will be needed from the system in order to detect them.

12.5.2 Initial Evaluation

In this section we show how the trustworthiness run-time maintenance tool described in Section 12.5.1 is used to monitor selected trustworthiness attributes in the AAL case study (described in Chapter 5). The system model from Figure 11.10 for AAL scenario is considered as the managed element. The goal of this evaluation was to validate that our tool can in fact increase a system's trustworthiness. The prototype implementation in the context of the OPTET project (OPTET Consortium, 2013b), (OPTET Consortium, 2014c) demonstrates the feasibility of our trustworthiness maintenance approach.

The AAL system consists of several assets: the elderly person who needs help in an emergency situation, the PERS (personal emergency response system) which is installed in the elderly person's home, the EMHT (emergency monitoring and handling tool) used by the alarm call center staff, and the Ambulance Service hosted by an ambulance station. The run-time maintenance tool monitors the trustworthy behavior of the AAL system with the goal of detecting misbehavior (untrustworthy behavior).

We consider a simplified scenario by focussing only on availability and performance as trustworthiness attributes of the trustworthiness vector (see Table 12.1).

Table 12.1: Trustworthiness attributes and exemplary metrics

Trustworthiness Attribute		Description	Possible Metrics
Availability		Is the service available at any time and every day (24/7/365)?	1. Number of refused server connection (connection initiated by device) or 2. Percentage of the time the server is up
Performance	Throughput	The system is trustworthy if it can handle all incoming requests. Related to: Dependability - Scalability	Percentage of incoming requests that are handled by system
	Response time	Measure the response times of each party (including 3rd parties). The system is trustworthy if the response times are as promised. The variation of response times may also be an indicator of trustworthiness. Related to: Performance - Latency	1. Overall response time (e.g. fall detection to resolution) 2. Device response time from the time a fall is detected until contact with server 3. Alarm Call Center response time (e.g. call received until call answered, call received until action is taken) 4. Alarm call center action time (e.g. ambulance response time)

Under normal conditions, the availability of the PERS and the ambulance service should be relatively high. We describe some cases in which mitigation actions (controls) can be applied, e.g. when the availability or performance of the ambulance service is lower than expected. The alarm call center normally uses one ambulance station. However, it has the possibility to use one more ambulance station (cf. Chapter 10, design decision for redundant asset instances). We assume that each ambulance station covers the entire area. Possible controls and mitigation actions for underperforming or unavailability are: 1) Replace ambulance service with the another ambulance service, 2) involve the second ambulance station in an on-call-basis and distribute emergency calls according to availability or proximity.

The alarm call center provides each elderly person with one mobile device for fall detection. It has more than one alternative (different mobile devices, multiple stationary devices etc. as described in Chapter 5). The following controls and mitigation actions are possible when, for example, the false alarm rate exceeds its threshold: 1) Update mobile device with a newer, more accurate fall detection software, 2) Replace mobile device with a more accurate device (replace hardware), 3) Introduce additional devices (video sensors to detect falls) that can complement fall detection at home.

Table 12.2 provides an overview of the scenarios, and exemplifies the concepts used in this chapter.

Table 12.2: Overview of scenarios for AAL

	Availability	Performance
Asset	**PERS**	**Ambulance Service**
Atomic event	"Available" event indicates the availability or unavailability of the PERS at a certain point in time	"StatusReport" event reports the status of an ambulance service (i.e. either underway or arrived)
Measurement by Monitor	Relation of uptime and downtime in a certain time frame, i.e. the percentage of availability time	Number of periodically polled status reports of an ambulance in a time slot (indicating the time elapsed to arrive at elderly person's home)
Identification of Misbehavior	Current availability below a certain threshold	Ambulance not arrived after a certain number of status reports, i.e. response time exceeds a certain threshold
Misbehavior	Unavailable	Underperforming
Threat	Client software malfunction	Underprovisioning
Control	Asset replacement, Software updates	Scale the service by increasing the number of available ambulances
Metrics for Analyzing Control	Average technician response time, average technician availability in percentage	Average response time of an ambulance service, average availability of an ambulance service in milliseconds
Control Selection	Select a speedy method to patch software or replace the hardware by sending a cost-effective technician	Select a cost-effective ambulance service to add to the current pool of ambulance services

The Monitor component receives atomic events from the AAL. The event producer stubs and respective interfaces are specified to simulate the AAL behavior. These event producer provides stimuli to the TW Maintenance tool. Specifically, we provide exemplary atomic events that allow for assessing the availability and the response time of the simulated assets (i.e. a PERS and an ambulance service).

The monitor component receives the "Available" (see Table 12.2) event with the following parameters: 1) A boolean value which indicates the current availability at a certain point in time. 2) A string value (sourceAssetType) that indicates the type of the asset from which this event is observed. 3) A string value (sourceAssetId) indicates the concrete identification of the asset instance, from which this event is observed. The time of the event is also documented (OccurrenceTime).

The monitor component receives the "StatusReport" event from the "Ambulance Service" with the following parameters: 1) A boolean value (taskComplete) that indicates that a specific asset achieved a specific task. Concerning the ambulance service, we assume that the ambulance tracking mechanism allows the ambulance service to send out notifications about the execution and achievement of some task.

As an example for such a task, we consider the arrival at an elderly person's home upon a request. 2) A string value (sourceAssetType) that indicates the type of the asset from which this event is originated. 3) Another string value (sourceAssetId) indicates the concrete identification of the asset instance, from which this event is observed. 4) The time of observing this event (OccurrenceTime) is documented as well.

These events are used for two purposes: First, to monitor the current availability of a PERS asset and the current response time of an ambulance asset. Second, to provide a basis for control selection by describing events that indicate the previous availability and response times for the potential controlling assets. The events are provided in the JSON (JavaScript Object Notation) format. The CPS adapter forwards each atomic event to both the CEP and the Measurement DB. We use the CEP as an interim solution for calculating response time metric values. Availability metrics can be calculated directly from the atomic events that are stored in the Measurement DB, while the response time values require pre-processing by the CEP. The outputs of the the TW Maintenance tool prototype is a list of possible controls that can be chosen by the operator for mitigating certain threats. To guide the operator in the decision process; the Control Selector calculates and enhances the list of controls with optimality values for each control, according to the metrics for analyzing the proposed controls (cf. Table 12.2).

The sensors send events to the monitor component every ten seconds. If based on measurements performed by the CEP, unavailability of PERS is identified, the CEP triggers an *Unavailable* misbehavior (see Figure 12.7), which is forwarded to the TWE. The TWE outputs several relevant threats, of which the one with the highest likelihood is *Client Software Malfunction*, and proposes *Software Update and Asset Replacement* (hardware replacement) as controls to mitigate it. If the operator selects asset replacement, the TW Maintenance tool prototype identifies a technician as the optimal one that should be requested and sent to the elderly person's home to fix the problems that have caused unavailability of the PERS.

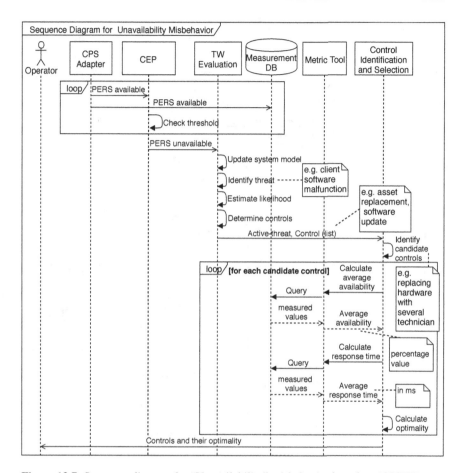

Figure 12.7: Sequence diagram for "Unavailability" misbehavior based on (OPTET Consortium, 2014c)

When a high load is detected on a sensor from the ambulance station, the *Underperforming* misbehavior is triggered (see Figure 12.8). This can lead to two possible threats: either the ambulance service is simply under a high load, which can be mitigated by adding an additional ambulance station to the pool. In the case of *Underperforming*, adding alternative ambulance stations to the current pool will achieve the best mitigation action. Consequently, the TW Maintenance tool lists the available ambulance services, with an indication of the optimality value (e.g. current load of each ambulance service).

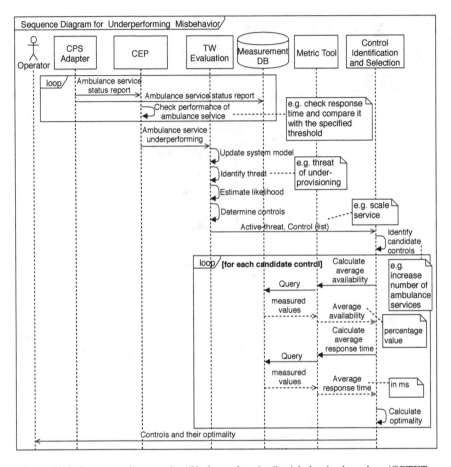

Figure 12.8: Sequence diagram for "Underperforming" misbehavior based on (OPTET Consortium, 2014c)

In the OPTET project, we conducted a small-scale experiment with 27 live operators (Goldsteen et al., 2015; OPTET Consortium, 2014c). Each operator used two alternative versions of the CPS, one integrated with the maintenance tool and one not. Results showed that the integrated system was better in early detection of misbehavior and performing mitigation actions on affected assets (it was able to mitigate 80% of the misbehavior vs. 63% in the regular CPS without integration of trustworthiness maintenance). Furthermore, operators and users perceived the integrated system to be more trustworthy (91% of the operators preferred the integrated version over the regular one). This demonstrates that a system's trustworthiness, as well as the users' perceived trustworthiness and acceptance of a system can be substantially increased by using such a tool. Please not that in the AAL scenario, the operator is the staff in the alarm call center (administrator).

12.6 Contribution and Summary of this Chapter

Maintaining trustworthiness of CPS at run-time is a complex task for service providers. In this chapter, we have addressed this problem by proposing a framework for maintaining trustworthiness. The framework is generic in the sense that it is based on a domain-specific meta-model suitable for all kinds of CPS. This meta-model provides key concepts for understanding and addressing run-time trustworthiness issues. Our framework defines reference processes for trustworthiness monitoring and management, which guide CPS providers in realizing run-time maintenance. As the first step towards realizing trustworthiness maintenance processes in practice, we presented results of a use case analysis, in which high-level functional requirements of maintenance systems have been elicited, as well as a general architecture for such systems.

We developed a prototype of a trustworthiness maintenance system that implements our reference architecture. We defined concrete scenarios that further detailed the abstract functional requirements presented in this chapter and also serve as a reference for validating the system in order to show the applicability of our approach. We demonstrated a tool for run-time monitoring of software systems, and specifically cyber-physical systems, to enable automatic detection and mitigation of active threats that may threaten the system's trustworthiness. Within the OPTET project, the tool was tested and validated on two trustworthiness-critical applications: a fall management system for ambient assisted living (as shown here) and a distributed attack detection and visualization system for cyber-crisis management. An initial proof-of-concept was also performed on real sensor data from an electric company (Goldsteen et al., 2015).

The tool covers a large range of trustworthiness metrics and can be adapted to many types of systems. It supports run-time adaptation and self-healing of critical systems, thus reducing the overall upkeep costs as well as complexity and increasing system uptake and retention. This approach requires detailed knowledge about the system to configure the different components, sensors able to accurately observe events that may affect trustworthiness, as well as "hooks" into the system to support automatic deployment of the mitigating actions.

13 Towards Preparation for the Trustworthiness Certification using Trustworthiness Cases

The development process of a trustworthy system and the evaluation phase (TWby-Design practices) produce evidence that the CPS is trustworthy. In this chapter[1], we introduce so-called trustworthiness cases which allow for documenting this evidence in a structured and systematic way. Our trustworthiness cases will guide the system development process toward evidence-based assurance of trustworthiness. Trustworthiness cases are based on assurance cases that have been successfully applied in safety- and security-related systems.

13.1 Motivation

The idea of creating trustworthiness cases is based on the creation of assurance cases for certification. *Certification* generally refers to the process of assuring that a product (e.g. a system) or a process has certain specified properties, which are then recorded in a certificate (National Research Council et al., 2007). In accordance to that, *assurance* is defined as justified confidence in a property of interest, and an *assurance case* attempts to demonstrate that sufficient assurance has been achieved (Hawkins et al., 2013). Assurance cases have long been established in the safety domain, where they are called safety cases (although they are not restricted to that domain). The task of a *safety case* is to communicate a clear, comprehensible and defensible argument that a system is acceptably safe to operate in a particular context (Kelly, 1998). The explicit presentation of the argument is fundamental, since it is used to demonstrate why the reader should conclude that a system is acceptably safe from the evidence available. For presentation, the Goal Structuring Notation (GSN) (GSN Working Group, 2011) is frequently used.

---

[1]This chapter partially adapts Gol Mohammadi et al. (2018b) © Springer Nature Switzerland AG 2018, and Di Cerbo et al. (2015) © Springer International Publishing Switzerland 2015, with the permission of the publishers.

© Springer Fachmedien Wiesbaden GmbH, part of Springer Nature 2019
N. Gol Mohammadi, *Trustworthy Cyber-Physical Systems*,
https://doi.org/10.1007/978-3-658-27488-7_13

The task of the *trustworthiness cases* that we introduce in this chapter is to communicate a clear, comprehensible and defensible argument that a system is acceptably *trustworthy* to operate in a particular context. For presentation of our trustworthiness cases, we also use GSN. However, we need to extend the notation of GSN.

Our contribution in this chapter not only consists in the trustworthiness cases that we suggest. In previous chapters, we developed methods which support the development of a trustworthy system, i.e. *trustworthiness-by-design* (cf. Chapter 6). An important characteristic of these methods and techniques is that they do not prescribe a certain development process. They can be combined with any development process. Therefore, as a further contribution, we show how our trustworthiness-by-design methods can be used to generate the artefacts that are required for documentation in trustworthiness cases. Thus, our co-development approach supports evidence collection in different phases of the development process. This allows for guiding developers in building the to-be-expected trustworthiness, and thus to steer and manage development activities and correspondingly focus necessary efforts towards satisfying trustworthiness goals.

The remainder of this chapter is structured as follows. In Section 13.2, we describe our trustworthiness cases and the artefacts that are required for documentation. In Section 13.3, we illustrate the creation of trustworthiness cases using the AAL case study (cf. Chapter 5). In Section 13.4, we present and discuss related work. In Section 13.5, we finally draw conclusions.

13.2 Trustworthiness Cases

Assessing a development process and the resulting system to identify its intrinsic qualities is not a trivial task. An assessment methodology must take into account multiple aspects and factors at the same time: some indications may come from an analysis starting from an observation of the activities conducted by developers, like for instance to assess whether risk assessment has been systematically conducted. Others may come from the generated developed system artefacts, for example, the measured availability of a service is 99.9% within a certain time frame. Therefore, the selection of the target for the assessment can be a complex task. For assessing a specific quality, typically two types of targets are defined: 1) definition of the target for the system under assessment and 2) definition of the target for the performed development activities.

In case of trustworthiness assessment, we also consider two types of targets: 1) trustworthiness goals or trustworthiness requirements that the system under development should satisfy in order to be trustworthy, 2) execution of certain trustworthiness enabling activities. The latter does not only have to be assessed with respect to whether they have been performed at all, but also how well they have been performed. However, defining product or process metrics is not the focus of this chapter. In Chapter 10, we focused on these aspects, but here, using trustworthiness cases, we aim at documenting the evidence that is produced during the development life cycle. Yet, both, product and process metrics, can be used to support the trustworthiness argument.

Evidence is presented by system providers or developers, and is verified by an evaluator. In the Common Criteria (CC), evidence is defined as "anything" that can prove the compliance with a mandatory CC requirement: evidence generally consists of documents, interviews as well as statements made by evaluators during the assessment (ISO/IEC 15408-1, 2009). We adopt this definition of evidence in our trustworthiness cases. Performed development activities and observable trustworthiness properties of the system that are objectively measurable may serve as trustworthiness evidence.

In the following, we first describe the conceptual model of our trustworthiness cases. Then, we describe how a trustworthy-by-design development process (which uses the methods that we developed in previous chapters) can be aligned with the process of documenting trustworthiness cases.

13.2.1 The Conceptual Model for Trustworthiness Cases

Figure 13.1 shows the conceptual model of a trustworthiness case. We developed the conceptual model based on the highly accepted assurance cases (Hawkins et al., 2013) and safety cases (Kelly, 1998). In this subsection, we briefly describe the core elements and their relations. A detailed explanation will follow in the next subsection.

The *trustworthiness goals and requirements* (describing the trustworthiness properties the system should possess) represent the target. The trustworthiness requirements must be addressed to assure the trustworthiness of the system under consideration. The *trustworthiness argument* logically states and convincingly demonstrates how and why trustworthiness requirements are met (by evidence). *Trustworthiness evidence* is information from the trustworthiness-by-design development process. This information supports the trustworthiness argument in order to demonstrate that the target is met. The *context* provides the basis for the whole trustworthiness case. We differentiate between two types of context: development process context and system context. The context of the development process includes facts and justifications about the performed development activities and the generated artefacts. The system context includes the general facts and assumptions about the system's (i.e. the CPS's) physical environment. We

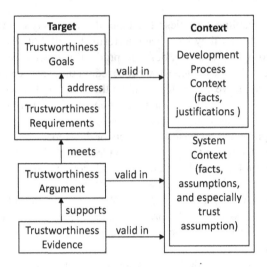

Figure 13.1: Conceptual model of Trustworthiness Cases (Gol Mohammadi et al., 2018b)

define trust assumptions as part of the system context information that should be included in trustworthiness cases, since the trustworthiness case will only be valid by consideration of the made trust assumptions.

For representing trustworthiness cases, we suggest using the GSN which is also used for assurance and safety cases. The notation is shown in Figure 13.3. The purpose of the modelled goal structure is to show how goals (claims about the system) are broken down into subgoals, until eventually they can be supported by evidence (solutions). As part of this structure, the strategies (that are adopted for assuring that a goal is met) may be modelled as well, just as the rationale (assumptions and justifications) and the context in which the goals are stated. In order to be able to model trust assumptions explicitly, we extend GSN with a corresponding modelling element (TA that stands for trust assumption) as shown in Figure 13.3. Examples related to trust assumptions will be presented in Section 13.3.

13.2.2 Approach for Co-developing the CPS and its Trustworthiness Cases

The amount and diversity of the information that flow into trustworthiness cases are high. As depicted in Figure 13.2, we present an approach for co-developing trustworthiness cases and the CPS.

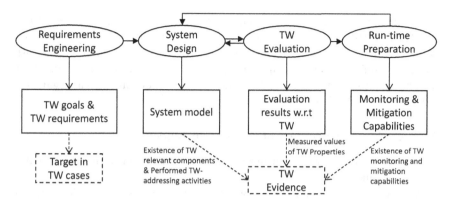

Figure 13.2: Co-development of trustworthiness cases with the development process (Gol Mohammadi et al., 2018b)

Requirements Engineering:

A requirements engineering (RE) process must lead to a list of trustworthiness goals and requirements which can be included in the trustworthiness cases as target.

As an example of such an RE process, we have developed two RE methods: one method that supports the elicitation and documentation of trustworthiness requirements using goal and business process models (cf. Chapter 7) and another method that is problem-based and supports the systematic derivation of trustworthiness requirements from end-users' trust concerns (cf. Chapter 9).

System Design:

The system design phase must lead to a system model. The system model must address the trustworthiness requirements (resulting from the RE phase).

Any design process can be selected to build the system model of the CPS. We recommend using a model-based method, since such a method will result in a system model. A further benefit of a model-based method is that model-based risk assessment approaches towards trustworthiness can then be used as well.

In Chapter 6, we have described a collection of methodologies, patterns, and practices which can be applied in order to achieve that the system under design is trustworthy. These trustworthiness-by-design methodologies ensure that trustworthiness is at the core of the software engineering practices so that the entire system and its individual components (standalone or chained) have high levels of trustworthiness through the implementation and maintenance of trustworthiness properties in the design process. The trustworthiness-by-design best practices can be adopted by any project. For example, risk-based design (Surridge et al., 2013; Lund et al., 2010) can be employed, and the result of this risk-based system design is the system model. The mitigation controls to block threats compromising trustworthiness (cf. Chapter 11) can be documented as evidence (solutions in GSN), and the use of such methods and best practices can be documented as arguments (strategies in GSN) in the trustworthiness cases.

Trustworthiness Evaluation of the System Model:

The trustworthiness evaluation must lead to an evaluation result that includes measured values of trustworthiness properties for the CPS.

As an example of such methods, we have developed the method described in Chapter 10 and its extension in Chapter 11.

However, other trustworthiness evaluation methods can be used as well in this step, e.g the method of Han (2018) that focuses on trustworthiness measurement for workflow management systems.

The result of the trustworthiness evaluation can be documented as evidence (solutions in GSN), and the use of trustworthiness evaluation methods can be documented as arguments (strategy in GSN) in the trustworthiness cases.

Preparation for Run-time Trustworthiness Maintenance:

Maintaining trustworthiness at run-time is a critical task in order to identify issues that could negatively affect the trustworthiness of the CPS. To this end, monitoring and mitigation capabilities for the CPS must be provided. Including these capabilities and interfaces for monitoring and adaptation might change the system model. In Chapter 12, we propose business processes for monitoring, measuring, and managing trustworthiness, as well as mitigating trustworthiness issues at run-time. In Chapter 12, we provide a reference architecture for trustworthiness maintenance systems. When this reference architecture is realized, trustworthiness maintenance capabilities for monitoring and managing the CPS's trustworthiness properties in order to preserve the overall established trustworthiness during runtime exist. Hence, these capabilities and artefacts that realize such a solution can be documented as evidence (solutions in GSN), and the practices leading to such monitoring and maintenance capabilities are valid arguments (strategies in GSN) in trustworthiness cases.

13.3 Application Example

This section demonstrates our approach of documenting trustworthiness cases in a development process that uses the trustworthy-by-design methods (cf. Chapter 6) that we developed. To illustrate the application of trustworthiness cases, we use again the AAL case study from Chapter 5 and the scenario used in Chapter 7.

In the following, we show some simplified trustworthiness cases for the AAL case study in the form of GSN diagrams. To recapitulate, there is the following mapping between the elements of our trustworthiness cases and GSN elements: trustworthiness goals and trustworthiness requirements map to GSN goals, trustworthiness evidence maps to GSN solutions, and trustworthiness arguments map to GSN strategies.

Figure 13.3 shows the top tier of the trustworthiness case for the AAL system. It starts with the top-level trustworthiness goal for the whole AAL system (i.e. the trustworthiness vector for the AAL system) and shows how this goal is achieved by a defensible trustworthiness argument. The high-level goal in this trustworthiness case is "AAL is trustworthy", which is refined into the two strategies "All TW goals are satisfied" and "All threats to TW are blocked". These strategies will assure that the "AAL is trustworthy" goal is met.

The strategy "All TW goals are satisfied" is solved by the solution "TW-by-design practices are performed". Figure 13.3 also illustrates the contributing factors to the trustworthiness of an AAL system. The "physical environment" has no impact on this level of abstraction, and therefore context information regarding the system context is not modelled. Yet, context information regarding the development process has to be considered. The context information related to the strategy "All TW goals are satisfied" is, that an appropriate requirements engineering method has been performed and the result of the requirements engineering method is a list of trustworthiness goals (and, to be specific, the trustworthiness requirements). Hence, the GSN model in Figure 13.3 documents that the strategy "All TW goals are satisfied" is valid in the context that "TW goals are identified and listed in Tab. 1". Please note that here Tab. 1 is simply a fictitious reference to a table where the trustworthiness goals are listed. Due to space limitations, we do not provide a trustworthiness requirements specification. The strategy "All threats to TW are blocked" can be assured, for example, by using risk assessment approaches. This is modelled as the substrategy "Risk assessment analyses are performed". This substrategy is solved by performing the "CORAS" risk assessment methodology (see Lund et al. (2010) for details on CORAS). The context information related to "All threats to TW are blocked" is that there is a list of "Identified threats against trustworthiness".

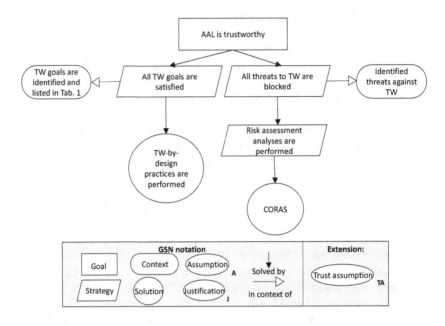

Figure 13.3: Trustworthiness case for entire AAL (Gol Mohammadi et al., 2018b)

In Figures 13.4 and 13.5, we present a breakdown of the abstract trustworthiness case goal presented in Figure 13.3. Since the latter is a vector of trustworthiness properties, we can break it down into these properties (e.g. reliability, usability, etc.). The trustworthiness properties can be assigned to relevant parts of the CPS, and each part can then be analyzed with respect to the trustworthiness properties from the vector that is relevant for that part. This trustworthiness goal breakdown structure represents the argument that is implicit in a trustworthiness refinement process. Specifically, it shows how the claims entailed by trustworthiness requirements can be developed and linked to the supporting evidence produced from the specified trustworthiness evaluation methods.

Figure 13.4 depicts the trustworthiness case for the trustworthiness property reliability of the AAL system. The goal "Reliability TW property is satisfied by AAL" is refined into three strategies: "Availability of emergency services", "Redundant sensors for incident detection", and "Correctness of medical treatments via service". As mentioned in the last section, it is important that, additionally to the context information regarding the development process, the operational or physical environment of the AAL is considered as well. Therefore, we documented

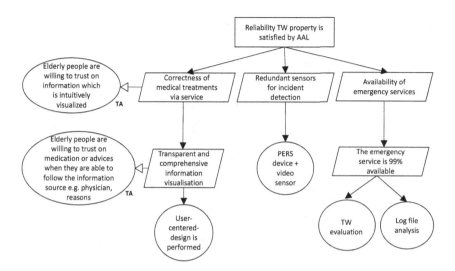

Figure 13.4: Trustworthiness case for TW property reliability (Gol Mohammadi et al., 2018b)

a trust assumption as contributing factor to the strategy "Correctness of medical treatments via service". The elderly persons' perception of correctness is dependent on intuitively visualized treatment information.

The strategy "Redundant sensors for incident detection" is solved by "PERS + video sensor" as solution. This solution for the strategy shows how the trustworthiness case is co-developed with the AAL, because the design decision of adding an additional sensor is only made in order to increase the reliability of the AAL in case of incidents.

The strategy "Availability of emergency services" is refined to the substrategy "The emergency service is available in 99% of the time". This can be assessed by conventional verification techniques such as testing or with the presented techniques in this book (cf. Chapters 10 and 12). Therefore, this substrategy is solved by "Trustworthiness evaluation" and "Log file analysis". The result of trustworthiness evaluation is, for example, that the service is available during 99.9% of the time.

Figure 13.5 shows the trustworthiness case for the trustworthiness property usability. The goal "Usability TW property is satisfied by AAL" is refined into three strategies that assure that this goal is met. These three strategies are: "Learnability", "Ease of use", and "Functioning indicators". For functioning indication, it is assumed that the elderly persons are willing to trust when they see explicit indica-

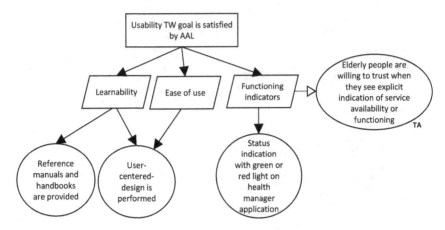

Figure 13.5: Trustworthiness case for TW property usability (Gol Mohammadi et al., 2018b)

tions of service availability or functioning. This should, for example, be realized in the *Health Manager* application. These three strategies are solved by having reference manuals and handbooks, performing user-centred design, and including status indication with color code.

13.4 Related Work

We analyzed related work from two perspectives: first, with regard to trustworthiness cases and, second, with regard to trustworthiness certification.

Trustworthiness cases are based on assurance and safety cases. Regarding assurance and safety cases, a lot of literature can be found. However, to the best of our knowledge, there are no existing approaches that define trustworthiness as a vector of trustworthiness properties (as we do) and create trustworthiness cases to demonstrate that a system is trustworthy. Nevertheless, we provide a short overview of important related work in the field of assurance and safety cases. Since assurance is defined as justified confidence in a property of interest (Hawkins and Kelly (2010a); Hawkins and Kelly (2010b); Hawkins et al. (2013)), assurance cases are not restricted to a specific property and are thus more general. In contrast, safety cases focus on one property, namely safety. However, the use of assurance cases is not restricted to the safety domain. They are also used in the security domain (Bloomfield et al., 2007; Weinstock et al., 2007; Patu and Yamamoto, 2013) and in general for software-based systems (Bloomfield and Bishop, 2010; Graydon et al., 2007).

Software certification can be used as a means to prove certain software product properties to potential consumers. There have been some efforts to automate the certification process, e.g. Lotz et al. (2012); Anisetti et al. (2016); Krotsiani et al. (2018), to facilitate the adoption of these processes in service-oriented environments. Kaluvuri et al. propose the concept of descriptive digital certification that can capture information emanating from the certification process. This conceptual model has been realized by an XML-based approach (Kaluvuri et al., 2013). The digital certificate contains information regarding the system that is being certified in a structured and machine-processable manner, thus providing transparency regarding the service architecture and implementation as well as its execution environment. However, in the above-mentioned works, the digital certificate concept is based on security certification schemes such as Common Criteria and, hence, have been used towards certification of security properties. Di Cerbo et al. (2014) extend the concept of digital certificate in order to certify the trustworthiness of software. Their trustworthiness digital certification concept provides a data structure for capturing the information emanating from certification processes and, thus, does not prescribe the content of the certifications. Di Cerbo et al. realize the concept of trustworthiness digital certificate using linked data vocabulary. In another paper (Di Cerbo et al., 2015), we propose an evidence-based trustworthiness approach through a controlled software development process. Similar to our method in this chapter, the intention is to collect evidence for trustworthiness. However, in that paper we did not aim at systematic generation and documentation of the evidence throughout the whole life cycle. Furthermore, the focus of that work is on evidence collected from coding, deployment, and operation phase.

All the above-mentioned approaches support post-design evaluation. Our trustworthiness cases cover the evidence generation and documentation in a co-development manner and cover the whole software development life cycle. They provide the content to the above-mentioned digital trustworthiness certificates, which - so far - do not include all the information that is provided in our trustworthiness cases.

13.5 Contribution and Summary of this Chapter

We have developed a new approach for assuring and documenting trustworthiness of cyber-physical systems in an evidence-based manner. We propose the co-development of trustworthiness cases along with the development of the CPS. Evidence that is documented in the trustworthiness cases is either product-oriented or process-oriented. Process-oriented evidence consists of the performed practices to build trustworthiness into the core of the CPS, e.g. by using a risk management method like the one presented in Chapter 11. Product-oriented evidence includes the quantitatively evaluated results of trustworthiness metrics for a component or other types of qualitative evidence. The benefit of trustworthiness cases is that they provide well-structured arguments and evidence. We have applied our approach in limited use cases and demonstrated its usefulness.

Part III

Achievements of the Book

14 Conclusions and Outlook

In this chapter, we conclude the work by summarizing our contributions. This chapter also discusses the book with respect to the specified research questions from Chapter 1. Furthermore, we revisit the requirements for the TW-Man (trustworthiness management) framework (presented in Chapter 3) and show how these are met. Finally, we provide an outlook on how further research could be pursued.

14.1 Summary of Contributions and Lessons Learned

In this book, we focused on Internet-based cyber-physical systems. CPS comprise individuals and organizations as well as software and hardware components, are distributed and connected via the Internet. The adoption and acceptance of cyber-physical systems by end-users are dependent on whether users have trust in these systems (Broy et al., 2012; Lotz et al., 2012). Hence, trustworthiness is a key concern that needs to be fostered and even engineered into these systems to maintain high levels of trust within society. Consequently, in this book, we aimed at providing necessary methods that support building trustworthiness into such systems.

First, we derived a definition of trust based on provided definitions by other researchers and extended it to include CPS. We defined trust as: "a bet about the future contingent actions of others, be they individuals or groups of individuals, or entire cyber-physical systems". Given our definition of trust, we argued that while trust is an act carried out by a person, trustworthiness is a quality of the system that has the potential to influence the trust this person has in the system in a positive way. CPS should exhibit objective properties to increase the confidence of their users that placing trust in the CPS will lead to an expected outcome.

We performed a systematic literature review to provide a common understanding on trustworthiness and provided a collection of trustworthiness attributes. A trustworthiness attribute is a property of the system that indicates its capability to prevent potential threats to cause an unexpected and undesired outcome. In other words, a CPS can be considered worthy of stakeholders' trust if it provides confidence in satisfying a set of relevant trustworthiness requirements.

© Springer Fachmedien Wiesbaden GmbH, part of Springer Nature 2019
N. Gol Mohammadi, *Trustworthy Cyber-Physical Systems*,
https://doi.org/10.1007/978-3-658-27488-7_14

To address trustworthiness in CPS, we identified key concepts and abstractions to address trustworthiness in cyber-physical systems regardless of the choice of development methodology. This enables designers to understand how to address trustworthiness. Specifically, with providing a collection of trustworthiness attributes as generic concepts, the provided methods can be used in a reusable and flexible manner. We defined a trustworthiness-by-design process using trustworthiness capability patterns that allows building CPS, while providing and documenting evidence about their trustworthiness. These methods can be used independently of each other. These methods involve:

1. Trustworthiness Requirements Analysis Methods: The trustworthiness requirements specification starts with high-level trust concerns which are refined to lower level trustworthiness properties on components of the cyber-physical systems.

2. Trustworthiness Evaluation Methods: We provided design-time trustworthiness evaluation methods for evaluating the overall trustworthiness of a CPS. The first method uses a computational approach to quantify the end-to-end trustworthiness (E2E TW Evaluation). The second method considers risks versus trustworthiness of a CPS and suggests controls to mitigate the corresponding threats. We enhanced our E2E TW Evaluation method by combining it with the risk-assessment method. However, each one of the methods can also be used also in isolation.

3. Run-time Trustworthiness Maintenance: We argued that trust relationships should be monitored in order to re-evaluate trustworthiness properties at run-time. For achieving this aim, a CPS should be delivered with the capabilities to monitor and maintain trustworthiness properties when the CPS is in operation. For this reason, we provided a reference architecture and the processes to develop such a run-time trustworthiness maintenance capability.

4. Co-development of Trustworthiness Cases: Based on the concept of the well-established assurance cases, we provided an evidence-based trustworthiness assurance. Trustworthiness cases can be used to ascertain whether the related trustworthiness artefacts are put in place, and they document these as evidence in a systematic and structured manner.

Figure 14.1 depicts how the methods provided in the TW-Man framework can contribute to the development lifecycle of a CPS.

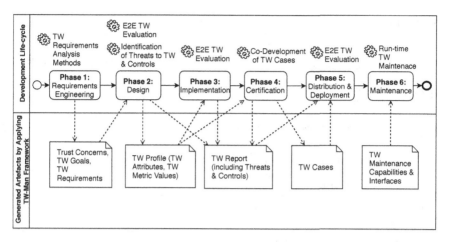

Figure 14.1: Our contribution along the development lifecycle of a CPS

14.2 Answers to the Research Questions

In this section, we address each research question identified in Chapter 1 and provide an answer to each demonstrating how the book contributed to exploring possible solutions. Table 14.1 gives a brief overview of research questions and contributions of the book.

RQ1: What are the contributing characteristics that can foster trustworthiness in cyber-physical systems? Is there any classification of these characteristics in the state of the art?

Answer to RQ1: To identify characteristics that foster trustworthiness, we performed a systematic literature review. No coherent classification of characteristics contributing to the trustworthiness of CPS could be identified. Furthermore, a collection of characteristics which need to be addressed and built into a CPS for being trustworthy could not be observed. In a literature review to define trustworthiness, we created a collection of trustworthiness attributes and a classification of these into different quality categories (cf. Chapter 4). Our collection of trustworthiness attributes can be used as a generic concept of trustworthiness and can be interpreted as generic trustworthiness requirements on a system-to-be-developed. Additionally, this collection enables developers to use the methods presented in this book (TW-Man framework) independently of each other. We discussed the relation of our trustworthiness attribute collection to other quality models used in literature.

Table 14.1: Contributions of this book to the research questions

Contributions of this book	RQ1	RQ2	RQ3	RQ4	RQ5	RQ6
Chapter 4: A Survey on Trustworthiness Attributes for CPS	✓					
Chapter 6: Trustworthiness-by-design (TWbyD)		✓				
Chapter 7: Systematic Refinement of Trustworthiness Requirements using Goal and Business Process Models			✓			
Chapter 8: Patterns for Documenting Trustworthiness			✓			
Chapter 9: Problem-based Derivation of Trustworthiness Requirements from Users' Trust Concerns			✓			
Chapter 10: Computational Approach towards End-to-End Trustworthiness Evaluation				✓		
Chapter 11: Enhancing Trustworthiness Evaluation with Risk Assessment				✓		
Chapter 12: Maintenance of Trustworthiness in a CPS and Preparation for Run-Time					✓	
Chapter 13: Evidence-based Trustworthiness and Preparation for the Certification						✓

RQ1: What are the contributing characteristics that can foster trustworthiness in cyber-physical systems? Is there any classification of these characteristics in the state of the art?

RQ2: Are the existing development processes appropriate in addressing trust and trustworthiness in the system under development? What are the gaps in these development processes and how can they be addressed?

RQ3: How to elicit the end-users' trust concerns? How can trustworthiness requirement analysis be performed in a way that is uniform and in conformance with the trust concerns of the end-users?

RQ4: Which evaluation methods can be used and extended so that they support the developers in the evaluation of the achieved trustworthiness?

RQ5: Do design-time activities suffice in guaranteeing trustworthiness? If not, which activities for run-time preparation are necessary?

RQ6: How can we generate and document evidence for the trustworthiness of the system under development throughout its lifecycle (design-time and run-time) in a systematic way and in alignment with the documentation demands of certification processes?

RQ2: Are the existing development processes appropriate in addressing trust and trustworthiness in the system under development? What are the gaps in these development processes and how can they be addressed?

Answer to RQ2: As another state of the art analysis, we analyzed development methodologies for addressing trustworthiness attributes (cf. Chapter 6). We considered also methodologies and best practices used by our industrial partners from the OPTET project in our analysis. We found out that none of them fully assures or addresses the development of a trustworthy CPS. Most of the existing development methodologies persued a one-dimensional approach, e.g. focus mainly on security or privacy. Consequently, we developed individual activities, so-called "trustworthiness-by-design (TWbyD) methodologies" (see Chapters 7 to 13) and provided support for incorporating them into development processes using the concept of capability patterns.

We provided six "trustworthiness capability patterns" that can be used in the different phases of a development process to objectively target building trustworthiness attributes into the core of a CPS. Furthermore, we provided guidance how these trustworthiness capability patterns can be tailored to the development process, i.e. in which phases which of these trustworthiness capability patterns can be adopted by the development team.

RQ3: How to elicit the end-users' trust concerns? How can trustworthiness requirements analysis be performed in a way that is uniform and in conformance with the trust concerns of the end-users?

Answer to RQ3: We addressed this research question in our two RE methods described in Chapter 7 and Chapter 9. We provided two alternative requirements engineering methods for the systematic derivation and refinement of trustworthiness requirements from trust concerns. We decided to provide two different RE methods since they are targeting two major RE communities (requirements engineers working with problem-based RE and requirements engineers who prefer goal and business process models). In this way, we provided support for both groups. In both methods, trust concerns are mapped to model elements and documented in a traceable way.

In addition to our requirements engineering methods for elicitation and refinement of trustworthiness requirements, we proposed two patterns (cf. Chapter 8): 1) trust concern identification pattern, and 2) trustworthiness requirement pattern. Our proposed pattern format follows the general guidelines that are suggested by the pattern community (Buschmann et al., 2007). The patterns are easy to learn, promote reuse, reduce ambiguities and avoid the lack of information related to trustworthiness. They are comprehensible to all stakeholders and maintain traceability between different model elements relevant for trustworthiness.

RQ4: Which evaluation methods can be used and extended so that they support the developers in the evaluation of the achieved trustworthiness?

Answer to RQ4: We proposed a method (cf. Chapter 10) that uses defined metrics to quantify trustworthiness properties and to evaluate the end-to-end trustworthiness of a CPS. We enhanced our computational evaluation method by combining it with a risk assessment approach (cf. Chapter 11). Therein, we first identify threats to trustworthiness and possible mitigating controls based on a system model. Then, the designer can evaluate the new configuration (including controls) and analyze the added value (trustworthiness value gained with the controls). To reason that a selected control acceptably mitigates the threats to trustworthiness, different possible configurations can be compared and documented as evidence. Hence, the controls for mitigating a threat and the implementation of controls can be compared by providing a comparative trustworthiness value. In our design-time trustworthiness evaluation, we took the system structure as well as the trustworthiness metric types into account. The result of the trustworthiness evaluation is documented either as a trustworthiness profile (for an asset) or as a trustworthiness report (for a system configuration). Both of these artefacts can be used to support making informed design decisions.

RQ5: Do design-time activities suffice in guaranteeing trustworthiness? If not, which activities for run-time preparation are necessary?

Answer to RQ5: For assuring the trustworthiness of a CPS, only design-time activities are not sufficient. This is because of various changes or issues that might happen in CPS or in its environment which affect trustworthiness. Therefore, we provided key concepts for addressing run-time trustworthiness issues. For trustworthiness maintenance during run-time, we provided a reference architecture which should be realized and delivered with the CPS (cf. Chapter 12). Moreover, we defined monitoring, management and mitigation processes to identify active threats to trustworthiness and managing and mitigating these threats. The reference architecture and the processes we developed guide CPS providers in realizing run-time maintenance.

RQ6: How can we generate and document evidence for the trustworthiness of the system under development throughout its lifecycle (design-time and run-time) in a systematic way and in alignment with the documentation demands of certification processes?

Answer to RQ6: In Chapter 13, we proposed the concept of trustworthiness cases and showed how the co-development of a CPS with its trustworthiness cases facilitates the documentation of all types of evidence generated by trustworthiness-by-design methodologies in a structured and systematic way. Considering evidence as objective elements generated during the trustworthiness-by-design methodologies makes it possible to demonstrate the arguments made on the trustworthiness of a product. These elements become evidences, i.e. elements able to provide assurance about a specific trustworthiness property. This concept is used in certification, where it is the cornerstone for supporting certificate claims. Therefore, with documenting these evidences in the form of trustworthiness cases we support the evidence-based trustworthiness of cyber-physical systems.

We illustrated the application of all of our proposed solutions using a case study. However, most of these methods have also been applied to at least one additional case study from the OPTET project. All these contributions are gathered and provided in the TW-Man framework.

In Chapter 3, we specified the requirements on the TW-Man framework based on a state of the art analysis. Moreover, these requirements were based on the research questions. Table 14.2 summarizes how the TW-Man framework meets its requirements.

To Address REQ1: We developed a well-structured method for the management of the development process of a trustworthy CPS. Trustworthiness-by-design allows a constructive, transparent, and traceable trustworthiness establishment. It includes best practices and methods for building trustworthiness into a CPS. Furthermore, it leaves enough flexibility and freedom to the development team in their choice of development methodology. We defined our trustworthiness-by-design methodologies based on the SPEM[1] (software process engineering meta-model). We also described how by means of the EPF[2] (Eclipse process framework) we could provide tool support. Thereby, a traceable and transparent process can be generated.

To Address REQ2: We developed two clear and well-defined methods for specifying trustworthiness requirements, i.e. two alternative trustworthiness requirements elicitation and modelling approaches. Different modelling techniques are used to allow the documentation of trustworthiness. Furthermore, we provided two patterns

---

[1]SPEM is used to define software and systems development processes and their components. http://www.omg.org/spec/SPEM/2.0/ (accessed on 17 August 2018)

[2]Eclipse Foundation: Eclipse Process Framework, https://www.eclipse.org/epf/ (accessed on 23 July 2018)

for supporting the requirement engineer in systematically identifying trust concerns and documenting trustworthiness requirements.

Table 14.2: Requirements for the TW-Man framework revisited

Part of TW-Man Framework	REQ1	REQ2	REQ3	REQ4	REQ5
Trustworthiness-by-design methodology	✓				
TW Requirements Refinement Method using Goal and Business Process Models		✓			
Documentation Pattern for Trust Concerns and Trustworthiness Requirements		✓			
Problem-based TW Refinement Method		✓			
End-to-End Trustworthiness Evaluation Enhanced with Risk Assessment			✓		
Run-Time Trustworthiness Maintenance				✓	
Trustworthiness Cases					✓

REQ1: A well-structured method is required for the management of the development process of a trustworthy CPS. This method should allow a constructive, transparent, and traceable trustworthiness establishment. It should include best practices and patterns for building trustworthiness into CPS.

REQ2: A clear and well-defined method is required for specifying trustworthiness requirements, i.e. a trustworthiness requirements elicitation and modelling approach. This modelling should also be expressive enough to allow the documentation of trustworthiness that requires a diverse combination of trustworthiness goals. These trustworthiness goals help later on to evaluate whether the required trustworthiness properties are obtained.

REQ3: An approach should be provided that supports the design-time evaluation of the achieved trustworthiness. The TW-Man framework should provide facilities for assessing trustworthiness properties of systems under development. The trustworthiness evaluation approach should provide the means to collect evidence for trustworthiness (e.g. information on implemented security mechanisms and performed privacy impact assessments).

REQ4: A method for considering the trustworthiness during run-time is required. This approach should support integrating some run-time trustworthiness maintenance capabilities into CPS, i.e. designing a supplementary monitoring and control system that updates the current state of trustworthiness properties to maintain the overall trustworthiness of the system. The trustworthiness evaluation approach should support discovering and eliminating unwanted situations that may happen during run-time.

REQ5: A systematic method is needed for generating and documenting evidence for trustworthiness of the system under development. The collection of evidence should take place throughout the whole development lifecycle in alignment with the documentation needs of certification processes.

To Address REQ3: We provided two complementary methods that support the design-time evaluation of the achieved trustworthiness. The TW-Man framework includes both of them to facilitate assessing trustworthiness properties of systems under development. The computational trustworthiness evaluation method is enhanced with a risk assessment technique to support discovering and mitigating the threats. The trustworthiness evaluation method provides input as evidence in trustworthiness cases.

To Address REQ4: A reference architecture and the necessary processes for considering the trustworthiness during run-time are provided in the TW-Man framework.

To Address REQ5: We provided a systematic method for generating and documenting evidence for trustworthiness of the system under development. The collection of evidence could be done throughout the whole development lifecycle, following our proposed co-development of a CPS and its trustworthiness cases.

14.3 Outlook on Future Research

Beyond the issues that have been addressed in the context of this book, there are still aspects for further research. This further research can extend in different directions as pointed out below.

Further User Experiments and Industrial Application. Similar to other approaches and developed concepts in research, there is the following general limitation: even though the developed methods were applied in case studies, there is no guarantee for an industrial success. One reason is that for a successful adoption by industrial practitioners the developed methods not only need to be applicable from a conceptual, theoretical point of view, demonstrated by use case studies and small-scale experiments. Their usability needs to be demonstrated by lager experiments with the participation of developers from industry.

Though we applied the TW-Man framework on real-life case studies from the OPTET project, the TW-Man framework was mostly developed and applied in a scientific context. In future work, the methods of the TW-Man framework could be applied in an industrial setting. Only in a realistic industrial setting with industrial practitioners, the applicability of the TW-Man framework can be evaluated. Using the results of such experiments, it can be further investigated what additional artefacts can be generated by the TW-Man framework to enhance the trustworthiness of the CPS under development. Such artefacts may also be generated by extending the TW-Man framework with new methods and artefacts.

It could also be interesting to investigate how the methods could be made more light-weight to better support agile development methodologies.

Furthermore, large-scale user experiments can address any remaining perceived trustworthiness issues. As has been introduced in Chapter 4, an area for future exploration includes the issue of reflecting operational trustworthiness attributes with the perceived trustworthiness attributes. It could be further analyzed what is the correlation between perceived and operational trustworthiness attributes and how operational trustworthiness attributes can be reflected with perceived trustworthiness attributes.

Extension of End-to-End Trustworthiness Evaluation and Trustworthiness Metric Definitions. In the End-to-End Trustworthiness Evaluation approach (presented in Chapter 10), we employ trustworthiness metrics for determining the overall trustworthiness of a CPS. However, the prototype described in Chapter 10 does not yet support all kinds of trustworthiness metrics. The end-to-end metric creation needs to be further extended to cover further metric types. In particular, the use of the specific metric tool and the trustworthy service marketplace were also assumptions we made. The detailed limitations of our approach are described in Section 10.7. The problems discussed may be handled by an appropriate definition and choice of trustworthiness metrics and end-to-end metric composition. In other words, re-classification and extension of trustworthiness metric types would allow for a more scalable formula composition.

For trustworthiness metrics, it is necessary to set targets, measure progress, and identify the best possible investment by, for example, using ROI (return on investment) calculations. While this book provided a collection of trustworthiness attributes that foster trustworthiness of a CPS, it did not focus on identifying trustworthiness metrics that could be appropriately applied. Such metrics require further analysis and study. For defining meaningful and expressive trustworthiness metrics the Goal-Question-Metric (GQM) (Basili and Rombach, 1988; Herrmann, 2007) may, for example, be applied.

Extending Capabilities of Run-Time Maintenance. In our run-time trustworthiness maintenance approach, we used techniques like complex event processing for monitoring and analyzing the current status of trustworthiness properties. However, this information could also be documented to create a run-time system model. The concept of run-time system models and updating these models during the run-time is an important piece of knowledge when conducting a proper risk analysis. In this context, a question to be answered is what changes might occur when the environment as well as the CPS itself changes and how these changes can be modelled. Another important question is what information a run-time system model needs to include. This is an open research problem related to risk assessment during run-time. In order to adequately trigger risk assessment during run-time, there is a need for a rich run-time model.

With respect to run-time maintenance, the integration of evidence-based trustworthiness management and policy-based enforcement is an obvious challenge. Here, it would be interesting to develop approaches which support the evaluation of trustworthiness of certificates that are capable of assessing the provided evidence. Furthermore, it is an important challenge to develop approaches that enforce the trustworthiness. To this end, one could extend the usage of sticky policies for enforcement of trustworthiness properties. However, not all of the trustworthiness attributes can be formulated in the form of a sticky policy. Further investigation is necessary to find out how sticky policies can be extended to cover all relevant trustworthiness attributes, e.g. data related qualities, privacy and security. It is planned that some of the above mentioned points are investigated as part of the EU Horizon 2020 project RestAssured[3] .

Knowledge Transfer to Social Media Applications. It is interesting to transfer the concepts that have been proposed for trustworthiness to social media applications. In social media systems, not only the trustworthiness of the system but also users and provided content (e.g. shared posts, news items) must be considered. In this work, we considered the established trust between a CPS and its end-users, but in social media applications this should be extended: from an end-user, to the application, to another end-user. Similar to the ambient assisted living system, it could be investigated which trustworthiness attributes need to be considered for a trustworthy social media application. A further extension of the work presented in this book could be the evaluation of the proposed methods in social media networks. Therein, the assessment of the provided trustworthiness properties (either operational or perceived trustworthiness) and the evaluation of the risk attitude of users in social media networks seems to be challenging.

Developing Further Trustworthiness Capability Patterns and Trustworthiness Design Patterns. The tool support of the provided trustworthiness capability patterns could be enhanced, and further trustworthiness capability patterns could be provided. As the tool support for the methods of the TW-Man framework consists so far of research prototypes, it can be further extended and improved, especially concerning its usability. As a consequence, the developers will benefit more from our methods.

One can also provide further design and architectural patterns. This would be especially helpful as design solutions. An analysis of alternative patterns would

---

[3]RestAssured project is funded by the EU's Horizon 2020 research and innovation programme under grant agreement 731678. `https://restassuredh2020.eu` (accessed on 10 August 2018)

also be important in order to further evaluate a rational choice of the level of trust-worthiness. A collection of design patterns could be provided to developers. Using this collection, the developers are supported in realizing trustworthiness attributes of a CPS under development. It would be necessary to analyze existing methods for architectural design with respect to their suitability for being extended with trustworthiness-related issues. TW requirements must be realized in the subsequent development phases and it has to be visible for the users how their trust concerns have been addressed during the entire development process. Therefore, it is valu-able knowledge to focus on architectural design and analyze how trustworthiness affects the artefacts that are produced during this phase and the way they need to be extended.

Trustworthiness Certification Process. For certifying the security or safety of a system, there are some well-established standards and clearly defined certification processes. However, certifying the trustworthiness is still in its infancy. So far, there is no standard defined for trustworthiness. There are only recommendations with respect to what should be considered and some self-certification processes. Therefore, a certification process could be developed to implement the indepen-dent validation of the trustworthiness cases that were provided by us in this book. To facilitate the acceptance of the proposed approach, a light-weight certification scheme can be developed where the deployment and operation of a CPS can receive a certification based on the existing and used evidence as well as used digital trust-worthiness certificates. In such a process, the only necessary step is a validation of the (quantitative or qualitative) assertions of the digital trustworthiness certificates by an independent body. To achieve a fast market adoption, a self-declaration may be an option as well. However, to support an open market development, that process should be as open as possible. Therefore, the certification process should allow different approaches in the following dimensions: (i) using different certification authorities (these are, in the language of certification processes according to ISO 17021 (ISO/IEC 17021-1, 2015), the certification bodies as well as the owners of the trustworthiness cases and different involved stakeholders in the certification pro-cess), thus allowing all from self-signed certificates, industrial certification bodies, up to nation-level certification authorities/bodies, if deemed necessary, (ii) using different evaluation laboratories that perform the actual assessment or verification of the metric values, thus allowing all from the manufacturers' own quality assurance department, industry-driven standards organizations, up to specialized accredited evaluation labs, (iii) using different scopes and context conditions as well as choice of metrics (and so evidence), thus allowing to adapt to different business and maybe also consumer scenarios in different verticals with different success factors and requirements for trustworthy CPS.

One important question that needs to be answered in an application of the above described scenario is the reliability of the overall process. We would recommend sticking to ISO 17021 (ISO/IEC 17021-1, 2015) and to apply software quality measurement techniques as described in ISO 25021 (ISO/IEC 25021, 2012), in order to benefit from the existing infrastructure for accreditation and certification that has been established and has proven to be successful in the market, for example, for quality management systems, information security management systems, and even Common Criteria certification schemes.

References

AAL Joint Programme. Active and Assisted Living Programme, ICT for ageing well. Objectives. http://www.aal-europe.eu/about/objectives/, 2013. Accessed on 15 August 2018.

Alfarez Abdul-Rahman and Stephen Hailes. Supporting Trust in Virtual Communities. In *Proceedings of the 33rd Annual Hawaii International Conference on System Sciences*, HICSS, pages 6007–6016. IEEE Computer Society, 2000. ISBN 0-7695-0493-0. 0.1109/HICSS.2000.926814.

Richards Adrion, Martha A. Branstad, and John C. Cherniavsky. Validation, Verification, and Testing of Computer Software. *ACM Computing Surveys*, 14(2): 159–192, June 1982. ISSN 0360-0300. 10.1145/356876.356879.

Ailixier Aikebaier, Tomoya Enokido, and Makoto Takizawa. Trustworthy Group Formation Algorithm Based on Decentralized Trust Management in Distributed Systems. In *15th International Conference on Network-Based Information Systems*, pages 58–65. IEEE, 2012. ISBN 978-1-4673-2331-4. 10.1109/NBiS .2012.113.

Christopher J. Alberts and Audrey Dorofee. *Managing Information Security Risks: The Octave Approach*. Addison-Wesley Longman Publishing Co., Inc., Boston, MA, USA, 2002. ISBN 0321118863.

Azadeh Alebrahim, Maritta Heisel, and Rene Meis. A Structured Approach for Eliciting, Modeling, and Using Quality-Related Domain Knowledge. In *Proceedings of 14th International Conference on Computational Science and Its Applications - Part V, ICCSA*, pages 370–386. Springer International Publishing, 2014. ISBN 978-3-319-09156-3. 10.1007/978-3-319-09156-3_27.

Azadeh Alebrahim, Nazila Gol Mohammadi, and Maritta Heisel. Challenges in Rendering and Maintaining Trustworthiness for Long-Living Software Systems. In *Gemeinsamer Tagungsband der Workshops der Tagung Software Engineering*, pages 103–105, 2015. URL http://ceur-ws.org/Vol-1337/paper14.pdf.

© Springer Fachmedien Wiesbaden GmbH, part of Springer Nature 2019
N. Gol Mohammadi, *Trustworthy Cyber-Physical Systems*,
https://doi.org/10.1007/978-3-658-27488-7

Mohammed Alhamad, Tharam Dillon, and Elizabeth Chang. Conceptual Service Level Agreement Framework for Cloud Computing. In *4th IEEE International Conference on Digital Ecosystems and Technologies, DEST*, pages 606–610. IEEE, 2010. 10.1109/DEST.2010.5610586.

Midhat Ali, Antonino Sabetta, and Michele Bezzi. *A Marketplace for Business Software with Certified Security Properties*, pages 105–114. Springer Berlin Heidelberg, 2013. ISBN 978-3-642-41205-9. 10.1007/978-3-642-41205-9_9.

Ibrahim A. Almerhag, A. A. Almarimi, A. M. Goweder, and A. A. Elbekai. Network Security for QoS Routing Metrics. In *International Conference on Computer and Communication Engineering, ICCCE*, pages 1–6, 2010. 10.1109/ICCCE .2010.5556868.

Amazon. AWS Marketplace, 2014. https://aws.amazon.com/ marketplace/.

Edward Amoroso, Carol Taylor, John Watson, and Jonathan Weiss. A Process-oriented Methodology for Assessing and Improving Software Trustworthiness. In *Proceedings of the 2nd ACM Conference on Computer and Communications Security*, CCS, pages 39–50, New York, USA, 1994. ISBN 0-89791-732-4. 10.1145/191177.191188.

Andrew Josey. TOGAF Version ® 9.1 Enterprise Edition: An Introduction, A white paper. The Open Group, January 2009. http://www.opengroup.org/ architecture/wp/.

Marco Anisetti, Claudio Agostino Ardagna, Filippo Gaudenzi, and Ernesto Damiani. A Certification Framework for Cloud-based Services. In *Proceedings of the 31st Annual ACM Symposium on Applied Computing*, SAC, pages 440–447, 2016. ISBN 978-1-4503-3739-7. 10.1145/2851613.2851628.

Nikolaos Argyropoulos, Shaun Shei, Christos Kalloniatis, Haralambos Moura-tidis, Aidan Delaney, Andrew Fish, and Stefanos Gritzalis. A Semi-Automatic Approach for Eliciting Cloud Security and Privacy Require-ments. In *50th Hawaii International Conference on System Sciences, HICSS*, 2017. URL http://aisel.aisnet.org/hicss-50/os/ enterprise_architecture/4.

Martin Arlitt, Diwakar Krishnamurthy, and Jerry Rolia. Characterizing the Scalability of a Large Web-based Shopping System. *ACM Transactions on Internet Technology (TOIT)*, 1(1):44–69, August 2001. ISSN 1533-5399. 10.1145/383034.383036.

Uwe Aßmann, Andreas Bartho, Falk Hartmann, Ilie Savga, and Barbara Wittek. Trustworthy Instantiation of Frameworks. In Ralf H. Reussner, Judith A. Stafford, and Clemens A. Szyperski, editors, *Architecting Systems with Trustworthy Components, International Seminar, Dagstuhl Castle, Germany, Revised Selected Papers*, pages 152–168. Springer Berlin Heidelberg, 2006. ISBN 978-3-540-35833-6. 10.1007/11786160_9.

Dave Astels. *Test Driven Development: A Practical Guide*. Prentice Hall Professional Technical Reference, 2003. ISBN 0131016490.

Sasikanth Avancha, Amit Baxi, and David Kotz. Privacy in Mobile Technology for Personal Healthcare. *ACM Comput. Surv.*, 45(1):3:1–3:54, December 2012. ISSN 0360-0300. 10.1145/2379776.2379779.

Algirdas Avizienis, Jean-Claude Laprie, Brian Randell, and Carl E. Landwehr. Basic Concepts and Taxonomy of Dependable and Secure Computing. *IEEE Transactions on Dependable and Secure Computing*, 1(1):11–33, 2004. ISSN 1545-5971. 10.1109/TDSC.2004.2.

Sulin Ba. Establishing Online Trust through a Community Responsibility System. *Decision support systems*, 31(3):323–336, 2001. 10.1016/S0167-9236(00)00144-5.

Torsten Bandyszak, Nazila Gol Mohammadi, Mohamed Bishr, Abigail Goldsteen, Micha Moffie, Bassem I. Nasser, Sandro Hartenstein, and Symeon Meichanetzoglou. Cyber-Physical Systems Design for Runtime Trustworthiness Maintenance Supported by Tools. In *Joint Proceedings of REFSQ Workshops, Research Method Track, and Poster Track co-located with the 21st International Conference on Requirements Engineering: Foundation for Software Quality*, pages 148–155, 2015. URL http://ceur-ws.org/Vol-1342/02-resacs.pdf.

Barry Barber. Patient Data and Security: An Overview. *International Journal of Medical Informatics*, 49(1):19–30, 1998. 10.1016/S1386-5056(98)00006-9.

Victor R. Basili and H. Dieter Rombach. The TAME Project: Towards Improvement-oriented Software Environments. *IEEE Transactions Software Engineering*, 14(6):758–773, 1988. ISSN 0098-5589. 10.1109/32.6156.

Kathryn Bassin, Shriram Biyani, and Padmanabhan Santhanam. Metrics to Evaluate Vendor-developed Software Based on Test Case Execution Results. *IBM Systems Journal*, 41(1):13–30, 2002. ISSN 0018-8670. 10.1147/sj.411.0013.

Kent Beck. *Test Driven Development: By Example*. Addison-Wesley, 2003. ISBN 0321146530.

Kristian Beckers, Stephan Fassbender, Maritta Heisel, and Santiago Suppan. A Meta-pattern and Pattern Form for Context-patterns. In *Proceedings of the 19th European Conference on Pattern Languages of Programs*, EuroPLoP, pages 5:1–5:23. ACM, 2014. ISBN 978-1-4503-3416-7. 10.1145/2721956.2721979.

Kristian Beckers, Stephan Fassbender, and Maritta Heisel. A Meta-model for Context-patterns. In *Proceedings of the 18th European Conference on Pattern Languages of Program*, EuroPLoP, pages 5:1–5:15. ACM, 2015. ISBN 978-1-4503-3465-5. 10.1145/2739011.2739016.

France Belanger, Janine S. Hiller, and Wanda J. Smith. Trustworthiness in Electronic Commerce: the Role of Privacy, Security, and Site Attributes. *Journal of Strategic Information Systems*, 11(3-4):245–270, 2002. 10.1016/S0963-8687(02)00018-5.

Steven J. Bleistein, Aybüke Aurum, Karl Cox, and Pradeep K. Ray. Linking Requirements Goal Modeling Techniques to Strategic e-Business Patterns and Best Practice. In *Proceedings of the 8th Australian Workshop on Requirements Engineering*, volume 3, pages 13–22, 2003.

Robin E. Bloomfield and Peter G. Bishop. Safety and Assurance Cases: Past, Present and Possible Future - an Adelard Perspective. In Chris Dale and Tom Anderson, editors, *Making Systems Safer - Proceedings of the 8th Safety-Critical Systems Symposium*, pages 51–67. Springer, 2010. ISBN 978-1-84996-086-1. 10.1007/978-1-84996-086-1_4.

Robin E. Bloomfield, Marcelo Masera, Ann Miller, O. Sami Saydjari, and Charles B. Weinstock. Assurance Cases for Security: The Metrics Challenge. In *Proceedings of 37th Annual IEEE/IFIP International Conference on Dependable Systems and Networks, DSN, Edinburgh, UK*, pages 807–808, 2007. 10.1109/DSN.2007.18.

Barry William Boehm, John R. Brown, and Myron Lipow. Quantitative Evaluation of Software Quality. In *Proceedings of the 2nd International Conference on Software Engineering*, ICSE, pages 592–605. IEEE Computer Society Press, 1976. URL http://dl.acm.org/citation.cfm?id=800253.807736.

Sissela Bok. *Lying: Moral Choice in Private and Public Life*. Pantheon Books, USA, 1999. ISBN 978-0-375-70528-1.

Pearl Brereton, Barbara Kitchenham, David Budgen, Mark Turner, and Mohamed Khalil. Lessons from Applying the Systematic Literature Review Process within the Software Engineering Domain. *Journal of Systems and Software*, 80(4): 571–583, 2007. 10.1016/j.jss.2006.07.009.

Paolo Bresciani, Anna Perini, Paolo Giorgini, Fausto Giunchiglia, and John Mylopoulos. Tropos: An Agent-Oriented Software Development Methodology.
Autonomous Agents and Multi-Agent Systems, 8(3):203–236, 2004. ISSN 1573-
7454. 10.1023/B:AGNT.0000018806.20944.ef.

Manfred Broy and Albrecht Schmidt. Challenges in Engineering Cyber-Physical
Systems. *IEEE Computer*, 47(2):70–72, 2014. ISSN 0018-9162. 10.1109/
MC.2014.30.

Manfred Broy, María Victoria Cengarle, and Eva Geisberger. *Cyber-Physical
Systems: Imminent Challenges*, pages 1–28. Springer Berlin Heidelberg, 2012.
ISBN 978-3-642-34059-8. 10.1007/978-3-642-34059-8_1.

Davide Brugali, Luca Gherardi, A. Biziak, Andrea Luzzana, and Alexey Zakharov.
A Reuse-Oriented Development Process for Component-Based Robotic Systems.
In *Proceedings of 3rd International Conference on Simulation, Modeling, and
Programming for Autonomous Robots, SIMPAR*, pages 361–374. Springer Berlin
Heidelberg, 2012. ISBN 978-3-642-34327-8. 10.1007/978-3-642-34327-8_33.

BSIMM. The Building Security In Maturity Model – BSIMM4. http://www
.bsimm.com/.

Frank Buschmann, Kevlin Henney, and Douglas C. Schmidt. *Pattern-Oriented
Software Architectur, 4th Edition, A Pattern Language for Distributed Computing*, volume 5 of *Wiley series in software design patterns*. Wiley,
2007. ISBN 9780470059029. URL http://www.worldcat.org/oclc/
314792015.

Cristina Cabanillas, David Knuplesch, Manuel Resinas, Manfred Reichert, Jan
Mendling, and Antonio Ruiz-Cortés. RALph: A Graphical Notation for Resource Assignments in Business Processes. In *Proceedings of 27th International
Conference on Advanced Information Systems Engineering, CAiSE*, pages 53–68,
2015. 10.1007/978-3-319-19069-3_4.

Jean Camp. *Trust and Risk in Internet Commerce*. MIT Press, Cambridge, USA,
2000. ISBN 0-262-03271-6.

Jorge S. Cardoso, Amit P. Sheth, John A. Miller, Jonathan Arnold, and Krys Kochut.
Quality of Service for Workflows and Web Service Processes. *Web Semantics:
Science, Services and Agents on the World Wide Web*, 1(3):281–308, 2004. ISSN
1570-8268. https://doi.org/10.1016/j.websem.2004.03.001.

Justine Cassell and Timothy Bickmore. External Manifestations of Trustworthiness in the Interface. *Communications of the ACM*, 43(12):50–56, December 2000. ISSN 0001-0782. 10.1145/355112.355123.

Cristiano Castelfranchi and Yao-Hua Tan. The Role of Trust and Deception in Virtual Societies. *International Journal of Electronic Commerce*, 6(3):55–70, April 2002. ISSN 1086-4415. 10.1080/10864415.2002.11044243.

Elizabeth Chang, Tharam S. Dillon, and Farookh Khadeer Hussain. Trust Ontologies for E-Service Environments. *International Journal of Intelligent Systems*, 22(5):519–545, March 2007. 10.1002/int.20212.

Chao Chen, Ke Wang, Shuren Liao, Qiuyan Zhang, and Yiqi Dai. A Novel Server-Based Application Execution Architecture. In *Proceedings of the 12th IEEE International Conference on Computational Science and Engineering, CSE, Vancouver, Canada*, volume 2, pages 678–683, 2009. 10.1109/CSE.2009.319.

Jin-Hee Cho, Ananthram Swami, and Ing-Ray Chen. A Survey on Trust Management for Mobile Ad Hoc Networks. *IEEE Communications Surveys and Tutorials*, 13(4):562–583, 2011. ISSN 1553-877X. 10.1109/SURV.2011.092110.00088.

Amit K. Chopra, Elda Paja, and Paolo Giorgini. Sociotechnical Trust: An Architectural Approach. In *Proceedings of the 30th International Conference on Conceptual Modeling*, ER, pages 104–117. Springer-Verlag, 2011. ISBN 978-3-642-24605-0. 10.1007/978-3-642-24606-7_9.

Lawrence Chung and Julio Cesar Sampaio do Prado Leite. *On Non-Functional Requirements in Software Engineering*, pages 363–379. Springer Berlin Heidelberg, 2009. ISBN 978-3-642-02463-4. 10.1007/978-3-642-02463-4_19.

Kassidy P. Clark, Martijn Warnier, Frances M. T. Brazier, and Thomas B. Quillinan. Secure Monitoring of Service Level Agreements. In *International Conference on Availability, Reliability and Security, ARES*, pages 454–461, 2010. 10.1109/ARES.2010.33.

Piotr Cofta, Hazel Lacohée, and Paul Hodgson. Incorporating Social Trust into Design Practices for Secure Systems. *Software Engineering for Secure Systems: Industrial and Research Perspectives: Industrial and Research Perspectives*, 1(4):1–24, 2010. 10.4018/jdtis.2010100101.

Cynthia L. Corritore, Beverly Kracher, and Susan Wiedenbeck. On-line Trust: Concepts, Evolving Themes, a Model. *International Journal of Human-Computer Studies*, 58(6):737–758, 2003. 10.1016/S1071-5819(03)00041-7.

Alberto Rodrigues Da Silva, Dušan Savić, Siniša Vlajić, Ilija Antović, Saša Lazarević, Vojislav Stanojević, and Miloš Milić. A Pattern Language for Use Cases Specification. In *Proceedings of the 20th European Conference on Pattern Languages of Programs*, EuroPLoP, pages 8:1–8:18. ACM, 2015. ISBN 978-1-4503-3847-9. 10.1145/2855321.2855330.

Yngve Dahl and Kristine Holbø. Value Biases of Sensor-based Assistive Technology: Case Study of a GPS Tracking System Used in Dementia Care. In *Proceedings of the Designing Interactive Systems Conference*, DIS, pages 572–581. ACM, 2012. ISBN 978-1-4503-1210-3. 10.1145/2317956.2318043.

Ralf Dahrendorf. *Reflections on the Revolution in Europe*. Transaction Publishers, USA, 2005. ISBN 978-0-7658-0828-8.

Weiqi Dai, T. Paul Parker, Hai Jin, and Shouhuai Xu. Enhancing Data Trustworthiness via Assured Digital Signing. *IEEE Transactions on Dependable and Secure Computing*, 9(6):838–851, 2012. ISSN 1545-5971. 10.1109/TDSC.2012.71.

Florian Daniel, Kamel Barkaoui, and Schahram Dustdar, editors. *Role Assignment in Business Process Models*, volume 99 of *Lecture Notes in Business Information Processing*, 2012. Springer. ISBN 978-3-642-28107-5. 10.1007/978-3-642 -28108-2.

José Luis De la Vara and Juan Sánchez. *Improving Requirements Analysis through Business Process Modelling: A Participative Approach*, pages 165–176. Springer Berlin Heidelberg, 2008. ISBN 978-3-540-79396-0. 10.1007/978-3-540-79396 -0_15.

Gero Decker, Oliver Kopp, Frank Leymann, Kerstin Pfitzner, and Mathias Weske. Modeling Service Choreographies Using BPMN and BPEL4Chor. In *Proceedings of the 20th International Conference on Advanced Information Systems Engineering*, CAiSE, pages 79–93. Springer-Verlag, 2008. ISBN 978-3-540-69533-2. 10.1007/978-3-540-69534-9_6.

Adela Del-Río-Ortega, Manuel Resinas Arias de Reyna, Amador Durán Toro, and Antonio Ruiz-Cortés. Defining Process Performance Indicators by Using Templates and Patterns. In *Business Process Management*, volume 7481 of *Lecture Notes in Computer Science*, pages 223–228. Springer, 2012. ISBN 978-3-642-32884-8. 10.1007/978-3-642-32885-5_18.

Department of Defense. *Trusted Computer System Evaluation Criteria, 5200.28-STD*. DoD Computer Security Center, December 1985.

Wil M. P. Van der Aalst and Akhil Kumar. A Reference Model for Team-enabled Workflow Management Systems. *Data Knowl. Eng.*, 38(3):335–363, September 2001. ISSN 0169-023X. 10.1016/S0169-023X(01)00034-9.

Morton Deutsch. Cooperation and Trust: Some Theoretical Notes. pages 275–320, 1962.

Guy Dewsbury, Ian Sommerville, Karen Clarke, and Mark Rouncefield. A Dependability Model for Domestic Systems. In *Proceedings of 22nd International Conference on Computer Safety, Reliability, and Security, SAFECOMP*, pages 103–115, 2003. 10.1007/978-3-540-39878-3_9.

Francesco Di Cerbo, Michele Bezzi, Samuel Paul Kaluvuri, Antonino Sabetta, Slim Trabelsi, and Volkmar Lotz. *Towards a Trustworthy Service Marketplace for the Future Internet*, pages 105–116. Springer Berlin Heidelberg, 2012. ISBN 978-3-642-30241-1. 10.1007/978-3-642-30241-1_10.

Francesco Di Cerbo, Pascal Bisson, Alan Hartman, Sebastien Keller, Per Håkon Meland, Micha Moffie, Nazila Gol Mohammadi, Sachar Paulus, and Stuart Short. Towards Trustworthiness Assurance in the Cloud. In Massimo Felici, editor, *Cyber Security and Privacy*, pages 3–15. Springer Berlin Heidelberg, 2013. ISBN 978-3-642-41205-9.

Francesco Di Cerbo, Samuel Paul Kaluvuri, Frederic Motte, Bassem Nasser, Willis X. Chen, and Stuart Short. Towards a Linked Data Vocabulary for the Certification of Software Properties. In *10th International Conference on Signal-Image Technology and Internet-Based Systems, SITIS*, pages 721–727, 2014. 10.1109/SITIS.2014.29.

Francesco Di Cerbo, Nazila Gol Mohammadi, and Sachar Paulus. Evidence-Based Trustworthiness of Internet-Based Services Through Controlled Software Development. In Frances Cleary and Massimo Felici, editors, *Cyber Security and Privacy - 4th Cyber Security and Privacy Innovation Forum, CSP Innovation Forum, Revised Selected Papers*, pages 91–102. Springer, 2015. ISBN 978-3-319-25360-2. 10.1007/978-3-319-25360-2_8.

Shuai Ding, Xi-Jun Ma, and Shan-Lin Yang. A Software Trustworthiness Evaluation Model using Objective Weight based Evidential Reasoning Approach. *Knowledge and information systems*, 33(1):171–189, 2012.

Earl Eugene Schultz, Robert W. Proctor, Mei-Ching Lien, Gavriel Salvendy. Usability and Security An Appraisal of Usability Issues in Information Security Methods. *Computers & Security*, 20(7):620–634, 2001. 10.1016/S0167-4048(01)00712-X.

Imed El Fray. *A Comparative Study of Risk Assessment Methods, MEHARI & CRAMM with a New Formal Model of Risk Assessment (FoMRA) in Information Systems*, pages 428–442. Springer, 2012. ISBN 978-3-642-33260-9. 10.1007/978-3-642-33260-9_37.

Golnaz Elahi and Eric S. K. Yu. Trust Trade-off Analysis for Security Requirements Engineering. In *Proceedings of 17th IEEE International Requirements Engineering Conference, RE*, 2009. 10.1109/RE.2009.12.

Hisain Elshaafi, Jimmy McGibney, and Dmitri Botvich. Trustworthiness Monitoring and Prediction of Composite Services. In *IEEE Symposium on Computers and Communications, ISCC*, pages 580–587, 2012. 10.1109/ISCC.2012.6249359.

Ivan Flechais, Martina Angela Sasse, and Stephen Hailes. Bringing Security Home: A Process for Developing Secure and Usable Systems. In *Proceedings of the Workshop on New Security Paradigms*, NSPW, pages 49–57. ACM, 2003. ISBN 1-58113-880-6. 10.1145/986655.986664.

Fred B. Schneider. *Trust in Cyberspace*. National Academies Press, 1999. ISBN 0309065585.

Diego Gambetta. Can We Trust Trust? In *Trust: Making and Breaking Cooperative Relations*, pages 213–237. Basil Blackwell, 1988.

Stefan Gärtner, Thomas Ruhroth, Jens Bürger, Kurt Schneider, and Jan Jürjens. Maintaining Requirements for Long-Living Software Systems by Incorporating Security Knowledge. In *IEEE 22nd International Requirements Engineering Conference, RE*, pages 103–112, 2014. 10.1109/RE.2014.6912252.

David Gefen. Reflections on the Dimensions of Trust and Trustworthiness Among Online Consumers. *ACM SIGMIS Database: the DATABASE for Advances in Information Systems*, 33(3):38–53, August 2002. ISSN 0095-0033. 10.1145/569905.569910.

Daniela Gerd tom Markotten. User-Centered Security Engineering. In *Proceedings of the 4th EurOpen/USENIX Conference – NordU2002*, 2002.

Jim Giles. US Internet Providers Hijacking Users' Search Queries. *NewScientist*, August, 2011. URL https://www.newscientist.com/article/dn20768-us-internet-providers-hijacking-users-search-queries/.

Paolo Giorgini, Fabio Massacci, John Mylopoulos, and Nicola Zannone. *Requirements Engineering Meets Trust Management*, pages 176–190. Springer Berlin Heidelberg, 2004. ISBN 978-3-540-24747-0. 10.1007/978-3-540-24747-0_14.

Paolo Giorgini, Fabio Massacci, John Mylopoulos, and Nicola Zannone. Requirements Engineering for Trust Management: Model, Methodology, and Reasoning. *International Journal of Information Security*, 5(4):257–274, 2006. ISSN 1615-5270. 10.1007/s10207-006-0005-7.

Nazila Gol Mohammadi and Maritta Heisel. Patterns for Identification of Trust Concerns and Specification of Trustworthiness Requirements. In *Proceedings of the 21st European Conference on Pattern Languages of Programs*, EuroPLoP, pages 31:1–31:20. ACM, 2016a. ISBN 978-1-4503-4074-8. 10.1145/3011784 .3011819.

Nazila Gol Mohammadi and Maritta Heisel. A Framework for Systematic Analysis and Modeling of Trustworthiness Requirements Using i* and BPMN. In *Proceedings 13th International Conference on Trust, Privacy and Security in Digital Business, TrustBus*, pages 3–18, 2016b. 10.1007/978-3-319-44341-6_1.

Nazila Gol Mohammadi and Maritta Heisel. Enhancing Business Process Models with Trustworthiness Requirements. In *Proceedings of 10th IFIP WG 11.11 International Conference on Trust Management X IFIPTM*, pages 33–51, 2016c. 10.1007/978-3-319-41354-9_3.

Nazila Gol Mohammadi and Maritta Heisel. A Framework for Systematic Refinement of Trustworthiness Requirements. *Information*, 8(2):46, 2017. 10.3390/info8020046.

Nazila Gol Mohammadi, Sachar Paulus, Mohamed Bishr, Andreas Metzger, Holger Könnecke, Sandro Hartenstein, and Klaus Pohl. An Analysis of Software Quality Attributes and Their Contribution to Trustworthiness. In *Proceedings of the 3rd International Conference on Cloud Computing and Services Science*, pages 542–552, 2013a.

Nazila Gol Mohammadi, Sachar Paulus, Mohamed Bishr, Andreas Metzger, Holger Könnecke, Sandro Hartenstein, Thorsten Weyer, and Klaus Pohl. Trustworthiness Attributes and Metrics for Engineering Trusted Internet-Based Software Systems. In *Cloud Computing and Services Science - 3rd International Conference, CLOSER, Revised Selected Papers*, pages 19–35, 2013b. 10.1007/978-3-319-11561-0_2.

Nazila Gol Mohammadi, Torsten Bandyszak, Micha Moffie, Xiaoyu Chen, Thorsten Weyer, Costas Kalogiros, Bassem I. Nasser, and Mike Surridge. Maintaining Trustworthiness of Socio-Technical Systems at Run-Time. In *Proceedings of the 11th International Conference on Trust, Privacy, and Security in Digital Business, TrustBus*, pages 1–12, 2014a. 10.1007/978-3-319-09770-1_1.

Nazila Gol Mohammadi, Torsten Bandyszak, Sachar Paulus, Per Håkon Meland, Thorsten Weyer, and Klaus Pohl. Extending Development Methodologies with Trustworthiness-By-Design for Socio-Technical Systems - (Extended Abstract). In *Proceedings of the 7th International Conference Trust and Trustworthy Computing, TRUST*, pages 206–207, 2014b. 10.1007/978-3-319-08593-7_14.

Nazila Gol Mohammadi, Torsten Bandyszak, Abigail Goldsteen, Costas Kalogiros, Thorsten Weyer, Micha Moffie, Bassem I. Nasser, and Mike Surridge. Combining Risk-Management and Computational Approaches for Trustworthiness Evaluation of Socio-Technical Systems. In *Proceedings of the CAiSE Forum at the 27th International Conference on Advanced Information Systems Engineering, CAiSE*, pages 237–244, 2015a. URL http://ceur-ws.org/Vol-1367/paper-31.pdf.

Nazila Gol Mohammadi, Torsten Bandyszak, Costas Kalogiros, Michalis Kanakakis, and Thorsten Weyer. A Framework for Evaluating the End-to-End Trustworthiness. In *Proceedings of the 14th IEEE International Conference on Trust, Security and Privacy in Computing and Communications (IEEE TrustCom), IEEE TrustCom/BigDataSE/ISPA*, pages 638–645, 2015b. 10.1109/Trustcom.2015.429.

Nazila Gol Mohammadi, Torsten Bandyszak, Sachar Paulus, Per Håkon Meland, Thorsten Weyer, and Klaus Pohl. Extending Software Development Methodologies to Support Trustworthiness-by-Design. In *Proceedings of the CAiSE Forum at the 27th International Conference on Advanced Information Systems Engineering, CAiSE*, pages 213–220, 2015c. URL http://ceur-ws.org/Vol-1367/paper-28.pdf.

Nazila Gol Mohammadi, Nelufar Ulfat-Bunyadi, and Maritta Heisel. Problem-based Derivation of Trustworthiness Requirements from Users' Trust Concerns. In *Proceedings of the 16th Annual Conference on Privacy, Security and Trust, PST*, pages 1–10, 2018a. 10.1109/PST.2018.8514183.

Nazila Gol Mohammadi, Nelufar Ulfat-Bunyadi, and Maritta Heisel. Trustworthiness Cases - Toward Preparation for the Trustworthiness Certification. In *Proceedings of the 15th International Conference on Trust, Privacy and Security in Digital Business, TrustBus*, pages 244–259, 2018b. 10.1007/978-3-319-98385-1_17.

Abigail Goldsteen, Micha Moffie, Torsten Bandyszak, Nazila Gol Mohammadi, Xiaoyu Chen, Symeon Meichanetzoglou, Sotiris Ioannidis, and Panos Chatziadam. A Tool for Monitoring and Maintaining System Thrustworthiness at Runtime. In *Joint Proceedings of REFSQ Workshops, Research Method Track, and Poster Track co-located with the 21st International Conference on Requirements Engineering: Foundation for Software Quality*, pages 142–147, 2015. URL http://ceur-ws.org/Vol-1342/preface-resacs.pdf.

R. Golembiewski and M. McConkie. The Centrality of Interpersonal Trust in Group Processes. *Theories of Group Processes*, pages 131–185, 1975.

Mario Gómez, Javier Carbó, and Clara Benac-Earle. *An Anticipatory Trust Model for Open Distributed Systems*, pages 307–324. Springer Berlin Heidelberg, 2007. ISBN 978-3-540-74262-3. 10.1007/978-3-540-74262-3_17.

Sonja Grabner-Kräuter and Ewald A. Kaluscha. Empirical Research in On-line Trust: A Review and Critical Assessment. *International Journal of Human-Computer Studies*, 58(6):783–812, 2003. ISSN 1071-5819. http://dx.doi.org/10.1016/S1071-5819(03)00043-0. Trust and Technology.

Tyrone Grandison and Morris Sloman. A Survey of Trust in Internet Applications. *IEEE Communications Surveys & Tutorials*, 3(4):2–16, 2000.

Patrick John Graydon, John C. Knight, and Elisabeth A. Strunk. Assurance Based Development of Critical Systems. In *Proceedings of the 37th Annual IEEE/IFIP International Conference on Dependable Systems and Networks, DSN*, pages 347–357, 2007. 10.1109/DSN.2007.17.

Stefanos Gritzalis. Enhancing Privacy and Data Protection in Electronic Medical Environments. *Journal of Medical Systems*, 28(6):535–547, 2004. ISSN 1573-689X. 10.1023/B:JOMS.0000044956.55209.75.

GSN Working Group. The 1st version of the Goal Structuring Notation (GSN) Standard, Version 1, November 2011. http://www.goalstructuringnotation.info/ (Accessed on 20 July 2018).

Jan Gurley, Nancy Lum, Merle Sande, Lo Bernard, and Mitchell H. Katz. Persons Found in Their Homes Helpless or Dead. *The New England Journal of Medicine*, 334(26):1710–1716, June 1996. 10.1056/NEJM199606273342606.

Charles B. Haley, Robin C. Laney, Jonathan D. Moffett, and Bashar Nuseibeh. The Effect of Trust Assumptions on the Elaboration of Security Requirements. In *12th IEEE International Conference on Requirements Engineering, RE*, pages 102–111, 2004. 10.1109/RE.2004.50.

Simin Hall and William McQuay. Fundamental Features of a Unified Trust Model for Distributed Systems. In *Proceedings of the 2011 IEEE National Aerospace and Electronics Conference, NAECON*, pages 139–145, 2011. 10.1109/NAECON .2011.6183091.

Qiang Han. Trustworthiness Measurement Algorithm for TWfMS Based on Software Behaviour Entropy. *Entropy*, 20(3), 2018. ISSN 1099-4300. 10.3390/ e20030195.

Bjarne Håkon Hanssen. The Coordination Reform, Proper treatment – at the right place and right time, 2008. URL https://www.regjeringen.no/ contentassets/d4f0e16ad32e4bbd8d8ab5c21445a5dc/en-gb/ pdfs/stm200820090047000en_pdfs.pdf. (Accessed on 7 August 2018).

Bernd Hardung, Thorsten Kölzow, and Andreas Krüger. Reuse of Software in Distributed Embedded Automotive Systems. In *Proceedings of the 4th ACM International Conference on Embedded Software*, EMSOFT, pages 203–210, 2004. ISBN 1-58113-860-1. 10.1145/1017753.1017787.

Christina Harrefors, Karin Axelsson, and Stefan Sävenstedt. Using Assistive Technology Services at Differing Levels of Care: Healthy Older Couples' Perceptions. *Journal of Advanced Nursing*, 66(7):1523–1532, 2010. 10.1111/ j.1365-2648.2010.05335.x.

Lloyd C. Harris and Mark M.H. Goode. The Four Levels of Loyalty and the Pivotal Role of Trust: A Study of Online Service Dynamics. *Journal of Retailing*, 80(2): 139–158, 2004. 10.1016/j.jretai.2004.04.002.

Wilhelm Hasselbring and Ralf H. Reussner. Toward Trustworthy Software Systems. *IEEE Computer*, 39(4):91–92, April 2006. 10.1109/MC.2006.142.

Denis Hatebur and Maritta Heisel. A UML Profile for Requirements Analysis of Dependable Software. In *Proceedings of the 29th International Conference on Computer Safety, Reliability, and Security, SAFECOMP*, pages 317–331. Springer-Verlag, 2010. 10.1007/978-3-642-15651-9_24.

Richard Hawkins and Tim Kelly. A Structured Approach to Selecting and Justifying Software Safety Evidence. In *Proceedings of the 5th IET International Conference on System Safety*, pages 31–37, 2010a. 10.1049/cp.2010.0825.

Richard Hawkins and Tim Kelly. A Systematic Approach for Developing Software Safety Arguments. *Journal of System Safety, Hazard Prevention*, 46(4):25, 2010b.

Richard Hawkins, Ibrahim Habli, Tim Kelly, and John McDermid. Assurance Cases and Prescriptive Software Safety Certification: A Comparative Study. *Safety Science*, 59:55–71, 2013. https://doi.org/10.1016/j.ssci.2013.04.007.

Ming He, Aiqun Hu, and Hangping Qiu. Research on Behavior Trust Based on Trustworthy Distributed System. In *International Conference on Networks Security, Wireless Communications and Trusted Computing, NSWCTC*, volume 1, pages 396–399, 2009. 10.1109/NSWCTC.2009.401.

Vigdis Heimly and Jacob Hygen. The Norwegian Coordination Reform and the Role of Electronic Collaboration. *electronic Journal of Health Informatics*, 6(4): 29, 2011.

Debra S. Herrmann. *Complete Guide to Security and Privacy Metrics: Measuring Regulatory Compliance, Operational Resilience, and ROI*. Auerbach Publications, Boston, USA, 1st edition, 2007. ISBN 0849354021, 9780849354021.

Ida Hogganvik and Ketil Stølen. *A Graphical Approach to Risk Identification, Motivated by Empirical Investigations*, pages 574–588. Springer Berlin Heidelberg, 2006. ISBN 978-3-540-45773-2. 10.1007/11880240_40.

Homeland Security. A Roadmap for Cybersecurity Research. Technical report, November 2009. URL www.dhs.gov/science-and-technology/csd-restructure.

Jennifer Horkoff, Tong Li, Feng-Lin Li, Mattia Salnitri, Evellin Cardoso, Paolo Giorgini, John Mylopoulos, and João Pimentel. Taking Goal Models Downstream: A Systematic Roadmap. In *IEEE 8th International Conference on Research Challenges in Information Science, RCIS*, pages 1–12, 2014. 10.1109/RCIS.2014.6861036.

Jennifer Horkoff, Fatma Basak Aydemir, Evellin Cardoso, Tong Li, Alejandro Maté, Elda Paja, Mattia Salnitri, John Mylopoulos, and Paolo Giorgini. Goal-Oriented Requirements Engineering: A Systematic Literature Map. In *24th IEEE International Requirements Engineering Conference, RE*, pages 106–115, 2016. 10.1109/RE.2016.41.

LiGuo Huang, Xu Bai, and Suku Nair. Developing a SSE-CMM-based Security Risk Assessment Process for Patient-centered Healthcare Systems. In *Proceedings of the 6th International Workshop on Software Quality, WoSQ*, pages 11–16. ACM, 2008. ISBN 978-1-60558-023-4. 10.1145/1370099.1370103.

Farookh Khadeer Hussain, Elizabeth Chang, and Tharam S. Dillon. Aspects Influencing Trustworthiness In Service Oriented Environments. In *Proceedings of the 22nd International Conference on Data Engineering Workshops, ICDE,* page 99. IEEE Computer Society, 2006. ISBN 0-7695-2571-7. 10.1109/ICDEW .2006.33.

Farookh Khadeer Hussain, Omar Khadeer Hussain, and Elizabeth Chang. An Overview of the Interpretations of Trust and Reputation. In *Proceedings of 12th IEEE International Conference on Emerging Technologies and Factory Automation, ETFA,* pages 826–830, 2007. 10.1109/EFTA.2007.4416865.

San-Yih Hwang, Haojun Wang, Jian Tang, and Jaideep Srivastava. A Probabilistic Approach to Modeling and Estimating the QoS of Web-services-based Workflows. *Information Sciences,* 177(23):5484–5503, December 2007. ISSN 0020-0255. 10.1016/j.ins.2007.07.011.

IBM. An Architectural Blueprint for Autonomic Computing, 2005. www-03.ibm.com/autonomic/pdfs/AC%20Blueprint% 20White%20Paper%20V7.pdf.

IEEE Standards Board. IEEE Standard for a Software Quality Metrics Methodology. *IEEE Standard 1061-1992,* 1993. 10.1109/IEEESTD.1993.115124.

Cynthia E. Irvine and Karl N. Levitt. Trusted Hardware: Can It Be Trustworthy? In *Proceedings of the 44th Design Automation Conference, DAC,* pages 1–4, 2007. 10.1145/1278480.1278482.

ISO/IEC 15408-1. Information technology – Security techniques – Evaluation criteria for IT security – Part 1: Introduction and general model. Technical report, December 2009. URL www.iso.org/iso/catalogue_detail .htm?csnumber=50341.

ISO/IEC 17021-1. Conformity assessment – Requirements for bodies providing audit and certification of management systems – Part 1: Requirements – Requirements. Technical report, June 2015.

ISO/IEC 21827. Information technology, Security techniques, Systems Security Engineering – Capability Maturity Model (SSE- CMM). Technical report, October 2008.

ISO/IEC 25021. Systems and software engineering – Systems and software Quality Requirements and Evaluation (SQuaRE) – Quality measure elements. Technical report, 2012.

ISO/IEC 27000. Information technology – Security techniques – Information security management systems – Overview and vocabulary. Technical report, International Organization for Standardization (ISO), October 2018.

ISO/IEC 27001. Information technology – Security techniques – Information security management systems – Requirements. Technical report, October 2013.

ISO/IEC 27005. Information technology - Security techniques - Information security risk management. Technical report, International Organization for Standardization (ISO), October 2011.

ISO/IEC 9126-1. Software engineering – Product quality – Part 1: Quality model. Technical report, june 2001. URL www.iso.org/iso/catalogue _detail.htm?csnumber=22749.

IT-innovation. OPTET Project Outcomes, 2013. URL http://www.it -innovation.soton.ac.uk/projects/optet.

Michael Jackson. *Problem Frames: Analyzing and Structuring Software Development Problems.* Addison-Wesley Longman Publishing Co., Inc., Boston, MA, USA, 2001. ISBN 0-201-59627-X.

Michael C. Jaeger, Gregor Rojec-Goldmann, and Gero Mühl. QoS Aggregation for Web Service Composition Using Workflow Patterns. In *Proceedings of the 8th International Enterprise Distributed Object Computing Conference*, EDOC, pages 149–159. IEEE Computer Society, 2004. ISBN 0-7695-2214-9. 10.1109/ EDOC.2004.19.

Pan Jing, Xu Feng, Xin Xianlong, and Lü Jian. A Personalized Trust-Based Approach for Service Selection in Internetwares. In *2008 International Conference on Advanced Computer Theory and Engineering*, pages 89–93, 2008. 10.1109/ICACTE.2008.88.

Audun Jøsang. *Computational Trust*, pages 243–270. Springer International Publishing, 2016. ISBN 978-3-319-42337-1. 10.1007/978-3-319-42337-1_14.

Audun Jøsang, Claudia Keser, and Theo Dimitrakos. Can We Manage Trust? In Peter Herrmann, Valérie Issarny, and Simon Shiu, editors, *Proceedings of the 3rd Trust Management International Conference, iTrust*, pages 93–107. Springer Berlin Heidelberg, 2005. ISBN 978-3-540-32040-1. 10.1007/11429760_7.

Audun Jøsang, Roslan Ismail, and Colin Boyd. A Survey of Trust and Reputation Systems for Online Service Provision. *Decision Support Systems*, 43(2):618–644, 2007. 10.1016/j.dss.2005.05.019.

Lalana Kagal, Timothy W. Finin, and Anupam Joshi. Communications - Trust-Based Security in Pervasive Computing Environments. *IEEE Computer*, 34(12): 154–157, 2001. 10.1109/2.970591.

Christos Kalloniatis, Evangelia Kavakli, and Stefanos Gritzalis. Addressing Privacy Requirements in System Design: The PriS Method. *Requirements Engineering*, 13(3):241–255, 2008. ISSN 0947-3602. 10.1007/s00766-008-0067-3.

Costas Kalogiros, Michalis Kanakakis, Shenja van der Graaf, and Wim Vanobberghen. Profit-Maximizing Trustworthiness Level of Composite Systems. In *Proceedings of the 3rd International Conference on Human Aspects of Information Security, Privacy, and Trust, HAS*, pages 357–368. Springer, 2015. ISBN 978-3-319-20375-1. 10.1007/978-3-319-20376-8_32.

Samuel Paul Kaluvuri, Hristo Koshutanski, Francesco Di Cerbo, and Antonio Mana. Security Assurance of Services through Digital Security Certificates. In *Proceeding of the 20th International Conference on Web Services, ICWS*, pages 98–102. IEEE, 2013. 10.1109/ICWS.2013.78.

Stephen H. Kan. *Metrics and Models in Software Quality Engineering*. Addison-Wesley, Boston, USA, 2nd edition, 2002. ISBN 0201729156.

Kristiina Karvonen. Creating Trust. In *Proceedings of the 4th Nordic Workshop on Secure IT Systems, NordSec*, pages 21–36, 1999. URL http://lib.tkk.fi/Diss/2007/isbn9789512287864/article1.pdf.

Kristiina Karvonen, Lucas Cardholm, and Stefan Karlsson. Cultures of Trust: A Cross-Cultural Study on the Formation of Trust in an Electronic Environment. In *In Proceedings of the 3rd Nordic Workshop on Security, NordSec*, 2000.

Timothy K. Keanini, Martin A. Quiroga, Brian W. Buchanan, and John S. Flowers. Network Security System Having a Device Profiler Communicatively Coupled to a Traffic Monitor, 2007. US Patent 7,181,769.

Timothy Patrick Kelly. Arguing Safety – A Systematic Approach to Managing Safety Cases, Dissertation. Department of Computer Science, The university of York, 1998.

Jeffrey O. Kephart and David M. Chess. The Vision of Autonomic Computing. *IEEE Computer*, 36(1):41–50, 2003. ISSN 0018-9162. 10.1109/MC.2003.1160055.

Siddhartha Kumar Khaitan and James D. McCalley. Design Techniques and Applications of Cyberphysical Systems: A Survey. *IEEE Systems Journal*, 9(2): 350–365, June 2015. 10.1109/JSYST.2014.2322503.

Rania Khalaf, Nirmal Mukhi, and Sanjiva Weerawarana. Service-Oriented Composition in BPEL4WS. In *Proceedings of the Twelfth International World Wide Web Conference - Alternate Paper Tracks, WWW*, 2003.

Barbara Kitchenham. Procedures for Performing Systematic Reviews. Technical report, Keele University and NICTA, 2004.

Barbara Kitchenham, Pearl Brereton, David Budgen, Mark Turner, John Bailey, and Stephen Linkman. Systematic Literature Reviews in Software Engineering – A Systematic Literature Review. *Information & Software Technology*, 51(1): 7–15, 2009. ISSN 0950-5849. 10.1016/j.infsof.2008.09.009.

Barbara Kitchenham, Pearl Brereton, Mark Turner, Mahmood Niazi, Stephen G. Linkman, Rialette Pretorius, and David Budgen. Refining the Systematic Literature Review Process - Two Participant-Observer Case Studies. *Empirical Software Engineering*, 15(6):618–653, 2010. 10.1007/s10664-010-9134-8.

Benjamin Klatt, Franz Brosch, Zoya Durdik, and Christoph Rathfelder. Quality Prediction in Service Composition Frameworks. In *Proceedings of the International Conference on Service-Oriented Computing*, ICSOC, pages 131–146. Springer-Verlag, 2012. ISBN 978-3-642-31874-0. 10.1007/978-3-642-31875-7.

Marios Koufaris and William Hampton-Sosa. The Development of Initial Trust in an Online Company by New Customers. *Information & Management*, 41(3): 377–397, 2004. 10.1016/j.im.2003.08.004.

Maria Krotsiani, George Spanoudakis, and Khaled Mahbub. Incremental Certification of Cloud Services. In *7th International Conference on Emerging Security Information, Systems and Technologie, SECURWARE*, 2018.

Ihor Kuz, Liming Zhu, Len Bass, Mark Staples, and Xiwei Xu. An Architectural Approach for Cost Effective Trustworthy Systems. In *Joint Working IEEE/IFIP Conference on Software Architecture (WICSA) and European Conference on Software Architecture (ECSA)*, pages 325–328. IEEE, 2012.

Axel Van Lamsweerde. Elaborating Security Requirements by Construction of Intentional Anti-Models. In *Proceedings of the 26th International Conference on Software Engineering*, pages 148–157, 2004. 10.1109/ICSE.2004.1317437.

Axel Van Lamsweerde. *Requirements Engineering — From System Goals to UML Models to Software Specifications*. John Wiley and Sons, 2009.

Edward A. Lee. Cyber Physical Systems: Design Challenges. In *11th IEEE International Symposium on Object-Oriented Real-Time Distributed Computing, ISORC*, pages 363–369, 2008. 10.1109/ISORC.2008.25.

Helena K. Leino-Kilpi, Maritta Välimäki, Teo Dassen, María Gasull, Chryssoula Lemonidou, Anne Scott, and Marianne Arndt. Privacy: A Review of the Literature. *International Journal of Nursing Studies*, 38(6):663–671, 2001. ISSN 0020-7489. http://dx.doi.org/10.1016/S0020-7489(00)00111-5.

Gabriele Lenzini, Andrew Tokmakoff, and Johan Muskens. Managing Trustworthiness in Component-based Embedded Systems. *Electronic Notes in Theoretical Computer Science*, 179:143–155, 2007. ISSN 1571-0661. http://dx.doi.org/10.1016/j.entcs.2006.08.038. Proceedings of the Second International Workshop on Security and Trust Management, STM.

Gabriele Lenzini, Ynze van Houten, Wolf Huijsen, and Mark S. Melenhorst. *Shall I Trust a Recommendation? Towards an Evaluation of the Trustworthiness of Recommender Sites*, pages 121–128. Springer Berlin Heidelberg, 2010. ISBN 978-3-642-12082-4. 10.1007/978-3-642-12082-4_16.

Emmanuel Letier and Axel Van Lamsweerde. Agent-based Tactics for Goal-oriented Requirements Elaboration. In *Proceedings of the 24th International Conference on Software Engineering, ICSE*, pages 83–93, 2002. 10.1145/581352.581353.

Minglu Li, Jianping Li, Hao Song, and Dengsheng Wu. Risk Management in the Trustworthy Software Process: A Novel Risk and Trustworthiness Measurement Model Framework. In *5th International Joint Conference on INC, IMS and IDC*, pages 214–219. IEEE, 2009. 10.1109/NCM.2009.283.

Zhengping Liang, Xiaoli Liu, Guoqing Wu, Min Yang, and Fan Zhang. A Formal Framework for Trust Management of Service-Oriented Systems. In *IEEE International Conference on Service-Oriented Computing and Applications, SOCA*, pages 241–248, 2007. 10.1109/SOCA.2007.3.

Noura Limam and Raouf Boutaba. Assessing Software Service Quality and Trustworthiness at Selection Time. *IEEE Transactions on Software Engineering*, 36(4):559–574, July 2010. ISSN 0098-5589. 10.1109/TSE.2010.2.

Steve Lipner. The Trustworthy Computing Security Development Lifecycle. In *Proceedings of the 20th Annual Computer Security Applications Conference, ACSAC*, pages 2–13, Washington, USA, 2004. IEEE Computer Society. ISBN 0-7695-2252-1. 10.1109/CSAC.2004.41.

Lin Liu, Eric Yu, and John Mylopoulos. Security and Privacy Requirements Analysis Within a Social Setting. In *Proceedings of the 11th IEEE International Conference on Requirements Engineering*, RE '03, pages 151–161. IEEE Computer Society, 2003. ISBN 0-7695-1980-6. 10.1109/ICRE.2003.1232746.

Zhenyu Liu, Tiejiang Liu, Lizhi Cai, and Genxing Yang. Quality Evaluation and Selection Framework of Service Composition Based on Distributed Agents. In *5th International Conference on Next Generation Web Services Practices*, pages 68–75. IEEE, Sept 2009. ISBN 978-0-7695-3821-1. 10.1109/NWeSP.2009.18.

Russell Lock and Ian Sommerville. Modelling and Analysis of Socio-Technical System of Systems. In *Proceedings of the 15th IEEE International Conference on Engineering of Complex Computer Systems*, ICECCS, pages 224–232, 2010. ISBN 978-0-7695-4015-3. 10.1109/ICECCS.2010.40.

Volkmar Lotz, Samuel Paul Kaluvuri, Francesco Di Cerbo, and Antonino Sabetta. Towards Security Certification Schemas for the Internet of Services. In *Proceedings of the 5th International Conference on New Technologies, Mobility and Security*, NTMS, pages 1–5, May 2012. 10.1109/NTMS.2012.6208771.

Volkmar Lotz, Francesco Di Cerbo, Michele Bezzi, Samuel Paul Kaluvuri, Antonino Sabetta, and Slim Trabelsi. Security Certification for Service-Based Business Ecosystems. *The Computer Journal*, 58(4):709–723, 2015. 10.1093/comjnl/bxt101.

Pin Luarn and Hsin-Hui Lin. A Customer Loyalty Model for E-Service Context. *Journal of Electronic Commerce Research*, 4(4):156–167, 2003.

David C. Luckham. *The Power of Events: An Introduction to Complex Event Processing in Distributed Enterprise Systems*. Addison-Wesley Longman Publishing Co., Inc., Boston, MA, USA, 2001. ISBN 0201727897.

Niklas Luhmann. *Trust and Power: Two Works, Parts 1-2*. U.M.I., 1979. URL https://books.google.de/books?id=PS0OnQEACAAJ.

Mass Soldal Lund, Bjørnar Solhaug, and Ketil Stølen. *Model-Driven Risk Analysis. The CORAS Approach*. Springer, 2010.

Curtis L. Maines, David Llewellyn-Jones, Stephen Tang, and Bo Zhou. A Cyber Security Ontology for BPMN-Security Extensions. In *IEEE International Conference on Computer and Information Technology; Ubiquitous Computing and Communications; Dependable, Autonomic and Secure Computing; Pervasive Intelligence and Computing*, pages 1756–1763, 2015. 10.1109/CIT/IUCC/DASC/PICOM.2015.265.

Zaki Malik and Athman Bouguettaya. RATEWeb: Reputation Assessment for Trust Establishment Among Web Services. *The VLDB Journal*, 18(4):885–911, 2009. ISSN 1066-8888. 10.1007/s00778-009-0138-1.

Stephen Marsh. Formalising Trust as a Computational Concept. Technical report, University of Stirling, 1994.

Stephen Marsh and Mark R. Dibben. Trust, Untrust, Distrust and Mistrust – An Exploration of the Dark(er) Side. In Peter Herrmann, Valérie Issarny, and Simon Shiu, editors, *Trust Management*, pages 17–33. Springer Berlin Heidelberg, 2005. ISBN 978-3-540-32040-1.

Jim A McCall, Paul K Richards, and Gene F Walters. Factors in Software Quality. volume i. Concepts and Definitions of Software Quality. Technical report, DTIC Document, 1977.

Gary McGraw. *Software Security: Building Security In*. Addison-Wesley Professional, 2006. ISBN 0321356705.

Harrison D. Mcknight and Norman L. Chervany. The Meanings of Trust. Technical report, Management Information Systems Research Center, University of Minnesota, USA, 1996.

Harrison D. McKnight, Vivek Choudhury, and Charles Kacmar. Developing and Validating Trust Measures for e-Commerce: An Integrative Typology. *Information Systems Research*, 13(3):334–359, 2002. ISSN 1526-5536. 10.1287/isre.13.3.334.81.

Hong Mei, Gang Huang, and Tao Xie. Internetware: A Software Paradigm for Internet Computing. *IEEE Computer*, 45(6):26–31, June 2012. ISSN 0018-9162. 10.1109/MC.2012.189.

Per Håkon Meland, Karin Bernsmed, Martin Gilje Jaatun, Humberto Nicolás Castejón Martínez, and Astrid Undheim. Expressing Cloud Security Requirements for SLAs in Deontic Contract Languages for Cloud Brokers. *IJCC*, 3(1):69–93, 2014. 10.1504/IJCC.2014.058831.

Daniel Mellado, Carlos Blanco, Luis E. Sánchez, and Eduardo Fernández-Medina. A Systematic Review of Security Requirements Engineering. *Computer Standards & Interfaces*, 32(4):153 – 165, 2010. ISSN 0920-5489. http://doi.org/10.1016/j.csi.2010.01.006.

Mukhtiar Memon, Stefan Rahr Wagner, Christian Fischer Pedersen, Femina Hassan Aysha Beevi, and Finn Overgaard Hansen. Ambient Assisted Living Healthcare Frameworks, Platforms, Standards, and Quality Attributes. *Sensors*, 14(3): 4312–4341, 2014. ISSN 1424-8220. 10.3390/s140304312.

Xianfu Meng, Yalin Ding, and Yue Gong. @Trust: A trust model based on feedback-arbitration in structured P2P network. *Computer Communications*, 35 (16):2044–2053, 2012.

Microsoft.   Microsoft Security Development Lifecycle.   `http://www.microsoft.com/security/sdl/default.aspx`.

Lars C. Monkerud and Trond Tjerbo. The Effects of the Norwegian Coordination Reform on the Use of Rehabilitation Services: Panel Data Analyses of Service Use, 2010 to 2013. *BMC Health Services Research*, 16(1):353, 2016. ISSN 1472-6963. 10.1186/s12913-016-1564-6.

Lik Mui, Mojdeh Mohtashemi, Cheewee Ang, Peter Szolovits, and Ari Halberstadt. Ratings in Distributed Systems: A Bayesian Approach, 2001.

National Research Council, Daniel Jackson, and Thomas Martyn (editors). *Software for Dependable Systems: Sufficient Evidence?* Committee on Certifiably Dependable Software Systems, Computer Science and Telecommunications Board, The National Academies Press, Washington, USA, 2007. ISBN 0309103940, 9780309103947.

Afonso Araújo Neto and Marco Vieira. Untrustworthiness: A Trust-based Security Metric. In *4th International Conference on Risks and Security of Internet and Systems, CRiSIS*, pages 123–126. IEEE, 2009. 10.1109/CRISIS.2009.5411967.

Peter G. Neumann. Principled Assuredly Trustworthy Composable Architectures, Final SRI report to DARPA. Technical report, Computer Science Laboratory SRI International, 2004. URL `http://www.csl.sri.com/neumann/chats4.pdf`.

Bashar Nuseibeh. Weaving together Requirements and Architectures. *IEEE Computer*, 34(3):115–119, 2001. ISSN 0018-9162. 10.1109/2.910904.

Object Management Group. Business Process Model and Notation (BPMN) Version 2.0. Technical report, Object Management Group (OMG), January 2011. URL `http://taval.de/publications/BPMN20`.

Object Management Group: SPEM. Software & Systems Process Engineering Meta-Model Specification, Version 2.0. Technical report, April 2008. URL `http://www.omg.org/spec/SPEM/`.

OPTET Consortium. D3.2 – Initial Trustworthiness-by-design Process and Tool Support, Technical Report. OPTET Project, 2013a.

OPTET Consortium. D6.1 – Catalogue of trust and trustworthiness events and mitigation actions, Technical Report. OPTET Project, 2013b.

OPTET Consortium. D8.1 – Description of use cases and application concepts, Technical Report. OPTET Project, 2013c.

OPTET Consortium. D2.4 – Socio-economic Evaluation of Trust and Trustworthiness, Technical Report. OPTET Project, Available online: `https://eprints.soton.ac.uk/410775/`, 2014a. (Accessed on 10 August 2018).

OPTET Consortium. D3.3 – Trustworthiness Evaluation Techniques and Prototypes, Technical Report. OPTET Project, 2014b.

OPTET Consortium. D.6.4.1 – Measurement and Management tools (1st release), Technical Report. OPTET Project, 2014c.

OWASP. CLASP Project (Comprehensive, Lightweight Application Security Process), Open Web Application Security Project (OWASP), July 2009. `www.owasp.org/index.php/Category:OWASP_CLASP_Project/es`.

Elda Paja, Amit K. Chopra, and Paolo Giorgini. Trust-based Specification of Sociotechnical Systems. *Data & Knowledge Engineering*, 87:339–353, 2013. 10.1016/j.datak.2012.12.005.

Mike P. Papazoglou. Service-Oriented Computing: Concepts, Characteristics and Directions. In *Proceedings of the 4th International Conference on Web Information Systems Engineering, WISE*, pages 3–12, 2003. 10.1109/WISE.2003.1254461.

Mike P. Papazoglou, Paolo Traverso, Schahram Dustdar, and Frank Leymann. Service-Oriented Computing: State of the Art and Research Challenges. *IEEE Computer*, 40(11):38–45, 2007. ISSN 0018-9162. 10.1109/MC.2007.400.

David Lorge Parnas and Jan Madey. Functional Documents for Computer Systems. *Science of Computer Programming*, 25(1):41–61, 1995.

David Lorge Parnas, A. John van Schouwen, and Shu Po Kwan. Evaluation of Safety-critical Software. *Communications of the ACM*, 33(6):636–648, 1990. ISSN 0001-0782. 10.1145/78973.78974.

Vishwas Patil and Rudrapatna K. Shyamasundar. Trust Management for E-transactions. *Sadhana*, 30(2):141–158, 2005. ISSN 0973-7677. 10.1007/ BF02706242.

Vaise Patu and Shuichiro Yamamoto. How to Develop Security Case by Combining Real Life Security Experiences (Evidence) with D-case. *Procedia Computer Science, 17th International Conference in Knowledge Based and Intelligent Information and Engineering Systems - KES*, 22:954–959, 2013. ISSN 1877-0509. https://doi.org/10.1016/j.procs.2013.09.179.

Sachar Paulus, Nazila Gol Mohammadi, and Thorsten Weyer. Trustworthy Software Development. In *Proceedings of the 14th IFIP TC 6/TC 11 International Conference on Communications and Multimedia Security, CMS*, pages 233–247, 2013. 10.1007/978-3-642-40779-6_23.

Michalis Pavlidis, Haralambos Mouratidis, Shareeful Islam, and Paul Kearney. Dealing with Trust and Control: A Meta-model for Trustworthy Information Systems Development. In *6th International Conference on Research Challenges in Information Science (RCIS)*, pages 1–9, 2012. 10.1109/RCIS.2012.6240441.

Marbin Pazos-Revilla and Ambareen Siraj. Tools and Techniques for SSE-CMM Implementation. In *The 12th World Multi-Conference on Systemics, Cybernetics and Informatics, Jointly with ISAS*, 2008. URL www.iiis.org/cds2008/ cd2008sci/SCI2008/PapersPdf/S268BG.pdf.

Peter Haumer. Eclipse Process Framework Composer, Part 1: Key Concepts. www.eclipse.org/epf/general/EPFComposerOverviewPart1 .pdf, April 2007. (Accessed on 23 July 2018).

Klaus Pohl. *Requirements Engineering: Fundamentals, Principles, and Techniques*. Springer Publishing Company, Incorporated, 1st edition, 2010. ISBN 3642125778, 9783642125775.

Klaus Pohl, Günter Böckle, and Frank van der Linden. *Software Product Line Engineering*. Springer Berlin Heidelberg, Germany, 2005. ISBN 978-3-540-24372-4.

Eileen J. Porter. Wearing and Using Personal Emergency Respone System Buttons. *J. Gerontol Nurs.*, 31(10):26–33, October 2005. URL https://www.ncbi .nlm.nih.gov/pubmed/16262088.

Princeton Survey Research Associates. A Matter of Trust: What Users Want From Web Sites. Technical report, 2002. URL consumersunion.org/wp-content/uploads/2013/05/a-matter-of-trust.pdf.

Thomas B. Quillinan, Kassidy P. Clark, Martijn Warnier, Frances M. T. Brazier, and Omer Rana. Negotiation and Monitoring of Service Level Agreements. In Philipp Wieder, Ramin Yahyapour, and Wolfgang Ziegler, editors, *Grids and Service-Oriented Architectures for Service Level Agreements*, pages 167–176. Springer, 2010. ISBN 978-1-4419-7320-7. 10.1007/978-1-4419-7320-7_15.

Basit Qureshi, Geyong Min, and Demetres Kouvatsos. Trusted Information Exchange in Peer-to-Peer Mobile Social Networks. *Concurrency and Computation: Practice and Experience*, 24(17):2055–2068, 2012. 10.1002/cpe.1837.

Dev G. Raheja and Louis J. Gullo. *Design for Reliability*. Wiley, USA, 2012. ISBN 978-0-470-48675-7.

Mohammadreza Rahimpour, Nigel H. Lovell, Branko G. Celler, and John McCormick. Patients' Perceptions of a Home Telecare System. *International Journal of Medical Informatics*, 77(7):486 – 498, 2008. ISSN 1386-5056. https://doi.org/10.1016/j.ijmedinf.2007.10.006.

Ragunathan Rajkumar, Insup Lee, Lui Sha, and John Stankovic. Cyber-Physical Systems: The Next Computing Revolution. In *Proceedings of the 47th Design Automation Conference, DAC*, pages 731–736. ACM, 2010. 10.1145/1837274.1837461.

Omer Rana, Martijn Warnier, Thomas B. Quillinan, and Frances Brazier. *Monitoring and Reputation Mechanisms for Service Level Agreements*, pages 125–139. Springer Berlin Heidelberg, 2008. ISBN 978-3-540-85485-2. 10.1007/978-3-540-85485-2_10.

Li-Ping Rao, Ming He, Song Huang, and Rui Bao. Behavior Trust Prediction and Control Based on Electronic Commerce System. In *International Conference on E-Business and Information System Security*, pages 1–4, 2009. 10.1109/EBISS.2009.5137946.

Parisa Rashidi and Alex Mihailidis. A Survey on Ambient-Assisted Living Tools for Older Adults. *IEEE Journal of Biomedical and Health Informatics*, 17(3):579–590, May 2013. ISSN 2168-2194. 10.1109/JBHI.2012.2234129.

Indrajit Ray and Sudip Chakraborty. *A Vector Model of Trust for Developing Trustworthy Systems*, pages 260–275. Springer Berlin Heidelberg, 2004. ISBN 978-3-540-30108-0. 10.1007/978-3-540-30108-0_16.

Mark Reith, Jianwei Niu, and William H. Winsborough. Engineering Trust Management into Software Models. In *Proceedings of the International Workshop on Modeling in Software Engineering*, MISE, page 9. IEEE Computer Society, 2007. ISBN 0-7695-2953-4. 10.1109/MISE.2007.5.

Robert Richardson. Computer Security Institute (CSI), Computer Crime and Security Survey. Technical report, 2011. URL cours.etsmtl.ca/gti619/ documents/divers/CSIsurvey2010.pdf.

Jens Riegelsberger, M. Angela Sasse, and John D. McCarthy. The Mechanics of Trust: A Framework for Research and Design. *International Journal of Human-Computer Studies*, 62(3):381–422, 2005. ISSN 1071-5819. http://dx.doi.org/ 10.1016/j.ijhcs.2005.01.001.

Alfonso Rodríguez, Eduardo Fernández-Medina, and Mario Piattini. A BPMN Extension for the Modeling of Security Requirements in Business Processes. *IEICE - Transactions on Information and Systems*, E90-D(4):745–752, March 2007. ISSN 0916-8532. 10.1093/ietisy/e90-d.4.745.

Robert Ellis Roush, Thomas A. Teasdale, Jane N. Murphy, and Stella Kirk. Impact of a Personal Emergency Response System on Hospital Utilization by Community-residing Elders. *South Med Journal*, 4(88):917–922, 1995. URL https://www.ncbi.nlm.nih.gov/pubmed/7660208.

Walker W. Royce. Managing the Development of Large Software Systems: Concepts and Techniques. In *Proceedings of the 9th International Conference on Software Engineering*, ICSE, pages 328–338. IEEE Computer Society Press, 1987. ISBN 0-89791-216-0. URL http://dl.acm.org/ citation.cfm?id=41765.41801.

Nick Russell, Wil M. P. van der Aalst, Arthur H. M. ter Hofstede, and David Edmond. *Workflow Resource Patterns: Identification, Representation and Tool Support*, pages 216–232. Springer Berlin Heidelberg, 2005. ISBN 978-3-540-32127-9. 10.1007/11431855_16.

S-Cube. Quality Reference Model for Service-Based Applications. Technical report, December 2008.

Mattia Salnitri, Elda Paja, and Paolo Giorgini. From Socio-Technical Requirements to Technical Security Design: An STS-based Framework. Technical report, DISI, University of Trento, 2011. URL http://www.secbpmn.disi.unitn .it/documentation/RE15.pdf.

Mattia Salnitri, Fabiano Dalpiaz, and Paolo Giorgini. Designing Secure Business Processes with secBPMN. *Software & Systems Modeling*, pages 1–21, 2015. ISSN 1619-1374. 10.1007/s10270-015-0499-4.

Sonia San-Martín and Carmen Camarero. A Cross-National Study on Online Consumer Perceptions, Trust, and Loyalty. *Journal of Organizational Computing and Electronic Commerce*, 22(1):64–86, 2012. 10.1080/10919392.2012.642763.

Koh Song Sang and Bo Zhou. BPMN Security Extensions for Healthcare Process. In *IEEE International Conference on Computer and Information Technology; Ubiquitous Computing and Communications; Dependable, Autonomic and Secure Computing; Pervasive Intelligence and Computing*, pages 2340–2345, 2015. 10.1109/CIT/IUCC/DASC/PICOM.2015.346.

Gerry W Scheffelmaier and John F Vinsonhaler. A Synthesis of Research on the Properties of Effective Internet Commerce Web Sites. *Journal of Computer Information Systems*, 43(2):23–30, 2003.

Alice C. Scheffer, Wilma J. Scholte op Reimer, Nynke Dijk, Barbara C. Munster, Ameen Abu-Hanna, Marcel Levi, and Sophia E. Rooij. Effect of a Mobile Safety Alarm on Going Outside, Feeling Safe, Fear of Falling, and Quality of Life in Community-Living Older Persons: A Randomized Controlled Trial. *Journal of the American Geriatrics Society*, 60(5):987–989, May 2012. 10.1111/j.1532-5415.2012.03932.x.

Douglas C. Schmidt. Model-Driven Engineering. *IEEE Computer*, 39(2), February 2006.

Susan P. Shapiro. The Social Control of Impersonal Trust. *American journal of Sociology*, pages 623–658, 1987. 10.1086/228791.

Li Shi, Shan-lin Yang, Kai Lia, and Ben-gong Yu. Developing an Evaluation Approach for Software Trustworthiness Using Combination Weights and TOPSIS. *Journal of Software*, 7(3):532–543, 2012.

SHIELDS. Detecting Known Security Vulnerabilities from within Design and Development Tools, July 2010. http://cordis.europa.eu/project/rcn/85431_en.html. (Accessed on 23 July 2018).

Stuart Short and Samuel Paul Kaluvuri. A Data-Centric Approach for Privacy-Aware Business Process Enablement. In *Proceedings of 3rd International IFIP Working Conference on Enterprise Interoperability, IWEI*, pages 191–203, 2011. 10.1007/978-3-642-19680-5_16.

Michael D. Siegel, Stuart E. Madnick, Hongwei Zhu, Michael D. Siegel, and Stuart E. Madnick. Information Aggregation - a Value-Added E-Service. In *Proceedings of the 5th International Conference on Technology, Policy, and Innovation – Theme: Critical Infrastructures*, pages 26–29, 2001.

Software Engineering Institute. Capability Maturity Model® Integration (CM-MISM), Version 1.1. Technical report, December 2002.

Bjørnar Solhaug and Dag Elgesem Ketil Stølen. Why Trust is not Proportional to Risk. In *The 2nd International Conference on Availability, Reliability and Security, ARES*, pages 11–18. IEEE, 2007. ISBN 0-7695-2775-2. 10.1109/ARES.2007.161.

Ian Sommerville. *Software Engineering*. Pearson, USA, 10th edition, 2016. ISBN 978-0133943030, 0133943038.

Ian Sommerville and Guy Dewsbury. Dependable Domestic Systems Design: A Socio-technical Approach. *Interact. Comput.*, 19(4):438–456, 2007. ISSN 0953-5438. 10.1016/j.intcom.2007.05.002.

Yu Song and Ling Wang. Software Trusted Comprehensive Evaluation Model Based on Fuzzy Grey Method. In *2nd International Conference on Networks Security Wireless Communications and Trusted Computing, NSWCTC*, volume 1, pages 513–516. IEEE, 2010. 10.1109/NSWCTC.2010.127.

Frederick Steinke, Tobias Fritsch, Daniel Brem, and Svenja Simonsen. Requirement of AAL Systems – Older Persons' Trust in Sensors and Characteristics of AAL Technologies. In *Proceedings of the 5th International Conference on PErvasive Technologies Related to Assistive Environments*, PETRA, pages 15:1–15:6. ACM, 2012. ISBN 978-1-4503-1300-1. 10.1145/2413097.2413116.

Frederick Steinke, Andreas Hertzer, Tobias Fritsch, Helmut Tautz, and Simon Zickwolf. Expected Reliability of Everyday- and Ambient Assisted Living Technologies – Results From an Online Survey. *International Journal of Advanced Computer Science and Applications (IJACSA)*, 4(6):17–22, June 2013. URL www.ijacsa.thesai.org.

R. Todd Stephens. A Framework for the Identification of Electronic Commerce Design Elements That Enable Trust Within the Small Hotel Industry. In *Proceedings of the 42nd Annual Southeast Regional Conference*, ACM-SE 42, pages 309–314. ACM, 2004. ISBN 1-58113-870-9. 10.1145/986537.986613.

Bernard Stepien, Amy Felty, and Stan Matwin. A Non-technical User-Oriented Display Notation for XACML Conditions. In Gilbert Babin, Peter Kropf, and Michael Weiss, editors, *E-Technologies: Innovation in an Open World*, volume 26 of *Lecture Notes in Business Information Processing*, pages 53–64. Springer Berlin Heidelberg, 2009. ISBN 978-3-642-01186-3. 10.1007/978-3-642-01187 -0_5.

James P.G. Sterbenz, David Hutchison, Egemen K. Çetinkaya, Abdul Jabbar, Justin P. Rohrer, Marcus Schöller, and Paul Smith. Resilience and Survivability in Communication Networks: Strategies, Principles, and Survey of Disciplines. *Computer Networks*, 54(8):1245–1265, 2010. ISSN 1389-1286. http://dx.doi.org/10.1016/j.comnet.2010.03.005. Resilient and Survivable Networks.

Mark Strembeck and Jan Mendling. Modeling Process-related RBAC Models with Extended UML Activity Models. *Information and Software Technology*, 53(5): 456–483, May 2011. ISSN 0950-5849. 10.1016/j.infsof.2010.11.015.

Luis Jesús Ramón Stroppi, Omar Chiotti, and Pablo David Villarreal. Extending BPMN 2.0: Method and Tool Support. In *Proceedings of 3rd International Workshop Business Process Model and Notation, BPMN*, pages 59–73, 2011a. 10.1007/978-3-642-25160-3_5.

Luis Jesús Ramón Stroppi, Omar Chiotti, and Pablo David Villarreal. A BPMN 2.0 Extension to Define the Resource Perspective of Business Process Models. In *XIV Congreso Iberoamericano en Software Engineering (CIbSE)*, 2011b.

Mike Surridge, Bassem I. Nasser, Xiaoyu Chen, Ajay Chakravarthy, and Panos Melas. Run-Time Risk Management in Adaptive ICT Systems. In *International Conference on Availability, Reliability and Security, ARES*, pages 102–110, 2013. 10.1109/ARES.2013.20.

Allistair G. Sutcliffe. *Convergence or Competition between Software Engineering and Human Computer Interaction*, pages 71–84. Springer, 2005. ISBN 978-1-4020-4113-6. 10.1007/1-4020-4113-6_5.

Ingrid Svagård and Elin S. Boysen. Electronic Medication Dispensers Finding the Right Users - A Pilot Study in a Norwegian Municipality Home Care Service. In *Proceedings of 15th International Conference on Computers Helping People with Special Needs - Part I, ICCHP*, pages 281–284, 2016. 10.1007/978-3-319 -41264-1_38.

Ingrid Svagård, Hanne Opsahl Austad, Trine M. Seeberg, Jon Vedum, Anders E. Liverud, B. M. Mathiesen, B. Keller, Ole Christian Bendixen, P. Osborne, and Frode Strisland. A Usability Study of a Mobile Monitoring System for Congestive Heart Failure Patients. In *Proceedings of the 25th European Medical Informatics Conferencee-Health - For Continuity of Care, MIE*, pages 528–532, 2014. 10 .3233/978-1-61499-432-9-528.

Frank Swiderski and Window Snyder. *Threat Modeling (Microsoft Professional) 1st Edition*. Microsoft Press, USA, 2004. ISBN 978-0735619913.

Piotr Sztompka. *Trust: A Sociological Theory*. Cambridge University Press, Cambridge, 2000. ISBN 9780521591447.

Mart Tacken, Fiorella Marcellini, Heidrun Mollenkopf, Isto Ruoppila, and Zsuzsa Széman. Use and Acceptance of New Technology by Older People. Findings of the International MOBILATE Survey: 'Enhancing Mobility in Later Life'. *Gerontechnology*, 3(3):126–137, March 2005. http://dx.doi.org/10.4017/gt.2005 .03.03.002.00.

Mihaela Teler and Valentin Cristea. Securing Vehicular Networks Using Deterministic Schemes for Computing Trust. In *4th International Conference on Intelligent Networking and Collaborative Systems, INCoS*, pages 214–221. IEEE, 2012. 10.1109/iNCoS.2012.123.

Nelufar Ulfat-Bunyadi, Rene Meis, and Maritta Heisel. The Six-Variable Model – Context Modelling Enabling Systematic Reuse of Control Software. In *Proceedings of the 11th International Joint Conference on Software Technologies, ICSOFT*, pages 15–26, 2016. 10.5220/0005944100150026.

U.S. Department of Defense. Trusted Software Methodology, SDI-SD-91-000007, Volumes 1 and 2. Technical Report, U.S. Department of Defense, Strategic Defense Initiative Organization. Technical report, 2007.

Ger Van den Broek, Filippo Cavallo, and Christian Wehrmann. *AALIANCE Ambient Assisted Living Roadmap*, volume 6 of *Ambient Intelligence and Smart Environments*. IOS Press, 2010. ISBN 978-1-60750-498-6.

Axel Van Lamsweerde and Emmanuel Letier. Handling Obstacles in Goal-Oriented Requirements Engineering. *IEEE Transactions on Software Engineering*, 26(10): 978–1005, 2000. ISSN 0098-5589. 10.1109/32.879820.

Lex Van Velsen, Thea van der Geest, Marc ter Hedde, and Wijnand Derks. Requirements Engineering for E-Government Services: A Citizen-centric Approach and

Case Study. *Government Information Quarterly*, 26(3):477–486, 2009. ISSN 0740-624X. https://doi.org/10.1016/j.giq.2009.02.007.

Frank M. F. Verberne, Jaap Ham, and Cees J. H. Midden. Trust in Smart Systems: Sharing Driving Goals and Giving Information to Increase Trustworthiness and Acceptability of Smart Systems in Cars. *Journal of Human Factors*, 54(5): 799–810, 2012. 10.1177/0018720812443825.

Warren Walker, Peter Harremoës, Jan Rotmans, Jan P. van der Sluijs, M.B.A. van Asselt, Peter Janssen, and M.P. Krayer von Krauss. Defining Uncertainty: A Conceptual Basis for Uncertainty Management in Model-Based Decision Support. *Integrated Assessment*, 4(1):5–17, 2003. 10.1076/iaij.4.1.5.16466.

Agustinus Borgy Waluyo, David Taniar, J. Wenny Rahayu, Ailixier Aikebaier, Makoto Takizawa, and Bala Srinivasan. Trustworthy-based Efficient Data Broadcast Model for P2P Interaction in Resource-constrained Wireless Environments. *Journal of Computer and System Sciences*, 78(6):1716–1736, 2012. 10.1016/j.jcss.2011.10.019.

MingXue Wang, Kosala Yapa Bandara, and Claus Pahl. Process as a Service Distributed Multi-tenant Policy-Based Process Runtime Governance. In *IEEE International Conference on Services Computing*, pages 578–585, July 2010. 10.1109/SCC.2010.33.

Ye Diana Wang and Henry H Emurian. An Overview of Online Trust: Concepts, Elements, and Implications. *Computers in Human Behavior*, 21(1):105–125, 2005.

Zheng Wang and Jon Crowcroft. Quality-of-Service Routing for Supporting Multimedia Applications. *IEEE Journal on Selected Areas in Communications*, 14(7): 1228–1234, September 2006. ISSN 0733-8716. 10.1109/49.536364.

Thomas Weigert and Frank Weil. Practical Experiences in Using Model-Driven Engineering to Develop Trustworthy Computing Systems. In *IEEE International Conference on Sensor Networks, Ubiquitous, and Trustworthy Computing, SUTC*, volume 1, pages 208–217, 2006. 10.1109/SUTC.2006.1636178.

Charles B. Weinstock, Howard F. Lipson, and John Goodenough. Arguing Security – Creating Security Assurance Cases, 2007. www.sei.cmu.edu.

Brian Whitworth. A Brief Introduction to Sociotechnical Systems. In *Encyclopedia of Information Science and Technology, Second Edition*, pages 394–400. IGI Global, 2009.

Stephen Withall. *Software Requirement Patterns*. Microsoft Press, Redmond, WA, USA, first edition, 2007. ISBN 9780735623989.

Christian Wolter, Michael Menzel, Andreas Schaad, Philip Miseldine, and Christoph Meinel. Model-Driven Business Process Security Requirement Specification. *Journal of Systems Architecture*, 55(4):211–223, 2009. ISSN 1383-7621. http://dx.doi.org/10.1016/j.sysarc.2008.10.002. Secure Service-Oriented Architectures (Special Issue on Secure SOA).

Wang Xin-zhi, Sun Le-chang, Liu Jing-ju, and Li Qiang. VISHNU: A Software Behavior Trustworthiness Control Method Based on DRTM. In *2nd International Symposium on Intelligence Information Processing and Trusted Computing, IPTC*, pages 169–172. IEEE, 2011. 10.1109/IPTC.2011.50.

Zheng Yan and Christian Prehofer. *An Adaptive Trust Control Model for a Trustworthy Component Software Platform*, pages 226–238. Springer Berlin Heidelberg, 2007. ISBN 978-3-540-73547-2. 10.1007/978-3-540-73547-2_24.

Kaifeng Yang. Trust and Citizen Involvement Decisions Trust in Citizens, Trust in Institutions, and Propensity to Trust. *Administration & Society*, 38(5):573–595, 2006.

Ye Yang, Qing Wang, and Mingshu Li. Process Trustworthiness As a Capability Indicator for Measuring and Improving Software Trustworthiness. In *Proceedings of the International Conference on Software Process: Trustworthy Software Development Processes*, ICSP, pages 389–401. Springer-Verlag, 2009. ISBN 978-3-642-01679-0. 10.1007/978-3-642-01680-6_35.

Ting-Fang Yen, Yinglian Xie, Fang Yu, Roger Peng Yu, and Martin Abadi. Host Fingerprinting and Tracking on the Web: Privacy and Security Implications. In *19th Annual Network and Distributed System Security Symposium, NDSS*, 2012.

Gao Ying and Zhan Jiang. Trustworthiness-based Controllable Delegation Trust Management Model in P2P. In *The 2nd IEEE International Conference on Information Management and Engineering, ICIME*, pages 503–507, 2010. 10.1109/ICIME.2010.5477920.

Pinar Yolum and Munindar P. Singh. Engineering Self-Organizing Referral Networks for Trustworthy Service Selection. *IEEE Transactions on Systems, Man, and Cybernetics - Part A: Systems and Humans*, 35(3):396–407, May 2005. ISSN 1083-4427. 10.1109/TSMCA.2005.846401.

Eric S. K. Yu. Towards Modelling and Reasoning Support for Early-Phase Requirements Engineering. In *Proceedings of the 3rd IEEE International Symposium on Requirements Engineering*, pages 226–235, 1997. 10.1109/ISRE.1997.566873.

Han Yu, Zhiqi Shen, Chunyan Miao, Cyril Leung, and Dusit Niyato. A Survey of Trust and Reputation Management Systems in Wireless Communications. *Proceedings of the IEEE*, 98(10):1755–1772, 2010. ISSN 0018-9219. 10.1109/JPROC.2010.2059690.

Tao Yu, Yue Zhang, and Kwei-Jay Lin. Efficient Algorithms for Web Services Selection with End-to-End QoS Constraints. *ACM Transactions on the Web*, 1 (1), May 2007. ISSN 1559-1131. 10.1145/1232722.1232728.

Weiwei Yuan, Donghai Guan, Lei Shu, and Jianwei Niu. Efficient Searching Mechanism for Trust-Aware Recommender Systems Based on Scale-Freeness of Trust Networks. In *IEEE 11th International Conference on Trust, Security and Privacy in Computing and Communications*, pages 1819–1823, 2012. 10.1109/TrustCom.2012.143.

Zabbix. The Enterprise-Class Monitoring Solution for Everyone, 2009. http://www.zabbix.com/.

Janusz Zalewski, Steven Drager, William McKeever, and Andrew J. Kornecki. Threat Modeling for Security Assessment in Cyberphysical Systems. In *Proceedings of the 18 Annual Cyber Security and Information Intelligence Research Workshop*, CSIIRW, pages 10:1–10:4. ACM, 2013. ISBN 978-1-4503-1687-3. 10.1145/2459976.2459987.

Pamela Zave and Michael Jackson. Four Dark Corners of Requirements Engineering. *ACM Transactions on Software Engineering and Methodology*, 6(1):1–30, 1997. 10.1145/237432.237434.

Jia Zhang and Liang-Jie Zhang. Web Services Quality Testing. *International Journal of Web Services Research (JWSR)*, 2(2):1–4, 2005.

Shenghui Zhao, Guoxin Wu, Yuemin Li, and Kun Yu. A Framework for Trustworthy Web Service Management. In *2nd International Symposium on Electronic Commerce and Security*, volume 2, pages 479–482. IEEE, 2009. 10.1109/ISECS.2009.226.

Zhiming Zheng, Shilong Ma, Wei Li, Wei Wei, Xin Jiang, ZhanLi Zhang, and BingHui Guo. Dynamical Characteristics of Software Trustworthiness and their Evolutionary Complexity. *Science in China Series F: Information Sciences*, 52 (8):1328–1334, 2009. 10.1007/s11432-009-0137-2.

Martina Ziefle, Carsten Rocker, and Andreas Holzinger. Medical Technology in Smart Homes: Exploring the User's Perspective on Privacy, Intimacy and Trust. In *IEEE 35th Annual Computer Software and Applications Conference Workshops*, pages 410–415, 2011. ISBN 978-1-4577-0980-7. 10.1109/COMPSACW.2011.75.

Miroslav Zivkovic, J. W. Bosman, J. L. van den Berg, Robert D. van der Mei, Hendrik B. Meeuwissen, and R. Núñez Queija. Dynamic Profit Optimization of Composite Web Services with SLAs. In *IEEE Global Telecommunications Conference, GLOBECOM*, pages 1–6, 2011. 10.1109/GLOCOM.2011.6133666.

Jiang Zuo-Wen, Ding Zhi-Jun, Tang Xian-Fei, and Jiang Chang-Jun. Evolutionary Behavior Verification to the Trustworthy Banking Software. In *Computer Engineering and Technology (ICCET), 2010 2nd International Conference on*, volume 6, pages V6–92–V6–99, 2010. 10.1109/ICCET.2010.5486319.

Mary Ellen Zurko. User-Centered Security: Stepping Up to the Grand Challenge. In *21st Annual Computer Security Applications Conference, ACSAC*, pages 187–202, 2005. 10.1109/CSAC.2005.60.

Printed in the United States
By Bookmasters